THE COMPLETE GUIDE TO
RRIFs and LIFs

Also by Gordon Pape

INVESTMENT ADVICE

6 Steps to $1 Million

Retiring Wealthy in the 21st Century

Gordon Pape's 2002 Buyer's Guide to Mutual Funds
(with Eric Kirzner)

Gordon Pape's 2002 Buyer's Guide to RRSPs
(with David Tafler)

Secrets of Successful Investing
(with Eric Kirzner)

Making Money in Mutual Funds

The Canadian Mortgage Book
(with Bruce McDougall)

The Best of Pape's Notes

Head Start
(with Frank Jones)

Building Wealth in the '90s

Low-Risk Investing in the '90s

CONSUMER ADVICE
Gordon Pape's International Shopping Guide
(with Deborah Pape)

HUMOUR
The $50,000 Stove Handle

FICTION
(with Tony Aspler)

Chain Reaction

The Scorpion Sanction

The Music Wars

NON-FICTION
(with Donna Gabeline and Dane Lanken)

Montreal at the Crossroads

Also by David Tafler

David Tafler's 50-plus Survival Guide

Gordon Pape's 2002 Buyer's Guide to RRSPs
(with Gordon Pape)

THE COMPLETE GUIDE TO
RRIFs and LIFs

How to Make the
Best Investment
Decisions for
Retirement

David Tafler
Gordon Pape

A Pearson Company
Toronto

National Library of Canada Cataloguing in Publication Data

Pape, Gordon, 1936–
    The complete guide to RRIFs and LIFs : how to make the best investment decisions for retirement

Includes index.
ISBN 0-13-064756-X

1. Retirement income–Canada–Planning. 2. Retirees–Canada–Finance, Personal. I. Tafler, David, 1943– II. Title.

HD7129.P356 2002   332.024'01   C2001-903673-6

ISBN 0-13-064756-X

Editorial Director, Trade Division: Andrea Crozier
Acquisitions Editor: Andrea Crozier
Production Editor: Catherine Dorton
Copy Editor: Linda Cahill
Proofreader: Ian MacKenzie
Art Direction: Mary Opper
Cover and Interior Design: Sarah Battersby
Author Photo: Lorella Zanetti
Production Manager: Kathrine Pummell
Page Layout: B.J. Weckerle

ATTENTION: CORPORATIONS
Books are available at quantity discounts with bulk purchase for educational, business, or sales promotional use. For information, please email or write to: Pearson PTR Canada, Special Sales, PTR Division, 26 Prince Andrew Place, Don Mills, Ontario, M3C 2T8. Email ss.corp@pearsoned.com. Please supply: title of book, ISBN, quantity, how the book will be used, date needed.

Visit the Pearson PTR Canada Web site! Send us your comments, browse our catalogues, and more. **www.pearsonptr.ca**

1 2 3 4 5 F 06 05 04 03 02

Printed and bound in Canada.

A Pearson Company

To all Canadians who hope to make their retirement years
the richest and most rewarding time of their lives

CONTENTS

ACKNOWLEDGMENTS

Every book is the product of the work and support of many people and organizations. The authors pull everything together, but without the help of others, none of this would be possible.

We would particularly like to acknowledge the contributions of the following people in the creation of this book: Lillian and Murray Morgenthau of CARP, for their ongoing encouragement; Jude Gravelle, for her superb editing; June Yee, for her invaluable research; Michelle Williams, our eagle-eyed proofreader; Deborah Pape, for her exhaustive mutual fund research; and Eric Kirzner, for his mutual fund analysis.

We also wish to thank the following people for their invaluable input and advice: Paul Gratias of Jones Heward Investment Management Inc., and Peter Gilchrist of Blake, Cassels & Graydon.

The statistical data on the pages that follow comes from a variety of sources. These include the mutual fund companies themselves, *The Globe and Mail*, the *National Post,* the *Mutual Fund SourceBook* published by Southam, PAL *Trak*, and Globefund.

A special thank you goes to the editorial and production staff at Prentice Hall Canada, who as always did a first-rate job in pulling everything together.

Finally, we would be remiss in not acknowledging the invaluable support of our families, who have had to put up with our absence while we sat at computer screens writing this book. David Tafler thanks his wife, Susan, and his sons, Jason and Jonathan, for their love and support in the creation of this book. Gordon Pape thanks his wife, Shirley, and his children, all of whom contributed in various ways to this and all his other books.

PREFACE

Retirement is one of the most important crossroads we face in life. It involves making a fundamental change in lifestyle—one that calls for a totally new outlook on how we approach each day. It also requires taking an entirely different approach to money management, a step many people are ill prepared for.

All our lives we have been conditioned to think in terms of saving for our retirement years. Now it's time to start drawing on that lifetime of savings. But how? Where should the money be invested? How often do you require payments? What are the tax implications?

We wrote this book to provide authoritative answers to these and many other questions people face in retirement. We want to make absolutely certain that Canadians who must make a decision on converting their RRSPs know about the various options they have available to them, so that they can choose the best method for their personal needs.

Registered Retirement Income Funds, known as RRIFs, are often the best choice for many people. But there are many other options to consider, such as LIFs, LRIFs, and annuities. However, choosing your retirement income vehicle is just the start of the process. Your decision must be accompanied by a solid financial plan. This plan can only be achieved by developing a proper financial strategy—one that fits your personal goals and circumstances and that evolves as you age and as your requirements change. So in addition to providing all the information you need to make the right retirement income choices, this book is also designed to give you the basic tools to develop the strategies you will need to create a successful RRIF or LIF—for the income you need now and in future years.

These are supposed to be the "golden years" of our lives. We hope this book will provide a contribution to making them exactly that.

David Tafler
Gordon Pape

1

Is Your Retirement Income Secure?

Retirement is being dramatically affected by the increasing social, political, and economic uncertainties facing mature Canadians. As governments attempt to cut spending, they are systematically phasing out tax benefits and programs for seniors. Unfortunately, they are making many of their cuts to financial and health programs just when an aging population needs them most.

And the politicians responsible—of all political stripes—make it worse by pretending these changes are part of an attack on the wealthy!

Who do they think they're trying to kid? We both present seminars across the country and have spoken to thousands of mature Canadians. It is clear to us that they are under no illusion.

It's obvious that governments have their eyes on the middle class, especially seniors and about-to-be seniors, who hold the largest remaining nest egg in the country, having saved for years and paid their full share of taxes. This money represents the last major pool available to cash-hungry governments, and they are going after it as quickly and avidly as they can without committing political suicide.

As both governments and corporations rush to save money by getting out of the retirement business, the onus is increasingly on us, as individuals, to take more responsibility for our security in later life. You might feel helpless, but the numbers are on our side: The number of Canadians over the age of 50 today is closing in on 9 million, and the numbers will continue to swell in this age group, the fastest-growing segment of the population.

Governments may be in for a surprise. For all of us, a secure retirement depends largely on proper planning, and a few systematic changes can have serious implications for our plans.

Fooling around with what they're dressing up as "tax reform" and "fair taxes" could create a severe backlash. When politicians attack the savings of seniors, they risk waking up a huge sleeping giant. Two changes, in particular, recently awakened many of us to the detrimental impact on our future of the government's apparent mandate.

Higher Mandatory Withdrawals on Registered Retirement Income Funds (RRIFs)

With the 1992 federal budget, the government changed the rules to allow RRIFs to extend through the life of the plan holder instead of being wound up at age 90. According to the policymakers, this change (which is positive for most Canadians) created the need for new, higher minimum annual withdrawal rates for RRIFs (a change that's not at all positive). The result is that the amount you must withdraw annually from age 71 forward is much higher for RRIFs established after January 1, 1993, than for older RRIFs. For instance, if you're 71 and set up your RRIF in 1993 or later, you must withdraw 7.38 percent of your RRIF assets annually, compared to 5.26 percent for older RRIFs.

For the government, the benefits of these new mandatory withdrawals are obvious: The sooner you take the money out, the sooner it gets its share of the tax revenues that arise from this income. For the average Canadian, the implications are just as serious but not as fortunate. In an environment of low interest rates, mandatory withdrawals can easily outstrip the growth of our RRIF investments. The result could be an income shortfall in later years. At the very least, it leaves many average Canadians struggling to maintain the capital in their RRIFs, even in periods of modest inflation.

When Finance Minister Paul Martin visited the national offices of Canada's Association for the Fifty-Plus (CARP) in February 2000, David Tafler, with input from Gordon Pape, raised the issue of RRIF withdrawal rates and suggested how the potential disaster inherent in the existing rules might be diffused. Instead of basing the withdrawal rates on short-term interest rates, index them to inflation. That would ensure that retirees were drawing enough income and would generate a fair amount of tax for government coffers. Alternatively, withdrawals could be based on historical averages for the 25 years immediately prior to the introduction of this policy, a broader representation of market trends.

Finance Canada took its time in reviewing our contentions–a response was six months in coming and, in the end, did nothing to address our concerns. The government argues that indexing would be too complex (not a good reason for failing to correct a bad policy); that lower withdrawal rates would serve only a minority of relatively wealthy seniors by allowing them to accumulate wealth (untrue, since the bigger the RRIF on the death of the RRIF holder or, in the case of a widow or widower, the surviving spouse, the better the government's chance of getting the top marginal tax); and that RRIF holders are required to take fewer retirement funds into income for tax purposes than people receiving annuities (true, but only because after-tax income is lower, partly because RRIF capital is being eroded). The arguments hold little water and CARP will continue to fight for fairer rules.

Earlier RRSP Conversion

The federal government's second attempt to get at the highly desirable tax revenues that lie dormant in the savings of older Canadians came in its 1996 budget, which reduced the age at which RRSP holders must convert their RRSPs from 71 to 69. The government had claimed in the past that its annual changes to rules regarding RRSP contributions were aimed only at high-income Canadians. Yet a reduction in the age limit for RRSP contributions affects everyone, wealthy or poor, and has an even greater impact on older people, who have less time to react and plan.

One of our reasons for writing this book is to help people who must convert their RRSPs this year and make decisions that will allow them to afford the most comfortable retirement possible. Not making any choice could lead to financial disaster, and none of us should lose a cent of our retirement savings to taxes simply because of a lack of knowledge or information. Our goals are also to increase awareness among the hundreds of thousands of RRSP holders who are within a mere five years of the conversion age of 69; to help them plan their affairs; and to help them choose their best investment options so that they will not suffer from a RRIF "crunch."

As you'll learn later in this book, RRIFs make sense for many people. However, annuities, which may be combined with RRIFs, can also be effective, and some of you will be more comfortable buying them. An annuity involves a one-time, irrevocable decision, and choosing one to match your situation is complicated and must be carefully evaluated, taking such factors as current interest rates into account (see Chapter 11, on annuities, for a guide to making the right choice).

From a broad perspective, we believe that the government's change to the cut-off age for RRSPs may be only the first step in a larger scheme. This is more than just a suspicion—it came directly from the horse's mouth.

Finance Minister Paul Martin's reaction to the question posed by co-author David Tafler more than five years ago, just after this crucial change was announced, remains telling. In March 1996, the minister addressed an audience of more than a thousand business people and Bay Street denizens at a combined Canadian and Empire Club luncheon in Toronto, his first stop on the post-budget speaking tour. During the question-and-answer period, David Tafler made his way to one of the microphones to ask the following question: "Your reasons for reducing the RRSP contribution limit from 71 to 69, and for freezing the maximum contribution at $13,500, sound plausible, but they sound plausible every year when you tinker with the retirement plan yet again. Will the government put a basic retirement plan in place and commit to keeping it the same for a period of 10 or 15 years?"

The question received a sustained round of applause, but Mr. Martin's answer did not: "That's a reasonable question and I'd like to give you a reasonable answer, but I can't." The comment (or non-comment) was ominous. Far from being carved in stone, the RRSP rules, which govern long-term retirement planning and saving, will continue to be subject to short-term political hocus-pocus. Now you see them, now you don't.

Later, in September 1997, Mr. Martin and several of his top advisors participated in a round-table workshop at the national office of CARP in Toronto. This time, in response to the same question, he gave a different answer. Still very much the politician, he now said he could not commit future finance ministers but that he, personally, would not lower the age limit again!

Despite the minister's effective evasion of the question, Ottawa may be beginning to realize that the 50-plus vote can pack a real punch: The last five federal budgets (1997 to 2001) have taken no backward steps in the retirement savings program, and some have even made improvements, such as allowing RRSP and RRIF assets to be passed on to dependent children and grandchildren and increasing the allowable foreign content in these plans.

Still, Ottawa's overall failure to maintain a stable set of RRSP rules fosters anxiety and uncertainty—scarcely the way to encourage or motivate people to plan and save for retirement.

Mr. Martin's refusal to commit to a longer-term RRSP arrangement may have a simple explanation: The government does not intend to stop at 69. It wants to go back to the well where it can save millions of dollars a year in tax deferrals now, without worrying about the tremendous problems this will cause for individuals and society as a whole in the future. In short, Ottawa is opting for short-term gain over long-term pain—but why should that come as a surprise where politicians are concerned?

At the same time, efforts to effect a particular change to RRSPs—one that could be of great benefit—have been futile so far. Annual contribution limits remain frozen at $13,500 until 2003, and will then increase to $14,500 in 2004 and $15,500 in 2005. So far, lobbying to increase these amounts has fallen on deaf ears, despite the fact that Members of Parliament voted themselves huge salary increases in June 2001. Apparently, the government doesn't feel we're entitled to the same opportunities for securing our retirements.

Based on the government's resolve on the issues of age and contribution limits, as well as other evidence, there may well be further reductions in the RRSP age limit, and RRSP contribution limits may not be adjusted upward.

If the rules continue to disregard the real situation of population aging, people will not be able to save properly for retirement. The result could be severe financial difficulties in the future. Then, the government of the day, pressured by the concern of the general public and aggressive aging baby boomers, will be charged with bailing us out.

Protecting Your Standard of Living

The overriding concern of Canadians as they get set to retire is whether they'll be able to maintain their standard of living without the benefit of their working-life income. As we have seen, while the government promoted its 1996 budget as containing no tax increases, in reality it made a variety of pension and retirement planning changes that resulted in a major tax grab from older Canadians. In particular, that budget contained a double whammy of concern to mature Canadians: The government cut benefits and moved to a means test on public retirement funding, and also reduced the flexibility of public retirement funds and the amount people could save on their own through registered plans. There is no question that these new policies translate directly into reduced incomes and a less comfortable lifestyle for many older and retired people.

The 1996 budget flagged a basic shift in policy concerning government pension payments. The proposed Seniors Benefit would have been based on income, and the deciding factor would have been family, rather than individual, income. As a result, fewer people would have collected this pension benefit, and less money would have been paid to many who do receive it.

Ottawa subsequently backed off on the Seniors Benefit, but the government's long-term taxation objectives remain in place.

In the coming years, we foresee changes to both the tax system and government benefit programs in Canada that will translate into even tougher times for seniors. That's why co-author David Tafler is involved with CARP. As the country's largest non-profit lobby group for people over 50, it brings many of these critical issues to the forefront, coordinates protest, and disseminates much-needed information.

Lobbying by CARP and other organizations may slow the damage and may even ensure that seniors as a group don't pay more than their fair share of government financial restructuring. However, the huge accumulated government debt, combined with demographic realities, makes this erosion inevitable. Governments, whatever their political bent, will be tempted to raise additional revenue and cut spending in this area even further to deal with what are perceived as more urgent priorities. As the age wave washes over this country, people will be moving into the seniors' age bracket in ever-increasing numbers, accelerating the costs of existing special benefits and social services.

The governments could deal with these demographic challenges in ways that don't bruise seniors, but they won't until enough pressure can be brought to bear.

This further underlines our point that those of us over the age of 50 will have to pay more attention to our financial affairs in the coming years to prevent our standard of living from being decimated. This book makes a number of suggestions to counterattack a potential decline in the lifestyle you worked hard for and deserve.

Life expectancy is higher than it's ever been, and while it's great that many of us will be living longer, we have to find ways to afford to enjoy those years without running any risk of outliving our capital. Many traditional investment strategies no longer make sense in today's environment. For example, interest rates—a sound foundation of many a retirement plan when they were high—touched their lowest levels in more than 40 years in 2001, and we expect them to stay that way for the foreseeable future. This means you can no longer simply buy interest-bearing securities and sit back and enjoy life. Adding to this climate of uncertainty is the fact that some of our venerable financial institutions—particularly life insurance companies—are either in trouble or have actually gone under.

This shifting political, economic, and business backdrop was very much taken into account in the writing of this book, with the goal of providing advice and suggestions on how to deal with each of these issues and how to plan in order to lessen their impact on your future—and on the futures of your children and grandchildren.

2

Cashing In Your RRSP

Not too many years ago, the letters *RRSP* almost always had to be followed by an explanatory phrase: Registered Retirement Savings Plan. Today, RRSPs have become so widely recognized as the most effective way for Canadians to save for retirement that the initials have been transformed into a household word—rare status for any financial term. The letters *RRIF* (Registered Retirement Income Fund) are fast attaining the status of everyday language as well.

Until recently, RRIFs, the best alternatives for most people when the law requires them to turn their RRSP savings into retirement income, have been of interest to only a small segment of Canada's population. However, changing government legislation and the growth of the aging population have resulted in increasing attention on both RRIFs and annuities, which are another common option for mature RRSPs.

If they are not looking seriously enough at RRIFs, RRSP holders in their mid-to-late 60s may be ignoring these vehicles at their own peril. Unfortunately, too many people are in just this boat.

In 1997, federal legislation reduced the age at which you must convert your RRSP to an income-producing vehicle, such as a RRIF. The mandatory deadline is December 31 of the year in which you turn 69; previously, the cut-off age for having an RRSP was 71.

Considering the fact that over one million people in Canada are between the ages of 65 and 69, a great number of Canadians will be trading in their RRSPs over the next few years.

In fact, the number of conversions will expand exponentially for many years to come, as the bulge of baby boomers continues to age. The reduction of the RRSP conversion age means that everyone under the age of 69 has been robbed of two full years of potential tax-sheltered RRSP contributions and earnings. We are all being forced to convert earlier, which means that, in effect, we will have fewer RRSP contributions and less tax-free compounding. As well, we have to start paying tax on the income from retirement savings at an earlier age. Depending on your finances when you reach age 69, this could translate into thousands of dollars in lost retirement savings, so thoughtful planning for converting your RRSPs is vital.

The RRSP Conversion Deadline: December 31

When the age for maturing our RRSPs was reduced, many Canadians were unaware of the change. In fact, a Scotiabank/Angus Reid Group study conducted at the time showed that more than 30 percent of Canadian RRSP holders between the ages of 50 and 70 knew nothing about the new rules. Even if that knowledge gap has closed somewhat recently, many people are still unaware of how the lower age limit will affect their retirement planning.

Most Canadian financial institutions keep close watch on RRSPs approaching maturity, and they do everything they can, through the mail and even by phone, to warn clients of this looming deadline—a far cry from the situation that existed when this book was first published in 1997. At that time, only a few firms provided a notification service for their clients. Now, some institutions even go so far as to switch maturing RRSPs into RRIFs automatically if they have not received instructions by a certain date, usually early November. This service is above and beyond the call of duty, and these institutions deserve a tip of the hat for saving unsuspecting clients from a terrible financial fate. If you or a younger member of your family is setting up an RRSP, we recommend using one of these "RRIF-default" institutions. Just ask the firm you deal with what its policy is. Better yet, get a confirmation in writing.

A lack of awareness about RRSP/RRIF rules can be dangerous. If you don't act by the December 31 deadline, you risk having your RRSP de-registered and all your assets treated by the Canada Customs and Revenue Agency (CCRA) as income earned in that year. That would mean paying tax on the money at your marginal rate (the rate you pay on the last dollar earned). In the most serious of cases, missing the deadline could mean losing as much as half of your retirement nest egg. This would be a devastating blow, especially for those whose RRSP makes up all or the bulk of their retirement savings.

A Crucial Financial Decision

Most of us remember the major financial commitments of our lives and often tell stories about them. When we were younger, it most likely involved the purchase of a car. As we moved ahead in the life cycle, it probably became buying a house. In retirement, by far the most important financial decision you make will be deciding what to do with your RRSP money.

The basic purpose of an RRSP, and the reason the government allowed you to make tax-sheltered contributions over the years and to earn all that income without having to pay tax, is to enable you to set up an ongoing stream of retirement income. Determining your RRSP conversion strategy may appear to be simple on the surface. But within the alternatives lies a myriad of choices and potential combinations of investments.

The right choices will lead to the most comfortable retirement your finances will allow. Poor decisions will not only affect you adversely for the rest of your life, they will also affect the lifestyles of your spouse and your heirs. We use the terms *spouse* and *surviving spouse* often in the text that follows. Before going any further, therefore, it is important to provide you with the method by which the CCRA determines who is and who is not a spouse. The term *spouse* applies to a legally married spouse. A common-law partner is defined as a person of the opposite sex who is living with you in a common-law relationship, and to whom any of the following applies. He or she

- is your child's natural or adoptive parent (legal or in fact); or

- has been living with you in such a relationship for at least 12 continuous months; or

- had lived with you previously in such a relationship for at least 12 continuous months and you are living together again (when you calculate the 12 continuous months, include any period of separation of less than 90 days).

An important development was the passage of Bill C-23 in the House of Commons in April 2000. Though it stops short of according the term *marriage* to partnerships of same-sex couples, it accords these unions the same rights and responsibilities—including the tax rules as they relate to RRIFs—that apply to common-law opposite-sex couples.

Three Conversion Options

Considering your options is the first step in converting your RRSP. There are three choices, but only two merit serious consideration:

1. Take the Money and Run Ottawa will gladly allow you to take all the cash in a lump sum. And why not? This step has the same effect as de-registering your RRSP. The full amount will become taxable as income in the year you cash in, and you will give a big chunk of your retirement savings back to the government, defeating the basic purpose of saving all those years. This option makes sense only if you have a relatively small RRSP and need the cash right away.

2. Buy an Annuity By purchasing an annuity, in essence, you trade your savings to a life insurance company in return for a guaranteed, fixed income, usually monthly, for life or for a set term. Some people like the simplicity and certainty of this option. There are no complicated investment or money management decisions involved; you get a regular monthly cheque and know exactly how much it will be. You certainly know where you stand. But this option also has drawbacks you should take into consideration.

Loss of control. Annuities are based on interest rates in effect at the time of purchase. Long-term rates are low at present and are likely to stay around these levels for some time. So be aware that if you buy an annuity at these rates, you'll be locking in a relatively low return for the rest of your life. In effect, you lose control of the money–if interest rates go up, you can't change your mind and switch to an annuity that pays a higher rate of interest. (Although some annuities allow you to switch or to commute your plan under certain conditions, the cost of doing so is considerable.)

Little or no estate value. If estate planning is important to you, this is certainly not the best way to leave something to your heirs. When you die, or when your surviving spouse dies in the case of a joint annuity, the insurance company that issued the annuity keeps all the proceeds and nothing is left for your estate. There are provisions for guarantee periods, which will keep payments coming for a time after death, but the cost is exacted in lower payments.

No inflation protection. Annuity payments almost always remain the same as long as you live, affording no protection against cost-of-living increases. Even if inflation remains at the current modest levels, you will lose buying power over time. You can opt for inflation-indexed annuities, but at a significant trade-off, in that your initial payments will be much lower.

3. Switch to a RRIF RRIFs have become the most popular RRSP conversion option in recent years for several reasons. A RRIF is essentially a continuation of your RRSP, providing the same tax sheltering of principal and earnings, with one key difference: Instead of making tax-deductible contributions, you have to take out a minimum taxable amount every year, based on your age. The withdrawal rate increases annually before levelling off at 20 percent for those who are 94 and older. The process is appealingly simple. You don't have to sell any of your RRSP holdings when you convert. Instead, you merely sign a simple form and the transfer is complete. Compare the advantages that RRIFs have over annuities:

Retention of control. You can hold the same securities in a RRIF as you can in an RRSP, including GICs, bonds, stocks, mutual funds, and the important allowance of 30 percent investment in foreign content. The money in a RRIF belongs to you, and you can take out more than the minimum if you wish. As well, you are not precluded from buying an annuity in the future, should higher interest rates make this a good option, or should you need other sources of income. So there is no need to rush into an annuity decision. As the minimum withdrawals increase with age, and since returns will differ based on investment choices, you may find that you're encroaching on your capital when you reach your mid-70s and certainly by the age of 80. It may then make sense to convert all or part of a remaining RRIF to a life annuity. Doing so may ensure that you have a regular income for as long as you live. As well, because you will be buying when you're older, your annuity payments will be higher.

Estate benefit. When you or your surviving spouse dies, any funds remaining in the RRIF become part of your estate. You will have the satisfaction and peace of mind of knowing that your spouse and other beneficiaries, rather than a huge, anonymous insurance company, will benefit from whatever is left.

Potential for inflation protection. The greatest advantage of a RRIF may be that your investments keep working for you, tax-sheltered, allowing your capital to continue to grow and providing protection against the ravages of inflation. This safety net is significant, although inflation may seem a minor concern these days. We have all seen the damage inflation has inflicted in the past, and there is no guarantee that it will not move back to higher levels down the road. Even if inflation rates remain relatively low, the buying power of your retirement income will be eroded. People can expect to live 20 to 30 years in retirement these days, and even a little inflation can hurt a lot over time.

Income Erosion

Details of a sobering projection can be found in the accompanying chart, "Income Erosion," which shows the effects of various inflation rates on income over the years. If you are retired and you need $40,000 in income to cover expenses, inflation averaging only 2 percent per year will mean that you will need almost $49,000 to pay the same expenses in just 10 years. In 20 years, at the same rate, you will need close to $60,000! If, heaven forbid, inflation were to average 5 percent over those 20 years, you would need more than $100,000 to pay the same bills. Where will that additional money come from if you are not earning income? Your RRIF can provide the relief you need. It can be set up to increase your cash flow each year to ensure that your needs are adequately covered. A well-balanced equity component in your RRIF will generally outpace any inflation drain on your purchasing power.

INCOME EROSION

The amount you would require to maintain $40,000 in purchasing power if inflation averages...

YEARS	2%	3%	4%	5%
0	$40,000	$40,000	$40,000	$ 40,000
5	44,163	46,371	48,666	51,040
10	48,760	53,757	59,210	65,160
20	59,438	72,244	87,645	106,120

Along with the potential for greater earnings with RRIFs comes the possibility that weak market conditions, low interest rates, or poor investment decisions will make your RRIF unprofitable. This could lead you to outlive your capital. However, thoughtful financial planning, often with the help of a professional advisor, can protect you against this eventuality.

Therefore, annuities and RRIFs have certain advantages and drawbacks that depend on many factors, including market conditions, your financial situation, and your choice of goals. Both options continue the tax-sheltered advantage of RRSPs in that you pay tax only when monies are paid out. Of course, there is no restriction on having both RRIFs and annuities, and such a combination may make sense in some cases.

3

What Are the Three Stages of RRIF Planning?

Before you can choose intelligently from the various products and services available to you, you will need to devote some time to understanding the RRIF planning process. What's more, if you plan to convert in the near future, you should undertake a number of strategies immediately. In fact, RRIF planning should start well before age 69, or at whatever age you plan to convert. We recommend you begin your planning four to five years before you intend to make the move. Of course, planning and management should continue long after—as long, indeed, as you have a RRIF.

Following is an outline of what we call the three stages of RRIFs—before, during, and after—and the steps you need to take during each phase in order to ensure RRIF success.

Stage One—Before: Planning to Convert Your RRSP

In your early- to mid-60s, and certainly before you reach 65, you should revise your financial plan to reflect retirement realities, consolidate your RRSPs, and reorganize your portfolio.

Come Up with a Financial Plan

If you don't have a financial plan to revise, don't panic—it is never too late to put one together. It is always best to work through this exercise with a qualified professional you trust. If such a person is not on your list of advisors, your first priority should be to find one as soon as possible.

At this stage, your plan should be based on answers to questions such as the following, plus others that are specific to your own circumstances. Here are the 10 key questions:

1. How much money will I need to pay my monthly bills?

2. What will my needs be in the future, taking into account such factors as inflation, increased health care costs, and preferred lifestyle?

3. What one-time cash expenditures would I like to make? A special trip? A new car? A golf club membership?

4. Where do I want to live? In my present house? In a retirement community? Outside the country?

5. How much travelling do I want to do?

6. What will my spouse and family's needs be in the event of my death?

7. How much would I like to leave to my beneficiaries?

8. What is a realistic or even conservative estimate of all my sources of retirement income?

9. What is my investment personality? What risks am I prepared to take in order to achieve better returns?

10. Am I in good health, and is there a history of long life expectancy in my family?

With this picture clearly in place, your financial plan becomes a simple exercise in budgeting. If you have insufficient income to achieve your goals, it is best to know now. This way, you can cut back on expenses or perhaps work with your financial advisor to adjust your investment mix in order to increase future income.

Consolidate Your RRSPs

Many of us have many RRSPs, set up with various companies or organizations over the years for different reasons and during changing economic climates. Spreading out your investments in this way can be convenient and prudent when you are saving for retirement. However, as you get closer to the conversion age limit, or to the date you wish to start drawing on your RRSP funds, it makes sense to consolidate them into one or two plans, ideally with the institution that will hold your RRIF. It is wise to do so because each RRIF must make a minimum annual payment—you cannot simply add up your

RRIF totals and take the minimum annual payment any way you wish. If you fail to consolidate your RRSPs, you could end up with 10 or even 20 monthly payments, a major headache from both bookkeeping and portfolio management points of view.

Adjust Your Portfolio

Working with your advisor, you should be adjusting your portfolio now to get the right mix of growth and income securities. It is probably a good idea to reduce holdings in more volatile mutual funds, replacing them, for example, with balanced mutual funds or blue-chip dividend-paying stocks.

You should also make sure the money in your RRIF is invested so that it will generate the cash flow you need when payouts begin. This can be a challenge in times of low interest rates. You may include GICs in a RRIF, but in selecting them you should ensure that they will provide steady income, and you should stagger maturities for maximum flexibility. For example, if you were to put all your money into five-year compounding GICs, you would find yourself with substantial assets but no income. A conservative, higher-return alternative to GICs is Government of Canada stripped bonds with staggered maturities, which will ensure that cash is flowing into the plan on a regular basis. This approach enables you to take advantage of higher long-term rates. However, it should be used with great caution when interest rates are low because stripped bonds lock in current rates until maturity.

Other favourite RRIF investments for generating cash flow are bonds and bond funds, mortgage funds, money market funds, mortgage-backed securities, Canada Savings Bonds, and Treasury bills. However, these will generate below-average cash flow during low-interest-rate periods and you may wish to explore some higher-yielding (but riskier) options to boost returns. We will discuss some of these later in the book. You will need a self-directed RRIF to hold most of these securities.

Ideally, when you convert your RRSP to a RRIF, you should not tackle the task of rearranging your portfolio at the same time. The conversion should be a smooth, simple change over, requiring nothing more than signing a single form. If you delay rearranging your portfolio until the deadline, you may find yourself with too little time to arrange your portfolio for maximum benefit, as the transfer can take a month or more if you set up your RRIF at a company other than the one that holds your RRSPs.

The process of setting up your portfolio also involves arranging GIC maturity dates to ensure an orderly transition. For example, if you are 65, should you put your money into a five-year GIC? Doing so would take you over the age 69 conversion deadline. Should you limit your GICs at this stage to only four years and under? The answer depends on personal circumstances and on your financial institutions—yet another reason why you need a financial plan and the help of an advisor who is familiar with your entire financial situation.

S P E C I A L   T I P

Open a Small RRIF Early. The first $1,000 of pension income receives a tax advantage, and payments from a RRIF qualify for the pension tax credit if you are 65 or older. Set up a small RRIF early to generate just enough income to allow you to take advantage of this credit. Keep the rest of your money in an RRSP until you have to convert.

Stage Two—During: Switching to a RRIF

If you are at the age at which you must convert your RRSP, or you wish to do so because you need the cash flow and have decided to go the RRIF route, you are moving from the savings phase to the income phase of retirement planning. This stage requires new strategies. Your goals are now to keep taxes at a minimum, to preserve capital, and to ensure that the income from the RRIF fits your spending needs. Following are some suggestions for getting the most out of your retirement savings and for maximizing your income in the years ahead, along with a list of things to do before December 31.

Fill Up That RRSP—Before December 31

The year in which you convert is your last chance to build your retirement nest egg, so make the most of it. Contribute as much as you can to your RRSP, even if you have to borrow to do so. Beware: Your RRSP deadline in your final year is December 31. Most people are accustomed to waiting until the regular deadline of March 1 of the following year, but if you go beyond the end of the year in this case, the door to contributions will be closed forever.

If you have any unused room for contributions carried forward from past years (you can now go all the way back to the 1991 tax year), this is the time to take advantage of them—use it or lose it. Combined with your regular entitlement, the carry-forward credits could add up to a significant last-time RRSP contribution and make an important difference in your retirement income.

Spousal contributions can continue after your 69th year if you have earned-income and if your spouse is 69 or younger.

Remember that you do not have to wind up your RRSP until December 31 of the year you turn 69. If you don't need income from your plan right away, delay shifting the funds into a RRIF until the summer or fall of the year in which you turn 69. As we described above, the only exception to this rule of thumb is opening a small RRIF to take advantage of the pension credit.

The objective is to tax shelter as much capital as possible for as long as you can. RRIFs are tax-sheltered as well, but once the first payment is made, money begins to flow out annually. Not only do you have to pay tax on those withdrawals, but they reduce the amount you have to invest.

Here's an example: You retire at 65. You have $250,000 in your RRSP, but you also have other sources of retirement income for at least the first few years. If you leave the money in your RRSP as long as you can, until age 69, and if you earn 7 percent per year, your capital will grow to almost $330,000, a tax-free increase of more than 30 percent in only four years. If you could increase that annual return to 9 percent, your capital would grow to almost $360,000, or more than 40 percent.

Don't Wait Too Long

It's likely that most of the financial advice you have read or received has urged you to wait until the very last minute before converting your RRSP to take full advantage of contributions and tax sheltering. But don't take the message literally—the last minute does not mean midnight on December 31!

Initiating a switch from an RRSP to a RRIF should be done no later than the fall. If you have to wait until the end of the year to make your final RRSP contribution, switch everything else in your plan to a RRIF and keep the RRSP open until you make the final contribution.

There's usually a run on demand for investment advice and financial services toward the end of the year because most people, despite the above recommendation, will leave their RRIF decisions to the last minute. Remember that, in general, investment advisors will have less time to pay attention to your affairs in December than they would earlier in the year. Also, if you transfer your holdings from one institution to another, you may need to allow several months for processing the move.

Choose the Right RRIF

The type of RRIF you choose can make a tremendous difference in the money it earns, yet many people convert without knowing what kind of RRIF they have, or even that there are various types. There are five basic types of plans. Here's how they work:

Savings This is the simplest and safest type of RRIF. It functions much like a bank deposit account. If your financial institution has deposit insurance, and most do, up to $60,000 is protected. However, because these RRIFs pay the lowest interest rates, they are the least desirable type to purchase.

Guaranteed Investment Certificates (GICs) This form of RRIF is also simple and is covered by the same deposit insurance, but it pays a better rate of interest than savings RRIFs. GIC-based RRIFs continue to be the most popular choice for conversions despite these inherent problems: They are inflexible, your money is locked in until maturity, and they are vulnerable to both inflation and interest-rate changes.

The Canada RRIF This is a no-fee RRIF that is sponsored by the Government of Canada. It is designed specifically for holding Canada Premium Bonds and Canada Savings Bonds.

Mutual Fund RRIFs Based on mutual fund investments, these RRIFs come in a wide range of options, with professional money managers making all the investment decisions. A properly selected mutual fund plan has more growth potential than a savings or GIC-based RRIF. It also provides the opportunity for diversification, as you spread your RRIF investment over a wide number of securities. The risk is higher, however, and mutual fund plans are not covered by deposit insurance.

Self-directed RRIFs Here is where you make all the decisions. The plan is really only a shell, holding whatever qualified investments you wish–GICs, bonds, mutual funds, stocks, etc. You are in full control, and a properly managed, self-directed plan, especially with professional input, can have far greater growth potential than any other type of RRIF. On the other hand, if you make poor decisions, you will diminish your own retirement income.

Of course, you can hold more than one RRIF and have more than one type of plan, but, as pointed out earlier, each RRIF has to make its own minimum annual payment, and keeping track of more than one or two can turn out to be a big administrative headache.

Build a Balanced Portfolio

Unlike in the early planning scenario, there is no need to restructure your investment portfolio when you move from an RRSP to a RRIF, unless your plan will not generate the cash flow you need or are required to take out under the minimum withdrawal rules. If your RRSP is not well diversified, opening a RRIF provides you with the chance to build a better, more balanced portfolio. Diversification through asset classes and categories spreads your risk and increases return on your investments.

Your needs will stay very much the same after December 31, so it makes sense to apply some of the old-fashioned chestnuts of financial wisdom. For instance, know that moving out of mutual funds into GICs does not make sense in today's retirement realities—many of us will likely live 20 to 30 years into retirement and will need growth securities in our RRIFs to protect capital and stay ahead of cost-of-living increases.

The ideal scenario would be to have the growth portion of your RRIF cover at least the required minimum annual withdrawal (you can arrange to make the mandatory withdrawals by setting up a systematic withdrawal plan). Because the minimum payouts climb, this goal becomes more difficult to achieve as you grow older, but it provides an interesting challenge for your investment advisor!

Delay the Payments

If you establish a RRIF in any given year, you are not required to take the minimum annual payment until December 31 of the following year. Take full advantage of this grace period and wait as long as you can before taking the money. This delay allows your capital to grow tax-free for as long as possible and puts off any tax payments.

Pick the Right Withdrawal Formula

Many people believe that RRIF payments are fixed by a federal government schedule, yet this could not be further from the truth. As explained earlier, the Canada Customs and Revenue Agency requires that a minimum amount be withdrawn each year. But as long as you meet that level, the actual amount of the payments is completely up to you.

You can tailor a withdrawal formula to suit your personal needs, and you can alter it in any way later on. For example, some people opt to take larger payments as soon as they retire so they can travel, buy a cottage or a Sunbelt second home, or spend more time golfing while they're in good health. Others decide to keep to the minimum withdrawals in those early years, leaving more in the plan to take care of medical or personal-care expenses that may arise in later years. Your situation and priorities will determine which strategy is right for you.

The amount of income you receive and the length of time the RRIF will maintain payments can vary considerably, depending on whether you choose to stick to the minimums or to increase your withdrawal rates over the years. Here again is where your trusted financial advisor can be a big help in selecting the formula that is right for you.

Take the Younger Age

The rules allow you to use your spouse's age as the base for your minimum withdrawals. If your spouse is younger and you do not need the income from your RRIF immediately, base the minimum payments on his or her age rather than on your own. The advantage can be significant, so use it if you can. The reason is obvious—the older you are, the greater the percentage that must be withdrawn from your RRIF each year. Using your younger spouse's age reduces the minimum amount, which means you will pay less tax. You can switch to using your spouse's age later, but it is much easier to do so when first opening a RRIF. If you find you need more money, you may increase the payments at a later date. This also allows more capital to remain sheltered and grow tax-free. There is no limitation on how young a spouse can be.

With the February 1992 budget, the federal government changed the rules so that RRIFs could extend throughout your lifetime, rather than the previous cutoff at the age of 90. This change necessitated creating two categories of RRIFs: those established before December 31, 1992, called "qualifying" RRIFs, and those established after January 1, 1993, called "non-qualifying" RRIFs. Qualifying RRIFs are subject to the old minimum withdrawal rates until age 78, when they become identical to the new non-qualifying rates. The table of minimum withdrawals for both classes of RRIFs appears on page 21.

SPECIAL TIP

The new rates translate into much higher minimums from the ages of 71 through 77. So if you have an old-rule RRIF, do not add any new RRSP funds to it. Doing so will make it ineligible for the lower rates.

MINIMUM RRIF WITHDRAWAL RATES*

AGE	OLD RULES	NEW RULES	AGE	OLD RULES	NEW RULES
69	4.76	4.76	82	9.27	9.27
70	5.00	5.00	83	9.58	9.58
71	5.26	7.38	84	9.93	9.93
72	5.56	7.48	85	10.33	10.33
73	5.88	7.59	86	10.97	10.97
74	6.25	7.71	87	11.33	11.33
75	6.67	7.85	88	11.96	11.96
76	7.14	7.99	89	12.71	12.71
77	7.69	8.15	90	13.62	13.62
78	8.33	8.33	91	14.73	14.73
79	8.53	8.53	92	16.12	16.12
80	8.75	8.75	93	17.92	17.92
81	8.99	8.99	94 and over	20.00	20.00

* Percentage of RRIF assets as of January 1 each year

Keep Extras Below $5,000

If you need a large sum from your RRIF for a special purpose such as buying a car, putting a down payment on a cottage, taking a trip around the world, or paying a club membership, try to take it out in increments of less than $5,000. In this way, you will pay the minimum amount of withholding tax, which is applied based on the formula in the table below. Remember, this is only a deferral of tax. The money is better off in your pocket for now, of course, but try to save some of it for when the tax payments come due.

You can increase RRIF withdrawals above the minimum whenever you wish, but exercise as much restraint as possible because larger withdrawals will shorten the life of your RRIF.

If you need money, cash in your non-registered investments first and keep your tax-sheltered RRIF money intact as long as possible.

WITHHOLDING TAX RATES ON RRIF WITHDRAWALS

WITHDRAWAL	TAX WITHHELD (CANADA, EXCEPT QUEBEC)	QUEBEC ONLY
Up to $5,000	10%	25%
Over $5,000, less than $15,000	20%	33%
Over $15,000	30%	38%

Stage Three—After: Keeping Your RRIF Alive and Well

After your reach age 69, investment strategy becomes at least as important for RRIFs as it was for RRSPs and, in some circumstances, is even more important. You should make sure your portfolio is broadly diversified and review your asset mix at least once a year. You will need to ensure, as well, that you have the necessary income to make the required minimum annual withdrawal. And, in your late 70s or early 80s, it could make sense to buy an annuity, depending on your circumstances. If you have not yet done so, now is the time for proper estate planning and the execution of a will. This will ensure that whatever remains of your retirement savings after you die will pass to your heirs according to your wishes–without delay or unnecessary tax payments.

RRIF Fees Revisited

The federal government has done a few flip-flops on the issue of how to pay RRIF (or RRSP) fees for administration, investment management, and investment counselling. As it stands, there are no tax implications if you pay any of these fees inside your plan. Fees paid inside the plan will not be included in your income, and fees paid outside the plan will not count as a contribution to the plan. Previously, fees for management or advice had to be paid from within the plan. So what should you do? Pay all such fees from outside your RRIF or RRSP if you have the cash to do so. Paying them from within the plan reduces its value over time. This is certainly the case for individuals with high net worth. While there is little advantage to paying these fees from inside any registered plan, it is a good option for those RRIF holders who have no other outside income.

Unfortunately, this policy change did not reverse the elimination of what was once a decent tax break. Such fees were tax-deductible before the 1996 budget, but that document decreed that this would no longer be the case. And that's too bad. For a $300,000 RRIF with an annual fee of 1.30 percent, for example, taxable income would have been reduced by $3,900, a substantial advantage for many people.

RRIF Assets Can Now Be Passed On

The 1999 federal budget made a dramatic change with regard to how RRSP and RRIF assets can be passed on at the time of your death.

Financially dependent children or grandchildren are now considered qualified beneficiaries and may inherit assets from RRSPs and RRIFs, even if there is a surviving spouse. Previously, a tax-free transfer of such assets on death could be made only to a surviving spouse. Now they can pass directly to dependent children or grandchildren and would be included in their income for tax purposes, meaning that, in most cases, the tax payable will be substantially less. This new rule applies in cases of deaths that occurred after 1998, but may also be applied retroactively to 1995, if the deceased's estate and beneficiaries wish to do so. In instances where a spouse is not in need of the monies, this could represent an effective estate planning strategy for reducing taxes.

4

WHAT ARE LIFs AND LRIFs?

The basic purpose of an RRSP is to help you accumulate retirement savings, but most plans are flexible in that you can withdraw any or all of the money you have saved, if and when you choose to do so. The catch, of course, is that withdrawals will be taxable as income in that year, but the main thing is that the plan is liquid–the cash is available to you.

Not so, however, with money that originates from a pension fund. When a person leaves an employer, he or she may have the option of transferring accumulated pension plan assets to a locked-in RRSP or a locked-in retirement account, called a LIRA. These are essentially the same thing but may have different names depending on the province. For purposes of this publication, we'll refer to them as LIRAs.

In the past, these funds were exactly what their names imply–they were locked in and could not be withdrawn until the prescribed age for any purpose, not even financial disaster. At retirement, LIRAs retain their own special features. For one thing, unlike a regular RRSP, there's generally no cash-out option for locked-in plans. In fact, the previous rules governing locked-in plans were overly restrictive.

However, the money in these plans has become more accessible in recent years. Some provinces–including Ontario, which introduced new legislation in March 2000–even allow individuals age 55 and over to withdraw or transfer small balances in locked-in plans to an RRSP or RRIF. The total in all locked-in accounts must be less than 40 percent of the "Year's Maximum Pensionable Earnings," a term used by the Canada Pension Plan to refer to the average earnings on which CPP contributions and benefits are based. For 2001, for example, the YMPE was $38,300, so eligible locked-in balances that would qualify for the small-account withdrawal would be a little over $15,000.

A more important development pertains to the income vehicle to which the locked-in plan can be converted. Prior to 1991, the only option you had was to buy a life annuity, which meant giving up control of your money to an insurance company in return for a guaranteed monthly cheque. Now, however, attractive alternatives are available to many Canadians in the form of Life Income Funds (LIFs) and Locked-in Retirement Income Funds (LRIFs), which are essentially types of RRIFs, each with special features and limitations. The important distinction is that LIFs and LRIFs are governed by provincial pension regulations, while RRIFs fall under the federal *Income Tax Act*.

Among the key advantages is the fact that LIFs and LRIFs offer estate-planning benefits that annuities do not have. The assets of the plan form part of your estate, as with a RRIF, and you can designate a beneficiary. You can also set up a LIF or LRIF with the money from your company pension plan if, and only if, the plan has been specifically amended for that purpose. It's well worth a call to the firm's human resources department to find out if you are eligible. Following is a description of how these plans work.

Life Income Funds (LIFs)

LIFs differ from RRIFs in three basic ways. The first difference is that LIF is a pension term governed by provincial pension legislation, whereas RRIF rules are set by the federal government in the Income Tax Act. This means that LIF regulations can differ from province to province.

There is a trend toward harmonizing pension rules across the country but it has been a slow one. The changes to Ontario's *Pensions Benefits Act* in March 2000, for example, mean that holders of locked-in plans in that province can now access the funds in pension plans and locked-in accounts for reasons of financial hardship or shortened life expectancy. Other provinces with similar rules include British Columbia, Alberta, Saskatchewan, Manitoba, and Quebec.

With a LIF, you must withdraw a minimum amount each year, based on the same formula as is used for RRIFs, but you may not base your withdrawals on the age of your younger spouse as you may with a RRIF. Also, with LIFs, there is an annual ceiling on how much you can take out, unlike RRIFs, which have no maximum. The reason for imposing maximum limits on annual payouts from LIFs and LRIFs is simple: It's a way to ensure that the LIF or LRIF provides income over your retirement lifetime. The accompanying table shows the Ontario scale as it applied for 2002.

MAXIMUM ANNUAL WITHDRAWAL FOR AN ONTARIO LIFE INCOME FUND (2002)

AGE ON JANUARY 1	MAXIMUM % WITHDRAWAL*
48	6.19655
49	6.23197
50	6.26996
51	6.31073
52	6.35454
53	6.40164
54	6.45234
55	6.50697
56	6.56589
57	6.62952
58	6.69833
59	6.77285
60	6.85367
61	6.94147
62	7.03703
63	7.14124
64	7.25513
65	7.37988
66	7.51689
67	7.66778
68	7.83449
69	8.01930
70	8.22496
71	8.45480
72	8.71288
73	9.00423
74	9.33511
75	9.71347
76	10.14952
77	10.65661
78	11.25255
79	11.96160

*Percentage of LIF balance on January 1 each year

As you can see from the table, the restrictions are pretty tight. You can never withdraw more than about 12 percent of the value of your plan in any given year. And the margin between the minimum and maximum withdrawal rates is very small. For example, at age 71, the minimum withdrawal from a LIF is 7.38 percent, while the maximum is set at 8.45 percent. That's a range of just over one percentage point. On a $100,000 LIF, that's a margin of about $1,070.

LIFs are available in most of the country, with minor variations in rules among the provinces and territories. In Newfoundland and Labrador, Nova Scotia, Ontario, Manitoba, Saskatchewan, and B.C., you must be 55 or older to set up a LIF. New Brunswick, Quebec, and Alberta have no age limit.

A note on LIF withdrawals: If you are thinking of moving a LIF from one company to another, effectively opening a new LIF, be aware of rules that could prevent you from withdrawing additional money from the LIF after you've made the transfer. In B.C., for example, you may not withdraw money from the new LIF in the first year it's open unless you have not made the mandatory minimum withdrawal. An easy way around this restriction is to withdraw as much as you wish to (for the year) *before* making the transfer.

Life Retirement Income Funds (LRIFs)

Another form of retirement income plan, a Life Retirement Income Fund (LRIF), is available in Alberta, Saskatchewan, Manitoba, Ontario, and Newfoundland and Labrador. LRIFs are similar to LIFs, but there are some key differences that make LRIFs more attractive.

One major difference is that, instead of being based on age and interest rates, the maximum withdrawal amount for LRIFs can be determined in a number of ways according to specific pension legislation. For instance, retirees in Ontario may base their withdrawals on their funds' previous year's investment return. Another important difference is that LRIF holders may carry unused withdrawal room forward from one year to the next.

Perhaps the biggest argument for an LRIF over a LIF is the fact that LRIFs allow plan holders to continue receiving payments until death, instead of having to buy a lifetime annuity upon turning 80. These features give LRIF holders greater flexibility and control over their precious retirement savings.

For the most part, whether you have the option of an LRIF depends on pension legislation, which tends to be provincial. It's an unfair situation that's slowly changing. Bowing to pressure from CARP (Canada's Association for the Fifty-Plus) and other groups, in the spring of 2000, Ontario introduced the LRIF option, and hopes are that more provincial pension legislators will adopt this policy in the near future. We can understand not allowing you to take the cash outright—after all, the money did originate from a pension plan—but why should you be forced to buy an annuity if you don't want to?

If your province does not allow LRIFs as an income option, it is generally best to wait until the maturity deadline of 80 years of age before buying your life annuity with the remaining proceeds of your LIF. Doing so allows you to take full advantage of your LIF's tax-sheltering benefits and will give you higher annuity payments when you do convert.

However, you may purchase an annuity at any time before the deadline, which gives you some room to manoeuvre with regard to interest rates. As we stressed earlier, annuities are fixed according to rates prevailing at the time of purchase, so you might consider making the move if interest rates climb when you are in your late 70s.

As with RRIFs, the greater control and flexibility of LIFs and LRIFs compared to annuities will make them increasingly popular with the growing number of Canadians moving into retirement in the years to come.

In the meantime, if you live in a province in which this option is not allowed, you can help by writing your provincial government. Every letter requesting greater flexibility will contribute to the overall effort.

5

How to Manage Your RRIF/LIF

It would be very nice if all you had to do was go through the paperwork of opening your RRIF or LIF and then forget about it. And you can do it that way if you really want to. However, if you're going to get the best results from your plan with the least amount of cost, you have to spend at least a little time managing it properly. In this chapter, you'll find some important tips and suggestions on how to do that.

The starting point is to ensure that the investments you hold in your RRIF are fully qualified from a legal point of view. If they're not, it will cost you money in unnecessary penalties.

Qualified Investments

Note that many qualified investments can be held only in a self-directed RRIF. Here's a list of what the federal government considers to be qualified RRIF holdings. As a general rule, if it's okay for a RRIF, it's also allowed in a LIF.

Agricultural Guaranteed Investment Certificates (AgGICs) These are offered to residents of rural Ontario through credit unions and caisses populaires. All invested money is used under Ontario's Rural Loan Pool Program for loans to farmers for agricultural financing. Interest rates are comparable to those paid for regular GICs.

Bankers' Acceptances These are short-term notes issued by financial institutions. They don't pay a high rate of return, but they are safe and are a good source of cash flow.

Call Options These options give you the right to purchase a security at a predetermined price for a certain period of time. They may be held in RRIFs provided they're listed on a recognized Canadian stock exchange. The option must allow you to acquire stocks or bonds that are qualified investments in their own right. This distinction, made by Ottawa, rules out holding commodity options in your RRIF (if you were willing to accept that degree of risk), since commodities themselves are not qualified investments. (See also Covered Call Options.)

Canada Premium Bonds Formerly known as Canada RRSP Bonds, these securities were introduced in 1997. They are designed specifically for registered plans and are backed by the federal government.

Canada Savings Bonds The interest rate is a little lower than for Premium Bonds, but CSBs have an advantage in terms of liquidity since they can be cashed any time.

Cash (Canadian) As long as the money is legal tender in Canada, it's okay. But direct cash deposits in a foreign currency, including U.S. dollars, may not be held in a RRIF. Any such contributions must be immediately converted to Canadian dollars.

Corporate Bonds (Canadian) Any debt securities (bonds, debentures, etc.) issued by a Canadian company with shares listed on a recognized stock exchange are eligible. This extends to securities of subsidiary companies. Debt securities issued by other Canadian companies, co-ops, and credit unions may also be eligible if certain conditions are met. In such cases, you should consult a tax expert who can assess the particular security you're considering.

Corporate Bonds (Foreign) Bonds and debentures of companies whose stock trades on an eligible foreign stock exchange may be held in RRIFs as foreign content.

Covered Call Options These are a particular type of call option, sometimes used by RRIF holders to generate additional revenue. The strategy involves selling options on shares you already own within the RRIF. The premiums received from selling the options add to the RRIF's cash flow and reduce the net price paid for the stock. However, some financial institutions do not permit such transactions within their self-directed plans because of the administrative problems they present, even though the Canada Customs and Revenue Agency says they're okay. So, if you want to use a covered call strategy, make sure the ground rules governing your self-directed plan will allow it.

Credit Union Shares Shares or similar interests in a credit union may be held in a RRIF.

Government Bonds (Canadian) These include all debt obligations (bonds, debentures, notes, mortgages, etc.) issued by a Canadian government or one of its agencies. This brings in the federal government, provincial governments, municipalities, Crown corporations (defined as at least 90 percent government owned), as well as educational institutions and hospitals if the security has a provincial guarantee.

SPECIAL TIP

Although foreign cash may not be held in a RRIF, you are allowed to hold qualifying Canadian bonds denominated in foreign currency. For example, the federal government often issues bonds denominated in Japanese yen, U.S. dollars, or other currencies. These are RRIF-eligible. Some mutual fund managers have used this rule to create fully RRIF-eligible bond funds that are partially or completely denominated in foreign currencies.

Government Bonds (Foreign) Only foreign government bonds with an "investment grade" rating from a recognized bond rating service are allowed. This means you cannot hold emerging market debt from economically unstable countries directly in your plan, although you may hold mutual funds that invest in them. For example, State of Israel bonds are often offered to Canadian investors. They have a lower safety rating than bonds issued by the Canadian or U.S. government, but the Israeli government has an excellent debt management record. However, continuing tensions in the Middle East are a risk factor associated with these bonds that needs to be taken into account. Most Israel bonds are denominated in U.S. dollars.

Guaranteed Investment Certificates (Canadian Currency) GICs are the most popular form of RRIF investment, although mutual funds are catching up fast. GICs are fully RRIF-eligible as long as they are issued by a Canadian financial institution.

Guaranteed Investment Certificates (Foreign Currency) GICs issued by Canadian banks, credit unions, and trust companies are fully eligible for RRIFs, no matter what their currency of denomination. So you can fill your plan with U.S.-dollar GICs (or GICs in any other currency, if you can find them).

i60 Units These index participation units track the performance of the S&P/TSE 60 Index. They trade on the TSE and are fully eligible for RRIFs. The old TIPS (Toronto Index Participation Shares) were merged into the i60s in early 2000.

International Bonds Bonds, debentures, and notes issued or guaranteed by a number of international banking organizations may be held in a RRIF without affecting the foreign property limit. These organizations include the International Bank for Reconstruction and Development (better known as the World Bank), the International Finance Corporation, the Inter-American Development Bank, the Asian Development Bank, and the Caribbean Development Bank.

Labour-Sponsored Venture Capital Funds These are investment funds—ostensibly sponsored by trade unions—that were created to raise capital for fledgling businesses. Money invested in such funds is eligible for tax concessions from the federal government and some provinces. Indeed, this is one of the main attractions of these funds for RRSP investors. However, there are some conditions with respect to RRIFs.

For one thing, the tax credits that accompany a labour-fund investment come with a minimum holding period of eight years—if you sell the investment before this time is up, the tax credit(s) will be clawed back by the government(s). Since RRIFs must pay out a set minimum annually, being locked in to any investment could create a problem.

Although you may roll labour fund units from an RRSP to a RRIF, a RRIF can't directly buy a labour fund. Technically, provincial rules will determine whether a RRIF may purchase a provincially sponsored labour fund but, even so, you won't be entitled to the tax credit because another part of the law says that RRIFs do not qualify for these credits.

Limited Partnership Units Until recently, these units counted against the foreign content of your plan if you held them in a RRIF, even if the company involved was 100 percent Canadian. Now, designated limited partnerships are RRIF-eligible as Canadian content under the following conditions: Principal activities of the LP must be based in Canada, and at least 80 percent of the full-time employees of the partnership must be employed in Canada. This new rule exempting qualified LPs from foreign-property status was passed in May 2000, retroactive to 1998. Among the largest eligible limited partnerships is the Mackenzie Master Partnership, which trades on the Toronto Stock Exchange.

Manitoba Rural Development Bonds These bonds are issued by the Government of Manitoba to encourage investment in rural areas of the province. Those purchased after July 1991 are eligible for inclusion in self-directed RRIFs.

Mortgages Mortgages on Canadian real estate are eligible RRIF investments. This includes your personal mortgage or mortgages on real estate owned by members of your family. Note that there is nothing in the rules that requires the investment to be a first mortgage, so second and third mortgages may also be held in your RRIF. Mortgage mutual funds are also eligible, as are shares in a mortgage investment corporation (MIC) that is listed on a stock exchange.

Mutual Funds Mutual funds that invest primarily in qualified RRIF investments are eligible in their own right. Funds that invest mainly in foreign securities will be limited by the foreign property rules. Before proceeding, check with the company selling the fund to determine if it is subject to these limitations. Real estate mutual funds (both open-end and closed-end) are RRIF-eligible, even though you're not allowed to hold real estate directly. The same principle applies to precious metals—you may hold mutual funds that invest in gold, but not gold itself.

Provincial Savings Bonds Several provinces, including British Columbia, Ontario, and Quebec, issue their own savings bonds. These securities may be held in self-directed RRIFs.

Rights Rights allow the holder to purchase a security at a set price within a specified time. As long as the rights relate to a security that in itself qualifies for a RRIF, they are eligible.

Royalty Trust Units Royalty trust units that trade on a recognized Canadian stock exchange and derive their value solely from Canadian resource properties are eligible RRIF investments.

Savings Certificates These are term deposits issued by some Canadian financial institutions (mainly smaller trust companies) that are cashable at any time. They may also be called cashable GICs. They are fully RRIF-eligible.

Small Businesses Shares in small businesses, including limited partnership interests, are allowed as long as a number of conditions are met. If you're interested in investing in a small business, consult a tax expert.

SPDRs (Standard & Poor's Depositary Receipts) Basket products for international investing, SPDRs are index participation units based on the S&P 500 Composite Index. They are RRIF-eligible as foreign content.

Stocks (Canadian) Common or preferred stocks listed on any Canadian exchange are fully eligible for RRIFs. Shares of any Canadian "public corporation" recognized by the *Income Tax Act* are also eligible. This includes shares in public companies that trade on Canada's newest stock exchange, CDNX, which was formed in 1999 by the merger of the Alberta and Vancouver Exchanges. CDNX lists primarily junior companies and includes the over-the-counter stocks of the Canadian Dealing Network, an over-the-counter market. If you're not sure whether a particular company qualifies, check with a tax expert before acquiring shares for your RRIF.

Stocks (Foreign) Shares in foreign companies traded on recognized stock exchanges may be included in your RRIF under the foreign-property rule. The recognized exchanges include a number in the United States (some you've probably never heard of): American, Boston, Cincinnati, Detroit, Mid-West, New York, Pacific Coast, Pittsburgh, Salt Lake, Spokane, and Washington. Stocks traded through the Philadelphia-Baltimore-Chicago Board of Trade and on the Nasdaq Stock Market—once a strictly over-the-counter market but now well known for its technology components—are also eligible. Overseas exchanges that qualify include the Amsterdam, Australia, Brussels, Copenhagen, Frankfurt, Helsinki, Hong Kong, Johannesburg, London, Madrid, Mexico City, Milan, New Zealand, Oslo, Paris, Singapore, Stockholm, Tel Aviv, Tokyo, Vienna, and Zurich exchanges.

Strip Bonds These bonds are eligible for RRIFs as long as the underlying debt security qualifies. However, since they do not provide any cash flow, they're generally better suited to RRSPs, although they could be used in a RRIF if maturities are staggered.

Term Deposits The definition of a term deposit is muddy. Some financial institutions allow early redemption of term deposits, with a penalty, but not of GICs. Others refer to certificates with a maturity date of less than a year as term deposits, while those maturing in one to five years are GICs. Still others use the terms interchangeably. Regardless of the definition (which you should inquire about before you invest), term deposits are fully RRIF-eligible as long as they're issued by a Canadian financial institution.

Treasury Bills These may be issued by the federal or provincial governments and are fully RRIF-eligible.

Warrants Like rights, warrants allow the holder to buy a security at a set price within a fixed time period. They are eligible for RRIFs as long as they meet the conditions outlined under Rights.

Non-Qualified Investments

The list of investments that do not qualify for RRIFs is fairly short. But pay close attention to it because the penalties for holding non-qualified investments in your RRIF can be costly. The government will hit you in three ways:

1. In the year you buy a non-qualified investment for your plan, your taxable income will be increased by the price you paid for it. For example, if you purchased a $5,000 gold bar (a non-qualified investment) for your RRIF in 2001, that amount would be added to your taxable income for the year. If you sold the bar in 2002, you could claim an offsetting deduction of $5,000 or the sale price of the gold, whichever was less.

2. Income or capital gains earned by non-qualified investments while they're held in a RRIF will be subject to a special tax. The rate will be the same as that paid by a person in the top tax bracket.

3. A penalty tax of 1 percent a month will be imposed on the fair market value of non-qualified RRIF investments held at the end of every month.

As you can see, mistakes can be expensive. And they are surprisingly easy to make. We know several people who held shares in companies traded on Nasdaq in the U.S. without realizing that, at the time, they were non-qualified investments. Ottawa has since changed the rules to make Nasdaq-listed shares eligible for registered plans.

The financial institution that holds your RRIF should stop you if you attempt to purchase a non-qualified investment for the plan. But don't rely on anyone to intervene. The rules relating to qualified and non-qualified investments are not well codified and are often loosely worded. It's not unusual to find junior staff at a bank, trust company, brokerage house, or credit union who aren't familiar with them or who don't fully understand them (in fact, it would be rare to find someone who does). If you have a self-directed plan and ask for an illegal trade to be made, it may be carried through without question—to your detriment.

So don't depend on someone else to sound the alarm. Check the list below carefully and monitor your investments closely.

Bonds and Debentures (Foreign) Only certain international bonds are eligible (see page 32 for details). All others are ineligible.

Coins You can, of course, get cash credit for any coins deposited in your RRIF that are legal tender in Canada. But you cannot deposit rare coins to your plan, nor are gold and platinum coins acceptable. The rule is that the value of a coin deposited in a RRIF cannot exceed its face value.

Collectibles You may have a valuable piece of art, a great stamp collection, or an antique clock, but it can't go into your RRIF.

Commodities No pork bellies, soybeans, oats, or any other type of commodity may be held in a RRIF. This includes options and futures relating to commodities. However, mutual funds that invest in such options and futures do qualify for RRIFs. You figure it out.

Foreign Currency Only Canadian cash is allowed, nothing else. Not even U.S. cash is permitted in your plan. However, you can hold GICs, stocks, and bonds denominated in foreign currencies, provided they are qualified investments in their own right. (See the entries on government bonds, page 31, and stocks (foreign), page 34.)

Futures The government appears to regard futures as too speculative for a retirement plan. This extends to financial futures as well as commodity futures. So you can't use your RRIF money to speculate on a drop in the value of the Canadian dollar or a rise in the yen. Stock index futures are also ineligible for individuals, although you can hold mutual funds that invest in them.

Mutual Funds (U.S.) U.S.-based mutual funds may not be held in a RRIF unless they are specifically licensed for sale in Canada and registered with the Canada Customs and Revenue Agency. Note the distinction between U.S.-based mutual funds, which are offered by U.S. issuers, and U.S. equity mutual funds, which invest in U.S. companies and are part of the lineups offered by most Canadian mutual fund companies.

Precious Metals You may not hold gold bullion, silver wafers, diamonds, or any other type of precious metal or gem in your plan. You may, however, own stocks in gold mines and similar companies, as well as precious metals mutual funds.

Put Options These are options that allow you to sell a security at a pre-determined price for a certain period of time. So on the option coin, they're on the side opposite calls, which give you a purchase right. However, while call options are acceptable in a RRIF, Ottawa says puts are offside.

Real Estate You may not hold any type of real estate directly in a RRIF under most circumstances. This includes both residential and commercial property as well as vacant land. You can, however, own real estate indirectly, either by purchasing shares in real estate companies or through units in a real estate mutual fund or real estate investment trust (REIT). You may also hold mortgages in your RRIF (see the entry on mortgages on page 33). The one exception to the no-real-estate rule is a case in which your RRIF has foreclosed on a mortgage and taken possession of the property. In such circumstances, your RRIF may temporarily hold the property, provided it is promptly offered for sale at a reasonable price and sold within a year.

Stocks (Foreign) You may hold stocks in foreign companies that are traded on one of the government's recognized exchanges; see the stocks (foreign) entry on page 34. Stocks traded on any other foreign exchanges are ineligible.

Substitutions

Many people don't know that you're allowed to substitute qualified assets from outside your RRIF for assets already in the plan. This option can be useful in a number of circumstances, but you need a self-directed plan to do it.

A substitution is exactly what it sounds like—you simply exchange one asset for another. Suppose, for example, you were in need of cash in excess of your minimum annual withdrawal amount. Your RRIF has some, but if you take out the money, you'll have to pay additional tax on it. If you have qualified securities available, you can simply put them into your retirement plan at fair market value and withdraw the equivalent amount of cash. This allows you to have your cake and eat it too—you don't have to sell any of your securities and you have the cash you require.

For tax purposes, a security is deemed to have been sold when it goes into the plan, triggering any capital gains taxes that may apply.

Some instances when you might want to make a substitution include

To Switch Interest-bearing Investments for Stocks or Equity Funds Stocks held in a RRIF can't benefit from the dividend tax credit or the lower capital gains tax rate. If you are holding securities that pay interest outside your RRIF, you'd be better off, at least from a tax point of view, swapping them for any equities inside the plan.

For Interest-free Loans You can't make direct use of the securities in your RRIF as collateral for a loan. But, through substitution, you can go one better. Suppose you have securities outside the RRIF and you need money. Instead of putting up those securities as collateral for a loan, make your RRIF your banker. By substituting the securities for cash in your RRIF, you are, in effect, providing yourself with an interest-free loan.

While substitution offers opportunities for some creative financial manoeuvres, be careful. There are bears lurking in the forest.

For example, don't try to get around the capital gains rules by selling securities to your RRIF for less than market value. The federal government has tough penalties for that.

Let's say you own shares in a small business, with a fair market value of $2,000. Since the stock isn't publicly traded, there's no easily accessible record of its value. So you decide to pull a fast one by setting the value at $5,000 and substituting the shares for that amount of cash. If the government finds out about it, you'll be deemed to have withdrawn $3,000 from your plan, which will be taxed as regular income.

Conversely, if shares worth $2,000 were already inside your RRIF and you sold them to yourself for $1,500 by using a substitution strategy, you'd be deemed to have withdrawn $500 from the plan and you'd be taxed accordingly.

Before you try using the substitution rule, check with the institution that holds your RRIF to see if it charges a fee for the transaction. And remember to consider the tax consequences before making the move.

Foreign Property

The Government of Canada wants RRIF holders to invest in this country. As a result, there have always been restrictions on the percentage of foreign assets you can hold in your plan, and the cost of transgression can be high: Going over the limit brings a penalty of 1 percent a month until the overage is eliminated. Fortunately, the allowable limits have been raised as a result of the budget presented in February 2000 by Finance Minister Paul Martin.

Under the revised rules, you are allowed to hold up to 30 percent of the assets of your RRIF in foreign securities. The foreign-property limit for registered plans rose from 20 percent to 25 percent in 2000 and has been at the current level since 2001. While we would have preferred to see the limits removed entirely, the higher limits are a distinct improvement.

Even with these higher limits, you still have to manage your RRIF so that you stay on side these new limits, and that can be more complex than with an RRSP, especially if you are making monthly or quarterly withdrawals from your plan. As a result, some financial institutions require you to maintain a foreign-content total that is somewhat below the legal limit. Check with the organization you are considering for your RRIF to see if it has its own rules in this regard.

Here's how the foreign-content limit works:

There are two ways in which the value of your RRIF is determined at any given time. One is market value—the price for which you could sell any of the assets in your plan today. The other is book value. This represents the original price you paid for a given asset and is defined as the original price of a security, including all acquisition fees. The foreign-property rule is based entirely on book value.

Calculating Book Value

Plan trustees, including your plan sponsor, must report periodically to the Canada Customs and Revenue Agency on the foreign property held by their clients. The limit applies to each plan, so you can't calculate the total you're allowed based on all your retirement plans (if you have more than one RRIF) and hold the sum in one plan only.

RRSP Conversion An oversight in government legislation used to mean that the assets in an RRSP were deemed to pass into the RRIF at fair market value—rather than at cost or book value—when an RRSP was converted to a RRIF. The result was disruptive and often expensive, because valuing everything at market price would often push the plan's foreign property over the limit, even though no changes had been made to the actual holdings.

This situation was the inadvertent result of some ambiguous legal drafting that's meant to deal with taxes on emigrating from Canada. But many of the Canadians caught by this rule were merely exchanging their RRSPs for RRIFs. The good news is that the government has dealt with the problem by allowing assets to pass between trusts—such as RRSPs and RRIFs—at book value.

Existing RRIFs While market value is not used to calculate foreign content in existing plans, you should be aware that a number of factors can affect the book value–and, consequently, the allowable foreign content–of your plan. For instance, if a foreign-property mutual fund makes distributions that are reinvested in additional units of the fund, this will bump up the percentage you hold in foreign content. As well, any redemptions or transfers will also affect the percentages of foreign and domestic content in a RRIF.

To avoid being pushed over the limit by distributions from a foreign-property mutual fund, consider having these distributions made in cash. You can then decide how to reinvest the money if you don't withdraw it.

Another thing to remember is that a mutual fund that's sold as fully RRIF-eligible is just that. No portion of such a fund counts in calculating the foreign content of your plan, regardless of whether it actually holds foreign stocks up to its own limit or is fully invested in Canada.

To illustrate the book value concept, we've prepared a sample portfolio for a self-directed RRIF, showing the book value of a plan and the market value as it stood on January 1, 2002 (we'll assume the plan was opened on December 31, 2001 for illustrative purposes). For the sake of simplicity, and because commissions will vary depending on how a security was purchased, we have not attempted to factor in sales charges.

In the examples that follow, we've assumed that the CSBs pay an average annual return of 4.5 percent and that the GIC pays 6 percent.

SAMPLE PORTFOLIO, JANUARY 1, 2002

Market value and book value are identical.

ASSET	NUMBER	PURCHASE PRICE (PER UNIT)	BOOK VALUE	MARKET VALUE (WITH ACCRUED) INTEREST)
Cash	—	$70,000.00	$70,000.00	$70,000.00
CSBs	30	1,000.00	30,000.00	30,000.00
GICs	10	5,000.00	50,000.00	50,000.00
Bond Fund	5,000	5.00	25,000.00	25,000.00
Canadian Equity Fund	1,000	20.00	20,000.00	20,000.00
Dividend Fund	2,000	15.00	30,000.00	30,000.00
Total	—	—	$225,000.00	$225,000.00

As you can see, the book value and market value of the cash holdings are the same, because this is a brand-new RRIF.

Now let's add some foreign property to this RRIF. The limit for calendar 2002, based on the book value of the assets in the plan, would be $67,500 (30 percent of $225,000). We'll take that amount from the cash reserves and buy units in a U.S. stock fund that is classified as foreign property for RRIF purposes.

The RRIF portfolio will now look like this:

SAMPLE PORTFOLIO WITH FOREIGN PROPERTY

Market value and book value are unchanged by purchase.

ASSET	NUMBER	PURCHASE PRICE (PER UNIT)	BOOK VALUE	MARKET VALUE (WITH ACCRUED) INTEREST)
Cash	—	$ 2,500.00	$ 2,500.00	$ 2,500.00
CSBs	30	1,000.00	30,000.00	30,000.00
GICs	10	5,000.00	50,000.00	50,000.00
Bond Fund	5,000	5.00	25,000.00	25,000.00
Canadian Equity Fund	1,000	20.00	20,000.00	20,000.00
Dividend Fund	2,000	15.00	30,000.00	30,000.00
U.S. Equity Fund	10,000	6.75	67,500.00	67,500.00
Total	—	—	$225,000.00	$225,000.00

The market value and book value of the RRIF remain unchanged because all we have done is convert part of the cash to a mutual fund. Now let's suppose that 11 months have gone by and it is now December 1, 2002. During that time, the U.S. equity fund performs extremely well, while everything else in the RRIF remains unchanged except for the interest on your CSBs and GIC (it won't happen that way, of course, but this is just an illustration). Here's how the RRIF would look on December 1, 2002.

SAMPLE PORTFOLIO, DECEMBER 1, 2002

Increase in market value has no impact on foreign-property limit.

ASSET	NUMBER	PURCHASE PRICE (PER UNIT)	BOOK VALUE	MARKET VALUE (WITH ACCRUED) INTEREST)
Cash	—	$ 2,500.00	$ 2,500.00	$ 2,500.00
CSBs	30	1,000.00	30,000.00	31,237.50
GICs	10	5,000.00	50,000.00	52,750.00
Bond Fund	5,000	5.00	25,000.00	25,000.00
Canadian Equity Fund	1,000	20.00	20,000.00	20,000.00
Dividend Fund	2,000	15.00	30,000.00	30,000.00
U.S. Equity Fund	10,000	6.75	67,500.00	100,000.00
Total	—	—	$225,000.00	$261,487.50

The market value of the RRIF has increased substantially, mainly because of your foreign property, which now has a market price of $100,000. At first glance, it may appear that we are now in violation of the foreign-property rule. The U.S. stock fund units are worth more than 30 percent of the book value of the RRIF.

In fact, we do not have a problem. Even though the market value of the foreign-content units has increased, the book value remains unchanged—and it is only book values that count in determining foreign-property holdings.

But now it's December 2002. We haven't taken any money out of the RRIF so far, so we must make our minimum annual withdrawal. Let's use age 70 as the benchmark, which means we must take out at least $11,250, based on the value of the plan back on January 1. To do this, we redeem 10 CSBs for $10,412.50 and take the other $837.50 from our cash reserve. Nothing else changes in the plan. Here's what we're left with on December 31, 2002.

SAMPLE PORTFOLIO, DECEMBER 31, 2002

Cash withdrawal reduces book value.

ASSET	NUMBER	PURCHASE PRICE (PER UNIT)	BOOK VALUE	MARKET VALUE (WITH ACCRUED) INTEREST)
Cash	-	$ 1,662.50	$ 1,662.50	$ 1,662.50
CSBs	20	1,000.00	20,000.00	20,825.00
GICs	10	5,000.00	50,000.00	52,750.00
Bond Fund	5,000	5.00	25,000.00	25,000.00
Canadian Equity				
Fund	1,000	20.00	20,000.00	20,000.00
Dividend Fund	2,000	15.00	30,000.00	30,000.00
U.S. Equity Fund	10,000	6.75	67,500.00	100,000.00
Total	—	—	$213,750.00	$250,237.50

Look closely at the book value total. The withdrawal has reduced the total book value to $213,750.

Under the foreign-property rule, that means the book value of any foreign assets in this plan cannot exceed $64,125 (30 percent of the total). But the U.S. equity fund units have a book value of $67,500. Even though we didn't do anything with those holdings, the withdrawal from the plan has put us in violation of the rule. We're offside by $3,375.

Unless we do something quickly, we'll be hit with a penalty tax of 1 percent a month on the excess foreign property in the account. And this special tax will have to be paid using cash held within the RRIF.

There are two ways to remedy the situation:

1. Sell enough units in the U.S. fund to bring the book value of your holdings down to the new limit.

2. Exchange cash or Canadian securities held outside the RRIF for part or all of the U.S. fund units. This is perfectly permissible, although many people don't realize it.

As you can see, withdrawals from a RRIF make managing the foreign-property limits even more tricky than in an RRSP. So if you're holding foreign property within the plan, you should review the situation any time you make a withdrawal or buy or sell securities.

The Costs

There is no such thing as a genuinely "free" RRIF. After all, the financial institution that holds your plan is in business to make money or, if it's a non-profit co-op or credit union, to at least recover its costs. So even if no charges are apparent when you set up your plan, they're present in one form or another. It's important to know what your costs are and to try to minimize them wherever possible.

In the case of savings and guaranteed investment RRIFs, the cost to you may be only an indirect one. When you invest money in these plans, you're providing the financial institution with additional assets. This money can be loaned out by the institution to generate profits for the company. Your "cost" is the difference between the interest rate you receive and the rate the financial institution charges when it lends funds.

For other types of RRIFs, the costs are more direct and can sometimes run high. Some may be one-time-only charges; others may be annual fees that can become a drain on your profits.

Not all the costs listed below apply to every plan. In fact, some RRIFs may impose only one or two of them. Just make sure you know exactly what expenses will be involved in the particular plan you're considering before going ahead. Here are some of the more common ones to look for:

Administration Fees Most self-directed plans and some mutual fund and insurance company plans charge administration fees. These are usually assessed annually, but some companies require semi-annual payments. Administration fees can vary tremendously, from as low as $15 a year to several hundred dollars, depending on the company and the type of plan. Most are charged as a flat rate but a few are calculated as a percentage of the assets in your plan.

Until the 1996 budget, administration fees were tax deductible if paid out of your own pocket—not withdrawn from the RRIF itself. However, Finance Minister Paul Martin axed this tax break. In doing so, however, he actually did some RRIF investors a favour. In an effort to grab more market share, several discount brokers launched a price war by reducing administration fees or eliminating them entirely. At the time, Bank of Montreal's InvestorLine Discount Brokerage was a leader in this trend, announcing that annual administration fees were being dropped from self-directed RRSPs and RRIFs forever. That represented an annual saving of $100 for clients. Several mutual fund companies also announced they were eliminating administration fees for RRSP and RRIF accounts.

So if you're moving to a self-directed plan, do some comparison shopping before you decide. Since the administration charges are no longer tax deductible, a no-fee plan would be a good choice.

If you're in a plan that charges administration fees, you may pay them from your RRIF assets without any penalty.

GST The GST applies to many of the charges relating to RRIFs. Administration costs of all types are subject to the tax. These include trustee fees, set-up charges, termination fees, transfer fees, and report preparation fees. If you hold mutual funds in your plan, you'll be taxed indirectly because of the imposition of GST on fund management fees. In the past, some fund companies showed their management fees without including GST, but it is now added in to all their numbers, making the true cost to the investor more transparent. Only a few RRIF-related expenses have escaped the GST. Most notable is the sales or brokerage commission on stocks, bonds, mutual funds, etc. Ask the company that handles your RRIF account for a list of costs to which the GST applies.

Investment Counselling Fees These would normally come into play only in the case of self-directed RRIFs for which a professional investment counsellor is employed. The charge would be either a flat fee or a percentage of the RRIF assets. The larger the plan, usually the smaller the percentage charged. The GST applies to these fees. Note that RRIF investment counselling fees, like administration fees, are no longer tax deductible as a result of the 1996 budget.

Management Fees These charges are levied against the total assets of all mutual funds. They pay for managerial salaries and bonuses plus other expenses. In most cases, the charge won't show up on your financial reports because it's taken directly from the fund's holdings. However, the fee is important to you because it reduces the return to individual investors. You should always take a close look at the management fee structure of any mutual fund you're considering, but pay special attention in the case of fixed income and money market funds.

For example, the Phillips, Hager & North Bond Fund had an average annual rate of return of 9.51 percent for the decade ending August 31, 2001. Its management expense ratio (MER) was among the lowest in the bond fund category, at 0.58 percent. In contrast, the Talvest Bond Fund had an average annual return of 7.84 percent in the same period. On the surface, it appears the PH&N managers were much better at their job. But in reality, much of the difference is accounted for by the fact that the management expense ratio (MER) of the Talvest fund is 1.98 percent, almost one and a half percentage points higher than the MER of the PH&N fund! If the Talvest fund had the same MER as the PH&N fund, its return would have been 9.24 percent, not much lower than the return on the PH&N fund. That's the impact high management fees can have!

Mortgage Charges Special fees, both one-time and ongoing, apply if you use your RRIF to hold a non-arm's-length mortgage. These can be very expensive.

Sales Commissions If you buy mutual funds for your RRIF, you may have to pay a sales commission. These fees can take a number of forms:

Front-end loads. These commissions are levied at the time of purchase. They can run as high as 9 percent, although you should never pay that much.

Back-end loads. These commissions are charged if you redeem mutual fund units within a certain time period (six to seven years is common, but it can be longer). The fee is usually based on a sliding scale and diminishes each year until it reaches zero. Also called deferred sales charges, redemption charges, or surrender charges, in the case of segregated funds.

Combination loads. A few mutual fund and insurance company plans levy sales charges at the time of purchase and again when you cash in—a sort of double whammy. Thankfully, the number of companies that indulge in this practice is diminishing.

Set-up Fees Some companies will charge you a one-time fee to establish a plan. This is to cover the paperwork involved in creating a new account and registering it with Ottawa. These fees vary but usually run between $25 and $50. Also known as new account fees.

Substitution (Swap) Fees Many RRIF plans allow substitution of assets at no cost (see substitutions on page 37). Some, however, charge a fee for these transactions.

Switching Fees These may apply to mutual fund-based RRIFs or to self-directed plans. Brokers or fund sales people are allowed by some mutual fund groups to charge a fee if you want to switch some of your assets from one fund to another in the same fund family (for example, from an equity fund to a bond fund in the same group). The amount you'll pay is negotiable (maximum is usually 2 percent) and some companies allow a set number of switches annually before the fee kicks in. Obviously, your goal is to get the best rate possible (preferably free), and, in fact, many financial advisors will waive these fees.

Systematic Withdrawal Fees Systematic withdrawal plans can be used to generate cash flow from equity mutual funds. A small handling fee is sometimes imposed.

Trading Commissions If you have a self-directed RRIF, you'll be charged commissions on many of your transactions, such as buying or selling stocks or bonds. Many stockbrokers offer low-cost self-directed plans with the idea of profiting from the commissions generated by trades. Discount broker plans charge less but you won't get as much in the way of guidance or advice about your investments.

Transfer Fees These fees are charged when a RRIF account is transferred to another financial institution.

Trustee Fees These are administration fees under another name. Most mutual fund RRIFs charge them; expect to pay up to $75 a year in such cases.

6

CAN YOU PROTECT YOUR
NEST EGG?

In recent years, many RRIF holders have become increasingly concerned about the safety of their investments. There are good reasons for this worry. Several financial institutions that offer RRIFs have run into serious problems, including companies once thought to be completely safe. Among them, Confederation Life, a giant of the insurance industry, went into liquidation, and Royal Trust, which was thought by most to be well established, had to sell out to the Royal Bank to avoid a similar fate.

On another level, there have been an increasing number of attempts by creditors to obtain access to retirement assets through legal action—and in some cases, the courts have gone along with them.

Add to these uncertainties another risk in the form of governments—if you owe them money and they can't collect, the tax people would like nothing better than to get their hands on your retirement savings. The government's claim can be based on section 160.2(1) of the federal *Income Tax Act*, which allows the Canada Customs and Revenue Agency to seize unpaid taxes from a retirement plan upon the plan holder's death. In such a case, the assets of the RRIF would be deemed income in the year of death and be taxed accordingly.

Thankfully, the CCRA has no strong claim against your plan while you're still alive, although not for lack of trying. Resistance to the government's efforts includes the Trust Companies Association's stand that its members will not surrender funds from registered plans unless they are served a court order to do so. This declaration to the CCRA came after an RRSP holder successfully sued a member company when it complied with a CCRA request.

Locked-in RRSPs are not subject to seizure, even under court order. However, annuity payments can be garnisheed; that is, amounts owed to the government can be deducted from this type of income by the CCRA or any other creditor who makes the appropriate claims.

Also safe from creditors are employee-sponsored pension plans, and life income funds (LIFs) and LRIFs that hold money from pension plans.

Unfortunately, most personal RRIFs aren't protected in any way. If your marriage breaks up (it does happen, even in later life), your ex-spouse is likely to have a claim on the assets of your plan. Even if your marriage is solid, your RRIF can fall prey to zealous bill collectors, who have come up with a number of ingenious approaches to separate you from your money if they feel you owe it to them or their clients.

The main justification used by creditors seeking to grab your retirement money is that, since RRSP and RRIF holders can dip into their plans whenever they want for consumer purchases, these plans are really just deposit accounts. As such, they should not be shielded from creditors. This argument has been used by creditors seeking access to the holdings of financial institutions and insurance companies that have gone bankrupt. In some cases, the courts have agreed.

There is one type of RRIF that creditors have greater difficulty seizing, however: the plans offered by life insurance companies that form part of an insurance contract. Retirement savings in this form are covered under provincial insurance legislation, which protects life insurance from the claims of creditors. That includes segregated funds, which are essentially mutual funds with an insurance component, and RRIFs issued by insurance companies.

But creditor-proofing laws may not cover retirement plans from banks, trust companies, or other financial institutions. Also be aware that there have been some court rulings recently that seem to undermine the creditor-proof status of even insurance company registered plans. The gist of these rulings is that a move into segregated funds can't be made for the sole purpose of avoiding creditors. The court decisions that allowed such plans to be seized looked at the length of time a plan was open before bankruptcy was declared. As a result, there are concerns that these plans aren't as secure as they appear, since RRIF assets have been seized by creditors under certain circumstances.

At the same time, a ruling by the Supreme Court of Canada in February 1996 asserted the creditor-proof status of the segregated fund holdings in registered plans. The case involved a Saskatchewan doctor and was extremely complicated. The bottom line, however, is that the Court upheld the creditor-proof status of insurance company retirement plans, and even appears to have strengthened this position.

A more recent ruling by the British Columbia Court of Appeal in January 1998 further strengthened the creditor-proof status of segregated funds and deferred annuity RRSPs, and presumably, by extension, of RRIFs. In this case, the court overturned three lower-court judgments that had denied creditor-proofing protection to these contracts.

Naturally, the insurance industry was delighted by these two rulings, since they confirmed one of the unique selling points of their retirement programs.

Taken together, however, these rulings underline a larger issue: the fact that the entire question of creditor-proofing and RRIFs is still up in the air. And it's made even more complex by the fact that authority in this field—as it pertains to insurance and pension-related plans—may be provincial. So the vulnerability of RRIF assets will vary from one province to another, at times turning on a technical phrasing in the law.

It's clear that creditor protection isn't the only factor to consider when you're setting up a retirement income plan. If you're in a high-risk business, however, it's important to take it into account. Doctors, for example, should be concerned about creditor-proofing their savings in general and their retirement assets in particular. We're seeing more malpractice suits in Canada. If you're on the losing side of one of these and don't have adequate insurance, you could be wiped out financially. But your RRSP or RRIF could be saved—if it were in the right place.

Other people who could be vulnerable include the self-employed, small-business owners, farmers, journalists, authors—in short, just about anyone who has assets at risk in a company or who works in a field where lawsuits are common or even possible.

We must emphasize that this doesn't mean you should run out and switch your registered plans to insurance companies in case creditors should breathe down your neck. Remember that bankruptcy laws include provisions that prevent people from shifting funds simply to avoid creditors. But it does mean that, in most cases, you'll get better protection from your insurance company than by holding your RRIF anywhere else, at least for now. And the varying legislation means that living in one province can give you more protection than living in another.

In general, court rulings have put provincial insurance laws ahead of federal bankruptcy laws in determining the level of creditor protection a RRIF enjoys. However, the issue of intent is most important. In other words, if it's clear that your intent in transferring your RRIF assets to an insurance company is to defraud your creditors, then creditor-proof status, as dictated by provincial regulations, will be superceded by federal bankruptcy laws and the RRIF assets could be seized.

Creditor-proofing legislation can vary by province, a situation that extends the protection accorded to life insurance RRSPs and RRIFs to some Canadians, no matter where they hold their plans, and not to others. Efforts by some industry organizations are aimed at promoting equal creditor protection, both during the life and at the death of the depositor, to all registered accounts. These efforts should be supported.

The Trust Companies Association of Canada, for one, believes this would be most fair. At the same time, it has conceded one point. Trust companies have accepted the "deposit account" argument, which holds that plan holders who voluntarily withdraw money from their plans for consumer purposes, like the federal Home Buyers' Plan in the case of RRSP investors, should be vulnerable to any creditor claims against them.

How Sound Is Your RRIF Carrier?

Even if your plan is with an insurance company, that won't necessarily guarantee you restful nights of sleep. There's another matter that may trouble your dreams: Will the company still be there the next day?

Consider the several thousand Canadians who woke up in 1994 to the chilling headlines that Confederation Life had gone belly up. Their registered plans were protected by a life insurance industry disaster pool known as the Canadian Life and Health Insurance Compensation Corporation (CompCorp). But CompCorp's protection limit for RRSPs and RRIFs is only $60,000. So any investors who had more in their Confederation Life retirement plan was at risk. Luckily, the company's segregated fund contracts were transferred to other companies.

The Confederation Life collapse wasn't an isolated case. In March 1993, the Quebec Court of Appeals froze payments to thousands of people who had registered plans with the Cooperants Mutual Life Insurance Society, a billion-dollar company that also folded. Creditors of the failed company claimed that the plans were deposit accounts, not insurance policies, and were therefore vulnerable to claims against the company's assets. That shook up a lot of investors, who had never dreamed they could lose their life savings in such a manner. Fortunately, an appellate court ruling in August 1993 upheld the industry's claim that the plans were indeed insurance contracts, and investors escaped the creditors' clutches.

There are more examples. Alberta's Sovereign Life collapsed in the mid-1990s. Two Alberta banks went out of business in 1985, and Standard Trust folded in 1991. Some companies are much more financially secure than others, and it's a solid assumption that the stronger ones will be among the survivors. So you certainly want to buy your life insurance products from the sound companies, even if you have to pay more or take a little less in payouts.

It seems obvious that your best source of information is the person who's selling you a policy or annuity, right? Well, not everything is as it appears. Is the agent working for you or, in fact, for the company? Most people are unaware that more than 90 percent of the life insurance agents, consultants, and brokers in Canada are employees of one life insurance company or another and are limited to selling that company's policies exclusively. Only the independent brokers offer the products of a number of different companies. In addition, many of the financial advisors employed by Canada's major investment dealers are licensed as independent insurance counsellors. So, in some cases, asking your agent for an objective evaluation is like asking Molson what they think of Labatt!

No one is suggesting you switch agents, but you need to realize that if your agent sells for only one company, he or she is not in a position to give you advice about others. At the very least, make sure to ask for a credit rating of the company that pays your agent's salary. Do some of your own homework. For example, once you've decided on the type and amount of policy or annuity you want, get quotes from at least three companies. Ask your insurance broker to give you the credit ratings for each. If your broker doesn't come up with that information, it may be wise to switch to someone who does.

The surest way to get unbiased information is from credit reports such as those issued by A.M. Best Canada (formerly TRAC Insurance Services). The Toronto-based firm rates and reports on the financial health of almost all of Canada's life insurance companies. You can contact them at 416-363-8266 or get the information online at **www.ambest.ca**. Some of this information is free and more detailed reports are available for a fee.

If you are still worried about the financial soundness of your financial institutions, you might consider joining a benefits society such as the Independent Order of Foresters (IOF) or the Knights of Columbus. They offer similar life insurance products to members, but they're considered safer, as the rules under which they operate are much tougher.

Another issue was raised by a Toronto-area investor after the 1995 Quebec referendum and, many years later, the question remains a valid one. What happens to RRSP, RRIF, or pension assets held by a Quebec-based company in the event of separation?

The good news here is that CompCorp coverage would apply up to the allowable limit, as long as the contract was expressed in Canadian dollars. Therefore, Canadians with pension, RRIF, and RRSP holdings in Quebec would have protection in the event the province ever votes to opt out of Confederation.

Less Risk in a Few Easy Steps

In the face of all this uncertainty, there are some things you can do to at least reduce the chance of your RRIF becoming the target of creditors, governments, corporate failures, and political unrest. Here are a few ideas:

Designate a Beneficiary If your RRIF has a named beneficiary (e.g., your spouse) instead of simply passing to your estate, it may help shield the plan from creditors. Unfortunately, this protection isn't absolute. In 1989, the CIBC won a court ruling that allowed the bank access to funds in an RRSP upon a plan holder's death. Even though the man had named his wife as the beneficiary, the bank was granted the legal right to the funds in order to satisfy an outstanding loan.

Familiarize Yourself with CompCorp As mentioned previously, RRIF assets up to $60,000 are protected under the CompCorp program, in the event of an insurance company bankruptcy. For a free brochure explaining how the coverage works, call 1-800-268-8099 (in the Toronto area, phone 416-777-2344), or send questions by e-mail to **info@compcorp.ca**.

Use an Insurance Plan Insurance company RRIFs have a higher degree of creditor protection than ordinary plans in most Canadian provinces. The Canadian Life and Health Insurance Association advises that if the plan has a designated beneficiary that is the parent, spouse, child, or grandchild of the policy holder, it's protected against creditors. Quebec's rules are even more liberal, extending the protection to family members who are even farther removed.

The growing concern over these issues is one of the reasons behind the move of many traditional mutual fund companies into segregated funds. You pay a higher annual management fee, but that buys you the benefit of creditor protection as well as guarantees against loss.

Keep the Assets in any One Insurance Plan under $60,000 This will protect your RRIF fully under the CompCorp rules in the event the insurance company goes under. Of course, the disadvantage of doing this is that you may end up with several RRIFs, which we do not recommend. You have to decide where your priorities lie.

All this raises a more basic question: Why should insurance company plans have special protection not accorded to anyone else? Shouldn't all RRSPs and RRIFs be treated the same way when it comes to creditor-proofing? Either they should all have it, or none.

It's time for the federal government and the provinces to take a look at this entire situation. There needs to be some consistency across the country and among different types of plans. It really doesn't make a lot of sense for one company's RRIF to offer a safe haven from the perils of bankruptcy, tax claims, and creditors, while another is open to seizure. (In fact, we now have an even more absurd situation in which the same fund, purchased from the same fund company, may or may not have creditor protection.) Nor is there any logical reason why an RRSP or a RRIF set up at a bank branch in Charlottetown should be safer than one opened at another branch of the same bank in Calgary.

There have been efforts to harmonize the rules. For instance, in May 1999, the Canadian Securities Administrators, which regulates mutual funds, and the Canadian Council of Insurance Regulators, which regulates segregated funds, published a detailed report comparing the two products. However, despite some important recommendations that would help level the playing field, change has been slow in coming.

7

When and How to Move Your RRIF

The time may come when you want to switch your RRIF from one company to another. The reasons for changing are many and varied. It may simply be that you've moved to a new location and want to switch your RRIF to a financial institution that's more conveniently located. Or it may be something more serious—investments that are underperforming, escalating fees, or a personality clash with your account representative. Whatever the reason, our advice is to think carefully before you act.

If you do undertake to move your RRIF, the rules state that the transferring institution is responsible for paying out the entire mandatory minimum withdrawal for the current year. So, if it's early in the year and you're used to dealing with a regular, say monthly, income stream from your RRIF, you could find yourself unexpectedly with a huge sum of money to handle.

Another thing to consider about RRIF transfers is the potential administrative difficulties you face. While the procedure for moving your registered assets—whether in the form of an RRSP or a RRIF—from one company to another is fairly straightforward, the actual execution of the move can sometimes be immensely frustrating. We have heard from many investors who have been forced to wait weeks and even months for a requested transfer of funds to take place. Some have actually brought suit in small claims court for lost revenue resulting from lengthy delays—and won.

Financial institutions have an annoying habit of burying the paperwork involved in these transfers. After all, if the account is being transferred to someone else, why break your back to service the customer? We'll get around to it—when everything else has been done.

The major financial institutions now charge fees to transfer your money among accounts or to other institutions. These range from $25 to $30 per transfer. So not only will they take their time moving your money, they'll penalize you as well.

This attitude is, unfortunately, very common in the industry. And besides being frustrating for RRIF holders, it can cost them money on top of the fees. That's because the transferring company will "freeze" your account once it receives the transfer instructions. That means you won't be able to conduct any transactions until the switch is completed. A transfer of funds that is delayed for several months could mean missed investment opportunities and lost income.

A 1993 court decision suggests that, if you can prove income loss, you may be able to win compensation from the company responsible for the delay, either by negotiation or through a lawsuit. The *Financial Post* reported in November 1993 that an investor had won a court decision in Toronto after claiming that he'd missed an investment opportunity because of delays in processing the transfer of funds in an RRSP held with Royal Trust. Maurice Chriqui told the court he had planned to reinvest the money from two GICs maturing in late February 1993 with Standard Life at 7 percent. That rate was guaranteed until Monday, March 1. His cheque wasn't ready on Monday, nor was it ready for him when he returned on Tuesday after securing a further guarantee of a day from Standard Life. When he went back to Royal Trust on Wednesday, his cheque was ready, but the guarantee had expired and he was forced to invest the funds at 6 3/4 percent. Mr. Chriqui calculated that the lost interest compounded over the four-year term of the investment amounted to $417, and filed suit for those funds plus court costs. He won.

Unfortunately, not every story has such a happy ending. In defence of Royal Trust, Mr. Chriqui's cheque was issued within their corporate standards—48 to 72 hours in normal periods, and three to five business days during peak investor periods, like RRSP season. A lawyer for Royal Trust added that had they been aware of the time-limited guarantee from Standard Life, they would have attempted to issue the cheque within the desired period. As a result of this case and others like it, several independent organizations are promoting guidelines to be adopted by the entire industry.

The Canadian Association of Financial Planners (CAFP) says that investors lose millions of dollars a year because of slow transfers. The CAFP, along with the Investment Dealers Association of Canada and the Canadian Bankers' Association, have set standards for their members of between 10 and 25 days for completing transfers of RRIFs. Along with time limits, there are recommendations for how interest lost due to delayed transfers would be paid by both the receiving and transferring organizations.

Another sign of the growing recognition by the industry that there is a need for improvements in this area is the introduction of new transfer forms by some financial institutions. The Canada Customs and Revenue Agency's T2033 form–which authorizes the RRIF transfer and is normally sent by the receiving organization to the relinquishing organization–is still in use, but some companies have devised less onerous, clearer forms. Hopefully, these developments will help change the way this part of the business is conducted.

The sooner real changes are implemented throughout the industry, the better. As things stand right now, however, lengthy delays still take place, occasionally as a result of corporate takeovers and mergers, but usually because of clerical error or inattention. You have to take measures to protect yourself. Here are some suggestions:

1. Find out what guidelines your financial institution has adopted for transfers to another organization. There are no standardized guidelines to cover the whole industry. Most industry associations have policies in place, but usually these are voluntary guidelines with no teeth.

2. Make sure the transfer is really necessary–ask yourself how you will benefit from the move.

3. Keep close track of the maturity dates of all GICs and term deposits in your plan. If you want to transfer assets from any of these sources, have the appropriate paperwork ready well in advance. This will ease the pressure on yourself and your financial institution.

4. Make it easy for them–don't initiate a transfer during January or February, the peak RRSP season when companies in the financial services sector are certain to be at their busiest. Wait for a quieter time (say, July), when your request is less likely to be put on hold.

5. Review all paperwork for accuracy before signing. If you've obtained a time-limited rate guarantee from another institution, make sure that you inform your broker, bank, or trust company both verbally and in writing. Attach a copy of the written notification to your paperwork.

6. Keep checking on the status of the transfer. If no action has been taken within a reasonable time, speak to the manager of the registered plan department of the transferring firm. If you do business with the company in other ways (deposit accounts, mortgages, etc.), say so–that might help to get their attention.

7. Consider a self-directed RRIF within the same company as an alternative to transferring your assets to another organization. You'll find the staff much more accommodating, and the entire transaction should be done quickly.

8. If you continue to have trouble, make a pest of yourself until the job gets done. We don't like having to give that kind of advice, but the actions of some financial institutions in this situation make it necessary.

8

WHAT ARE THE BEST INVESTMENT STRATEGIES?

When interest rates began to drop early in the 1990s, millions of conservative North Americans were taken by surprise. Rates had been high for so long that people who had money to invest or who were living on their savings, especially retired people, simply got used to making an easy 10 percent or so a year. When they opted for the overall safety of interest-bearing securities, many people didn't realize that there was an inherent risk in terms of interest rates themselves.

How would you feel if your income were cut in half? Unfortunately, many retirees can answer this question. Some were hit hard by the tremendous downward slide in rates in the 1990s. More recently, retired investors have been hit again by the fast and furious slashes to interest rates that began right after New Year's Day 2001, aimed at stimulating a faltering economy. The cuts accelerated following the terrorist attacks of September 2001, driving short-term rates to their lowest levels in more than 40 years.

Investors have seen the rates of return on five-year GICs fall drastically between the time the investment was originally made and the maturity date. When these GICs are rolled over for a new term, unfortunate retirees suddenly find their incomes slashed because of the drop in rates. For some people, such a decline means the difference between comfort and financial difficulty.

Short-term interest rates rose slightly in the late 1990s, but recent political and economic turbulence have sent rates plummeting again. There is so much uncertainty in our current economic environment that chances are low interest rates will continue for some time to come, although they will likely increase somewhat from the extremely low levels of early 2002. However, the days of the 10 percent GIC don't appear likely to return any time in the foreseeable future.

From a longer-term perspective, the current situation is more consistent with historic norms. No matter what you read in the media about the past few years bringing "unprecedented lows" for interest rates, it was actually the higher rates of the 1970s and 1980s that were out of the ordinary, created by the high-spending governments of that era. If you look back prior to that period, you will find that long-term rates ranged between 3 percent and 6 percent.

During the "deficits are good" era, governments created their own inflation by spending like there was no tomorrow. As most of you certainly remember, short-term interest rates skyrocketed. Late in the summer of 1981, short-term rates hit their staggering high of 22.75 percent. Too bad investors could not have locked in for 20 years back then!

Modern governments have taken a deficit-cutting, inflation-fighting approach. The 1998 federal budget was the first surplus budget to be brought down in Canada in 30 years, and the situation continued to improve until the attacks of September 2001 created a new dynamic that put public finances under pressure again. Now, with political instability around the globe reaching levels many people have never witnessed before and with deficit-wary baby boomers the major policymakers around the world, it is unlikely that any major power will tolerate double-digit inflation rates again in this generation.

It seems we are in for an extended period of low interest rates. This means that many investors will have to adopt new or different investment strategies in order to generate the income they need from their RRIFs. Our suggestions and advice can be found in the following pages.

Investing to Improve Returns and Reduce Risk— At the Same Time!

Older Canadians are sometimes too conservative for their own good when it comes to investing. Whether they choose their investments from habit or fear, their reliance on term deposits and other interest-bearing securities hurts them in the long run by hindering their ability to grow wealth and assets, especially given the current economic and interest-rate scenario.

Canadians are embracing growth securities. According to a Canadian Shareholder Study published by the Toronto Stock Exchange in 2000, more than 49 percent of Canadians hold stocks, directly or indirectly–not a surprising statistic given the great and prolonged market boom of the 1990s.

However, as volatility in financial markets reaches frightening levels, investors feel increasingly vulnerable. People over the age of 50 could hardly be faulted for veering toward conservatism. A movement to safety, away from the uncertainty of stock markets, is understandable. We are, after all, at a point in life when it is crucial to minimize risk. Yet too many Canadian investors operate under the mistaken belief that they can avoid risk altogether, that they can simply tuck their money away in "risk-free" investments. No such investments exist.

For one thing, short-term deposits don't pay what they used to pay, and they are certainly not risk-free. It is important to recognize that there is more than one kind of risk. If you are too conservative and take only interest-rate risk, you may end up with too little money to fund a long, comfortable retirement. We have heard too many horror stories about people whose income has been cut in half or more with declines in rates in recent years. You must protect yourself against cost-of-living increases, which can be dramatic even with low inflation rates. Growth, over time, is the answer.

If you look at demographic statistics, you will discover that people over 50 actually gamble more than any other age group–just visit any casino. So, deep down, they can't be all that conservative. It's probably truer that they just do not know how to gamble properly when it comes to investing, by taking whatever they do not or will not need and letting it ride for a while. A growth investment strategy is much more secure than playing slot machines, roulette, or blackjack, and it is certainly better than buying lottery tickets.

We are not suggesting that you gamble with your retirement money. But we are saying that you can be overly cautious. Now that you are near, at, or beyond RRIF age, what investment strategies are appropriate for you? How can you achieve growth without betting the farm?

With the minimum RRIF withdrawal rate being 7.38 percent at the age of 71, you have to earn 8 percent or better to keep your tax-sheltered assets from being eroded. If you are able to find a relatively secure way to increase your returns by just a few percentage points, it makes a tremendous difference to the value of your RRIF, to the amount of money you can draw from it, and to the number of years it will last.

Well, how can you accomplish that?

Winner by a Bay Street Mile

First, let's answer that question with another question–it's a multiple-choice pop quiz, so don't peek at the answer in the next paragraph.

The best way to achieve maximum long-term results in any investment portfolio is to

a. Stick with safe, secure term deposits and GICs;

b. Focus on equity funds;

c. Rotate into the "hot" mutual funds every quarter;

d. Mix your assets in a widely diversified portfolio; or

e. Carry a heavy component of emerging-market funds.

Anyone who chose "d" is far ahead of most Canadian investors. In fact, it's the winner by a Bay Street mile. Dubbed by the financial industry as "asset allocation" or "asset mix," this is the most powerful strategy you can utilize to achieve long-term performance. In fact, the strategy is more important than the actual selection of individual investments.

Most professional money managers have agreed for years that holding the right blend of investments can account for as much as 80 percent of gains in the long run. Now, strong evidence suggests that even this estimate is low. Analyzing the performance of 82 large U.S. pension fund managers, the prominent Chicago-based investment consulting firm of Ibbotson Associates found that, on average, asset allocation was responsible for a whopping 91.5 percent of their portfolio returns over time.

The proven impact of asset allocation is significant for RRIF investors. At this stage in life, you cannot be as aggressive as younger traders can. Even with 20 or 30 years in retirement, you do not have the time, nor can you likely afford, to ride out too many market cycles or fluctuations. That means you need to put together a carefully structured portfolio that will minimize risk while generating the cash flow you need to live on. Properly applied, asset allocation can both increase return and reduce risk. Who could ask for a better combination?

The asset mix strategy is relatively straightforward. You choose, ideally with the help of a good financial advisor and based on your individual needs and the current economy, a blend of three basic categories:

1. Cash and cash equivalents, such as savings accounts, Treasury bills, term deposits, and money market funds. These products feature safety and liquidity, but at the cost of low returns.

2. Income securities, such as GICs, bonds, mortgages, preferred shares, and mutual funds that invest in these instruments. Depending on what you choose, your money may be locked in for specific periods at fixed rates of return.

3. Growth securities, such as equities (stocks) and equity mutual funds. These carry higher risk but also higher return potential, and offer some protection against inflation.

Holding a blend is the best way to protect yourself. You can never be sure of what tomorrow will bring. Depending on the economy and business cycles, you may alter the percentage you hold in each category. Each of us has to choose the right mix for ourselves, based on our financial profile, goals or objectives, income needs, and tolerance for risk. In choosing a formula, good professional advice becomes invaluable.

Generally, the older you are, the more conservative your mix should be. But regardless of the mix, your age, or how conservative you are, you should always include some growth securities in your portfolio. The asset mix strategy is a basic investment philosophy that is not restricted to RRIFs. It will work just as effectively in a non-registered portfolio–but in that case, be sure to take taxes into consideration.

Your Personal Asset Mix

The following are guidelines to follow in setting up and maintaining your personal asset mix:

Step 1: Ask yourself some basic but key questions: What are your investment goals? What amount of risk can you tolerate? You can mix assets successfully in portfolios that range from the conservative to the aggressive. Only you can determine where you fit on the risk scale.

For example, on its upward climb during the 1990s, the stock market had "corrections" ranging from a 5 percent to a 25 percent drop. When the bear market took hold in 2000–01, the declines became much steeper. At one point, the volatile, technology-oriented Nasdaq Index was down more than 60 percent from its early 2000 high. A RRIF portfolio should not be subjected to potential losses of this magnitude, and this should be an important consideration in determining your personal risk tolerance level.

If you are a mutual fund investor, do you look up the unit prices every day? Although daily changes have little to do with your long-term plan, do small fluctuations make you nervous? In essence, any good investment plan will allow you to answer "yes" to the following: Will I be able to sleep well at night? Deciding exactly how much risk you are prepared to accept without abandoning your long-term goals is the key to structuring your RRIF investment plan–no matter what the current environment.

Many financial institutions have questionnaires or software to help you simplify the asset allocation process. The answers to the questions profile you as either maximum income, income and growth, balanced growth, or maximum growth. Ask your financial institution if it has such tools to help you. You'll also find an investment personality profiler in a companion book, *Secrets of Successful Investing*, by Gordon Pape and Eric Kirzner (Prentice Hall Canada).

Bear in mind that if your RRIF represents the only retirement savings you possess, you may have to be somewhat more aggressive to outperform cost-of-living increases.

Step 2: When you buy mutual funds, which often makes more sense than purchasing individual securities, ensure they are solid, core funds with consistent, long-term track records. Funds with a value orientation tend to be less risky and therefore may provide more comfort for investors in retirement. Choose funds that are suitable for a buy-and-hold approach. Avoid those that have a volatile history and/or that specialize in specific sectors of the economy.

It is one thing to decide on a buy-and-hold strategy, but quite another to stick to it in a downturn, such as the one we experienced in 2000–01. It's tough to sit by and watch your nest egg crack open, but don't panic and sell at what will likely turn out to be the bottom of a wave. On the contrary, a market downturn is often a good time to add to holdings. Here's where your professional financial advisor can keep you on track.

Step 3: For comfort's sake, measure the total return on your portfolio against an appropriate benchmark. Do not focus on any one fund.

Step 4: Make sure to include growth securities in your mix. If you select carefully, this can be done without incurring a great deal of additional risk. As pointed out previously, the adage about switching 100 percent of your assets into GICs or bonds at age 65 or 70 simply doesn't cut it any more. People are now living 20 to 30 years into retirement. To ensure that you don't outlive your capital, you need investments that grow after you start drawing down on them.

The Case for Equities

Until the economy started to slow in 2000, a trend that accelerated dramatically in 2001, we were in the midst of the longest economic upturn on record, with inflation tightly monitored and under control. Baby boomers are the policymakers now. They grew up during the difficult period of price controls and huge inflationary increases in the 1970s and early 1980s. As a result, they are committed to stable prices and moderate growth, not only in

Canada, but also in economically powerful countries such as the United States, Japan, and Germany. All these countries are supporting aging populations and no one wants dramatic cost-of-living increases.

These policies of stable prices and controlled growth translated into low inflation rates, low interest rates, strong economic growth, and higher corporate profits for most of the 1990s. That made stock markets more attractive as declines were short-lived, and gains were steady.

This idyllic situation ended in 2000–01, as world economies fell into recession and stock markets tumbled. Ironically, the result may have been to make stocks and equity mutual funds less risky for retirees going forward than they were during the boom times of the 1990s. That's because prices dropped sharply during the bear market, to much more reasonable levels. Any veteran money manager will tell you that the best time to buy is when markets are low, since it is at such times that profit potential is greatest and risk is lowest. Although history has proven that theory to be true time and again, many people are still reluctant to act on it because of fear of the future.

We believe that stock markets will rally strongly once economic and political uncertainties are behind us and that we will see an upward trend for another 10 to 15 years as a river of cash from pre-retirees and baby boomers flows into the market.

This prognosis suggests that everyone, even those who are retired, should hold at least some of their portfolio in stocks or equity mutual funds. Stocks historically outperform cash, bonds, and inflation, and are likely to continue doing so for the foreseeable future. Over time, the stock market is an attractive investment, despite the short-term volatility it can experience. Since the crash of 1929, the longest period it has taken the U.S. market to recover from any drop was 3.5 years, and the average recovery rate in all that time was only 2.5 years.

Over the past 50 years, stocks have outperformed bonds by over 6 percentage points annually–that's every year for 50 years, on average. This trend tells you that the long-term accumulation of wealth is still best achieved through stocks or equity mutual funds. Some of the latest studies even suggest switching the traditional 40/60 equity/debt portfolio mix to 60/40– that is, 60 percent stocks and 40 percent bonds. That may be too aggressive for a RRIF portfolio, but even the most conservative money managers agree that retired people must have some growth to offset even modest increases in inflation over the years and to deal with the investment challenge created by low interest rates.

Since 1946, the safety record of the traditional mix of 40 percent stocks or equity mutual funds and 60 percent bonds has been perfect over any five-year period; in other words, there have been no losses in well-constructed portfolios using that mix over any five-year time frame. And, out of all three-year periods since then, only twice would this mix have lost money. Thus, the wisdom of a 40/60 split between equities and bonds has been proven.

So here is a game plan to consider, given these facts: If you put money you will not need, say, for four years, out to grow in the market in good, value-based equity mutual funds, they will more than likely produce better returns than you can expect from any interest-bearing security. The reason equity mutual funds make the most sense is that they provide the diversification you could not match on your own, and the investment decisions are made by professionals who watch their corner of the market 12 hours a day, every day. Use this time-mix approach in addition to the asset-mix strategy. Invest whatever money you need to live on with complete safety in mind, and, beyond that three- or four-year cushion, put the rest in growth holdings.

If you need to generate cash flow from your equity holdings, you can use what's called a "systematic withdrawal plan," which will redeem enough units every month or quarter to meet your needs. We'll explain these in more detail in a moment.

You don't need a sophisticated portfolio for your equity holdings; an index fund or two, a value-oriented Canadian equity fund, a broadly based international fund, and a U.S. equity fund will do the trick.

Timing the Market

If you do take our advice and put more of your RRIF and non-registered investments into stock-based mutual funds, don't make the mistake of trying to time the market—that is, attempting to guess when it will go up or down and investing accordingly. Not even the investment gurus can perform that trick. Consider this amazing statistic: 95 percent of the major gains in stocks between 1963 and 1996 took place on a total of 31 different days. Who could be lucky enough to predict those 31 days? The answer is no one.

The only kind of market timing we like, because we believe in the long-term strength of the strategy, is to buy when you see a significant drop in any basic-value market. The market is likely to improve over time. Unfortunately, the average person reacts to a market drop by panicking and running. People who try to time the market too often end up buying high and selling low, which certainly does not fulfill anyone's investment goals. Try to take a long-term view of your investments and pay no attention to the inevitable day-to-day fluctuations.

Market volatility is a part of life and is affected by a vast number of factors, including economic cycles, elections, changes in government policies, natural disasters such as earthquakes or hurricanes, specific corporate industrial reports, frauds à la Bre-X, and, of course, acts of terrorism and war. Here's what Warren Buffett, chairman of multi-million-dollar Berkshire Hathaway, Inc., says about trying to time the market: "With enough inside information and a million dollars, you can go broke in a year."

TSE 300 TOTAL RETURN INDEX, SEPTEMBER 30, 1991 TO SEPTEMBER 30, 2001

PERIOD OF INVESTMENT GROWTH OF $10,000	AVERAGE ANNUAL RETURN (%)	TOTAL RETURN ($)
Fully invested (2518 days)	9.46	24,864
Miss the 10 best days	5.34	16,851
Miss the 20 best days	2.11	12,320
Miss the 30 best days	−0.60	9,418
Miss the 40 best days	−2.82	7,530
Miss the 50 best days	−4.82	6,142
Miss the 60 best days	−6.63	5,096

Source: Bloomberg/AIM Funds Management Inc.

The Price of Missing the Market

Market fluctuations have always been with us and always will be. Yet, you can both protect yourself from such volatility and profit from it. To protect yourself, spread your investments in a well-diversified portfolio, as suggested. It is most unlikely that any downturn will affect all of your holdings at the same time. As we saw in 2000–01, as the stock market fell, bond prices rose, especially those of short- and mid-term government issues.

As well, make a serious commitment to investing for the long term, although in the case of a RRIF, the time frame needs to be adjusted to take account of age. Doing so makes short-term hiccups less of a concern. You generally buy a GIC and put it away for five years, so why do you have to look up the value of a mutual fund every day? Again, remember to take into account the minimum withdrawal requirements of your RRIF and your income needs. If you cannot envision a term of at least five years, stock market investments are probably not for you.

You may use market "corrections" as bargain-hunting opportunities for adding to your portfolio at reduced prices. This procedure, called "dollar-cost averaging," lowers the average cost of your securities.

When we suggest dollar-cost averaging at seminars or in discussions with investors, the typical question is: How do I know if the market will come back? No one knows, of course, but if history is any measure, rest assured it will rebound. Since World War II, the market has been on a steady upward climb. As long as the world's industrial economies continue to grow, which appears likely, given continuing technology advances and productivity gains, this trend will continue. Most of the market downturns we have seen, despite all the frightening headlines they generate, are merely blips in that broad, upward spiral.

Well-known U.S. money manager Peter Lynch is famous for saying, "I'm not sure what direction the next 1,000 point movement in the Dow will be, but I'm certain the next 5,000 point move will be up."

Use Equity to Generate Cash Flow

Investing a portion of your RRIF in an equity fund does not necessarily mean that you cannot use those assets to produce income. If you need cash flow from that source—to create some or all of your minimum withdrawal requirement, for example—you could set up a systematic withdrawal plan (SWP) within the RRIF that will do the job very nicely.

Systematic withdrawal plans are very simple at the core, but some people have difficulty understanding them. Let's say you want to hold 30 percent, about $50,000, of your RRIF in growth securities. You have no other foreign content in your plan, so you decide to use the entire allocation here. After checking the options carefully, you decide to invest it all in the Fidelity International Portfolio Fund.

You tell your financial advisor that you want to establish an SWP for the fund that will produce $400 a month in cash flow for the RRIF. The necessary paperwork is done and the plan is set into place. Each month, that $400 will be there for you. It can be generated from several sources: realized capital gains within the fund, interest earned by cash holdings, and dividends. If your fund holdings do not generate enough cash to meet the monthly requirement, some of your units will be redeemed to make up the difference. That may appear to be a draw-down of capital, but it will likely be only temporary. Over time, a well-managed equity fund should generate a return that will more than cover the value of your withdrawals.

Here's another example: If you'd invested $100,000 in the Trimark Fund, with an initial deduction of 4 percent commission, when the fund was introduced in September 1981, and requested payment of $833 each month beginning October 1, 1981, you would have withdrawn a total of $200,000 to the end of September 2001. But, far from being exhausted, your investment would have actually grown to more than $843,000 in that time because of the fund's performance. In other words, you withdrew more than you put in but your original investment grew more than eight times in value.

You don't have to worry about the tax consequences of a systematic withdrawal plan inside a RRIF because all the money, whatever the source, is taxed at your standard marginal rate when it is withdrawn.

The "Segregated" Alternative

Life insurance companies offer segregated funds, which are investment vehicles similar to mutual funds but with several interesting differences. Generally, segregated funds are on a par with mutual funds when it comes to investment returns, although fees are generally higher for segregated funds.

The term *segregated* is used because laws governing life insurance require the companies to keep these funds separate from other assets and to hold them in trust for their owners, the unit holders. You can buy a RRIF based on various segregated funds, or you can add them to your mix within a self-directed RRIF—just as you can with mutual funds. Segregated funds are managed by professional money experts, in some instances the same people who manage major mutual funds.

The most attractive feature of these funds is that they can combine the growth aspects of a mutual fund with the principal guarantees of a GIC—guarantees that do not come normally with mutual funds or with any other growth investments.

The guarantee is two-fold. First, segregated funds offer partial or full return of your investment, less any withdrawals, of course, at maturity (usually your investment must mature at least 10 years in the future) no matter how the markets perform during that time. In other words, if the market goes up, the gains are yours. If the market falls, you get back all the money you invested.

Second, these funds offer full return of your investment, less any withdrawals, at death, regardless of the maturity date. In this case, your heirs receive whichever is greater, the total amount you invested or the current value of your holdings. (In some cases, the death benefit is phased in over time in the case of older people.)

Generally, investments in segregated funds do not have to be combined with any other life insurance policy or annuity. In some cases, however, there are potential tax savings if they are bought in tandem with certain life policies. Consult an independent expert before making any decision.

Segregated funds are offered in all the major fund categories: indexed, money market, bond, equity, balanced, and international. Some life insurance companies also offer the same range of purchase options and services on their segregated funds as are available with many mutual funds–a prime example being no-cost periodic withdrawal plans to provide investors with regular income. In addition, if you name a family member as your beneficiary, your investment in segregated funds will be protected from the claims of creditors.

If you are interested in segregated funds, it is best to "shop the market" by dealing with an advisor or broker who acts as agent for at least several insurance companies–avoid those who represent only one. Most investment dealer representatives are now licensed to sell such insurance products as well.

Choosing Fixed-Income Assets

There is a wide range of choices available when it comes to selecting fixed-income securities for your RRIF. The decisions you make here are critical, because income securities will form the backbone of your plan and will generate most of the cash flow needed to meet your withdrawal requirements. Selecting the right blend of fixed-income assets becomes especially difficult in times of low interest rates, because the returns from most of the available options will not be enough to produce adequate income to meet even the minimum withdrawal requirements.

Let's take a close look at the choices available to you here.

Mutual Funds

There was a time when the selection was simple–you could buy a bond fund or a mortgage fund. That was it. But now there is a wide range of fixed-income funds available, each of which meets a different need. They include:

Short-term Bond Funds These specialize in securities with maximum maturities of three (or sometimes five) years. Short-term bonds are highly defensive, which means their market value is not severely affected by interest-rate movements, up or down. As a result, these funds offer good protection in a rising interest-rate climate.

Mortgage Funds These fall into the same league as short-term bond funds in terms of defensiveness but their returns tend to be a bit higher over time.

Regular Bond Funds Most bond funds fall into the mid-term category, even though they don't explicitly say so. They hold maturities of varying durations, depending on the economic and financial situation, but they will usually stay reasonably close to the line of the SCM Mid-Term Bond Index or the SCM Universe Bond Index. If you are holding a "regular" bond fund in your portfolio, it probably falls into the mid-term classification.

Long-term Bond Funds This is where we enter higher-risk territory. These funds focus on bonds with long maturities, which means they will be more sensitive to interest-rate movements, up or down. When long-term rates are falling, such funds are capable of producing handsome capital gains. However, when rates are on the rise, long-term bond funds will be subject to above-average losses.

High-Yield Bond Funds These invest in so-called junk bonds, and they don't follow the general pattern of bond funds. Interest-rate movements aren't the primary force here. What counts is the credit-worthiness of the companies whose issues these funds hold. In times of economic stress, the risk of default mounts as credit ratings are downgraded and these funds become vulnerable to above-average losses. But when a recovery takes hold, we'll see a reverse phenomenon. Spreads between corporate and government bonds will narrow and these funds will do well.

Foreign Bond Funds These funds have a spotty record. Longer term, they have not generated much profit. But when interest rates and the value of the Canadian dollar fall in tandem, as happened in 2001, they can produce very good returns. Unhedged funds (those that don't hedge all or part of their foreign currency exposure back into Canadian dollars) can be useful in a RRIF because they offer protection against further drops in the value of the loonie. But if interest rates rise, you can get the same effect with less risk in a U.S.-dollar money market fund.

Dividend Income Funds Be careful here. There are actually two types of dividend funds. Type A is the most common—these are really blue-chip stock funds in disguise, with little or no preferred share content. They do not classify as fixed-income securities. Type B is the true dividend fund, one in which a sizeable chunk of the portfolio is invested in preferred shares. Type B funds were good performers when interest rates were falling. They will not do nearly as well in a rising-rate environment; in fact, the challenge will be to preserve capital.

Canadian Income Trust Funds These invest in anything from bonds to royalty trusts and have a history of high volatility. They produce above-average cash flow with tax advantages if held outside a RRIF, but the income is highly unpredictable and depends in large part on such factors as the world price of crude oil. Although they are designed as income products, they are right on the borderline with the equity category and should be treated accordingly. RRIF investors may use them as a way to boost cash flow, but they should represent only a small part of your fixed-income allocation.

Strip Bonds

Strip bonds have been popular with RRSP investors for many years, because they offer the opportunity to lock in interest rates for the long term. As a result, you may have some strips in your RRSP when the time comes to convert it to a RRIF.

There is nothing wrong with this, assuming that the strips will mature within a reasonable period of time. However, we do not recommend adding any new strips to a RRIF unless you are doing so as part of a well-planned strategy to maximize interest-rate returns by staggering your maturities.

The reason for our caution here is simple. At this stage, income generation becomes one of your prime goals. Strips do not generate any income. They are passive investments that do nothing for you until they mature. Few RRIF investors can afford to allow a portion of their plan to lie fallow in this way. So, in most situations, our advice is to cash in existing strips as they mature and to re-deploy the money.

Regular Bonds

Regular bonds, by contrast, are a valuable resource to RRIF investors. If you choose top-grade bonds with medium maturities (five to ten years), you will be investing in securities that combine steady and predictable income with a high degree of safety.

The best choices for a RRIF from a risk perspective are Government of Canada bonds. However, you'll get a higher return, with relatively little added risk, by investing in debt securities issued by the provinces or by major corporations, such as the chartered banks.

For cost efficiency, it's usually better to buy the bonds directly rather than investing in a bond mutual fund. This eliminates the annual management fees charged by the funds and any sales commissions that might apply. On the other hand, bond mutual funds offer the advantage of diversification—most bond funds hold a mix of bonds with various terms to maturity—and professional management. However, the major problem is that, with recent interest-rate levels, the management fees on bond funds can have a significant impact on returns.

Guaranteed Investment Certificates (GICs)

GICs used to be a very straightforward type of investment. Now they come in a wide variety of formats, some of which are better suited to a RRIF than others. To help you make the best choice, here's a rundown of some of the options you're likely to find when you go GIC shopping.

Redeemable GICs Also called cashable GICs, they're the financial community's equivalent of Canada Savings Bonds. They can be cashed at any time, although you won't receive interest if you redeem within the first 60 or 90 days, depending on the terms set by the issuer. You'll receive full interest up to the day you redeem (CSBs only pay up to the last day of the previous month). They're covered by deposit insurance. Plus, the interest rate may be slightly higher than that offered on CSBs, depending on where you buy them.

Almost all financial institutions, including the big banks, offer some type of redeemable GIC at certain times during the year. But be careful. In most cases, the sale period is limited. This means you won't be able to roll over your redeemable GICs if rates rise in a few months. A few trust companies and credit unions offer them year-round, however. Compare rates before you buy—they can vary considerably. These investments are recommended for a combination of reasonable return and maximum flexibility, both important within a RRIF.

Extendible GICs Here you lose some flexibility because you're locked in for a year. However, you have the option of extending the GIC for a second year at the same rate of return. Remember that the extra year will be of value only if one-year interest rates fall a year from now. If rates are higher, you wouldn't renew at the old rate. If you think lower rates are unlikely, this type of product is not a good alternative.

Escalating GICs This product is designed for long-term investors who are unhappy with present GIC rates. The idea is seductively simple: Your interest rises each year (or sometimes after the first two years) over a five-year term. By the time you get to the fifth year, your GIC is paying a rate that looks impressive by today's standards. It seems great, but if you analyze it carefully, it actually isn't. What really counts is the blended rate you'll receive over the full term. You'll probably find that figure isn't much more than you'd receive from a regular five-year GIC. However, to obtain that rate of return, you'll have to accept two disadvantages.

First, you're locked in for five years. It's never a good idea to tie up your money when interest rates are low; the probability is that they will rise during that time.

Second, if the certificate is held outside your RRIF, the Canada Customs and Revenue Agency will tax you on the blended interest rate over the five-year term. That means you'll pay disproportionately higher taxes in the early years, even though it usually works to your advantage to defer tax as long as possible.

For these reasons, this product should be held only within your RRIF. Buy it only if you get a clear interest-rate advantage over a standard five-year GIC and if there is a high probability that interest rates are about to decline.

Staggered Maturity GICs Financial advisors are always telling people that the best way to beat volatile interest rates is to stagger the maturity dates of their GICs. By having 20 percent of your GIC assets roll over each year, instead of 100 percent every five years, you smooth out interest-rate variations and prevent sudden drops in your investment income.

Some financial institutions now put that advice into practice by offering GICs that can be divided into separate components, each with a different maturity date. So, for example, you could invest $10,000 in a five-year GIC but have $2,000 come due on the anniversary date of each year.

If you want to be sure that the GIC section of your RRIF continues to generate returns at a relatively constant rate, this type of certificate is worth looking at. But keep in mind that you won't get the full benefit when interest rates are high, since a portion of your assets will be invested in lower-rate holdings.

Monthly-pay GICs These can be particularly useful in a RRIF where regular cash flow is essential. These GICs do exactly what the name suggests— generate income for your plan every month. The disadvantage is that the interest rate they offer is usually a little less than you would receive from an ordinary GIC.

And here's an important point to remember when investing in any GICs for your RRIF: Most bank and trust company branch managers have the discretion to improve on the posted rates. All you have to do is ask. They can usually give you up to a quarter point more, but we've heard of some bonuses of up to three-quarters of a percent where a lot of money was involved and the financial institution wanted to keep the business. So don't be afraid to do a little hard bargaining.

Look before You Link

Mutual funds reached new heights of popularity in the late 1990s as stock markets boomed and interest rates were low. Even the most conservative of investors, those usually attracted to GICs, felt the pull to put at least some money into funds.

Enter the index-linked, or market-linked, GICs. To pull some of those cautious people back into the fold, many financial institutions created a variety of these products. An index-linked GIC is simply a GIC whose rate of return is based on the performance of one or more of the world's major stock markets.

Index-linked GICs are similar to regular GICs in that full security of the original amount invested is guaranteed. But instead of your return being based on a set interest rate, it's linked to how well a particular stock market performs over a specific period, generally two or three years. If the market has gone up, say, 20 percent when your GIC matures, your payout will be based on that rate. If the market loses ground in that time period, your original investment is returned in full, but you get no interest at all.

These GICs have been tried before without attracting much interest. But the strong stock markets and low interest rates of the 1990s combined to make them extremely popular. Millions of dollars poured into these securities during that time.

On the plus side, you will do better than on a normal GIC if the markets do well. If they don't, you will have given away two or three years of interest. Some people were attracted to this trade-off when the markets were rising. They wanted to get in on the action but didn't wish to risk their capital. Unfortunately, many of these investors will realize a zero return on their money because of the stock market collapse in 2000–01. That's better than a loss, of course–they got their principal back at the end. But they would have been better off putting the money in regular GICs, even at low rates. The best time to buy this type of GIC is when markets are down and pessimism is rife. Ironically, that's when they attract the least interest.

Index-linked GICs have various restrictions that you should examine carefully before investing. Most institutions offer two types of these GICs, one tied to the Canadian market, the other to key foreign markets. Some are "capped," meaning that you cannot earn more than 20 percent or 30 percent no matter how high the market climbs. Others have a "participation" rate. If that's 80 percent, you would get only 80 percent of whatever your market index gains.

Index-linked GICs are very much a hybrid. In considering them as an investment, compare them to other GICs, not to mutual funds. Despite the fact that they are based on market performance, they are very much like ordinary GICs in that they have a basic guarantee, and their return is paid as interest, not dividends or capital gains. If held outside a RRIF, their earnings are fully taxable.

Some products allow investors to lock in growth at some point, protecting against a subsequent market drop. However, this also triggers a tax payment if the GICs are held outside a registered plan. Because the amount of the gain is known, it has to be reported–even if it has not yet been received. You may find it difficult, and you will certainly feel it's unfair, to pay tax on earnings without actually having the money in your hands.

Holding these hybrid GICs inside your registered plan avoids any tax and also provides another interesting advantage: Most of the foreign-index-linked GICs are RRIF-eligible as Canadian content, making them a relatively safe way of increasing your plan's foreign content beyond the mandated limit.

If you decide in favour of an index-linked GIC, do some shopping. Examine how the return is calculated, the length of time to maturity, the profit cap (if there is one), and whether it is possible to cash in early.

You may well find that your financial advisor can achieve results similar to those of an index-linked GIC without many of the disadvantages. One strategy that might work well for some people involves blending conventional GICs with a mutual fund.

Here's how it works:

Split your investment between a conventional GIC and one or more equity mutual funds. This approach offers several advantages, including downside protection for half your assets (your GIC principal is fully guaranteed), a competitive rate of return on the GIC portion, and favourable tax treatment for capital gains earned by the equity funds, if the securities are held outside a RRIF.

As a general rule, however, we do not recommend index-linked GICs inside a RRIF. Although they protect your principal, they do not provide steady cash flow and may end up generating zero profit at maturity. There are better fixed-income alternatives available.

Royalty Trusts

With interest rates continuing to be relatively low, GICs are unlikely to generate enough income in a RRIF to enable you to make a minimum withdrawal without dipping into your capital. For example, if your age was 71 on January 1, 2002, and you had $100,000 in a RRIF, you would need to withdraw at least 7.38 percent or $7,380 from the plan during the year under Canada Customs and Revenue Agency rules. But $100,000 invested in a

6 percent GIC will generate only $6,000 in cash flow. So, to meet the legal requirement, you would have to take out some capital–$1,380 in this case. That means that going into 2003, you would have only $98,620 in RRIF assets. If you're still invested in 6 percent GICs, this will mean less income from the RRIF in 2003 ($5,917). But your minimum withdrawal will continue to be higher (7.48 percent or $7,377 in this case). As you can see, this is a recipe for financial disaster as the assets in your RRIF are steadily depleted.

So the investment community came up with an answer to the capital-eroding effect of low interest rates: the royalty income trust (RIT). The concept had actually been around for some time, but didn't receive much interest or attention until low interest rates created the need.

Fundamentally, it's a simple idea. A trust is set up and acquires partial or full ownership of a revenue-producing asset. In doing so, it may also receive some accumulated tax benefits. It then sells shares (units) in the venture to the public. The attraction is that revenues will flow through to the unit holders, after management fees and other expenses have been deducted.

This is the same principle that lies behind real estate investment trusts (REITs) and dividend income mutual funds. But it's now been extended into totally new areas.

There are basically two types of royalty trusts. The first can be described as the commodity trust. It's based on a resource asset. The most common have been trusts specializing in the petroleum, iron ore, and coal sectors.

Early on, the returns were extremely attractive. Then this class of RIT ran into problems as commodity prices fell and the 1997–98 economic crisis in Asia reduced exports of such key products as metallurgical coal. The subsequent decline in cash flow and market valuations brought home one of the main problems with commodity RITs–they can be volatile and, unlike bonds and strips, the returns are not guaranteed.

The other type of royalty trust is what we call a commercial trust. These trusts own a commercial asset of some type–it could be anything from a hydro-generating plant to a tree nursery to a mattress factory. Again, the revenue from the asset is flowed through to investors. Yields are usually higher than you'll receive from a GIC or bond. Most commercial trusts don't have any tax advantages, but they have tended to be more dependable in cash flow and market price than the commodity-based RITs.

So should you consider using royalty trusts in your RRIF? Absolutely. These securities provide a way to improve cash flow to a level that allows you to draw income without jeopardizing your principal. Just be very careful in your selection, and understand exactly what you're doing.

Before you make a final decision on adding royalty trusts to your RRIF or selecting one or more such securities, here are five points to consider:

The Return Potential You'll see a lot of glowing numbers whenever a new offer comes along. But the reality has been something else, as commodity prices have fluctuated. Ask what happens to your return if the price of the commodity drops 10 percent, or the Canadian dollar rises or falls in value by 5 percent, or the commercial enterprise suffers a 10 percent shortfall in projected revenues. Base your return estimate on a realistic scenario, not on pie-in-the-sky figures. And remember that returns on RITs will fluctuate from year to year. They are not guaranteed.

Restrictions In assessing the potential return from a royalty trust against the other investment options available to you, remember to consider how a particular RIT will be classified in your plan. This is less likely to be a consideration since Ottawa introduced legislation in May 2000 that allows designated limited partnerships—including some royalty trusts—to be classified as full Canadian content and be 100 percent RRIF eligible. Previously, limited partnerships counted as foreign content.

The Risks By their nature, royalty trusts will be higher risk than GICs, Canada Savings Bonds, or even a well-managed equity mutual fund. But the degree of risk will vary from one trust to another. The volatility of resource prices is one critical variable. Oil and gas prices are highly vulnerable to political, economic, and climatic changes. A steep drop in the oil price will mean lower returns from an energy-based trust, as we saw in 1998. On the other hand, a big rise in petroleum prices would boost payouts considerably, a phenomenon that occurred in 2000.

Other risk factors include changes in the value of the Canadian dollar (a higher dollar is usually bad news for these deals, while a lower loonie works in favour of investors) and the depletion of reserves with a corresponding decline in future income.

The Time Factor The longer the time horizon of your RRIF, the more effective a royalty trust can be because of tax-sheltered compounding of your distributions and, if you sell at some point, your potential capital gains.

Income Needs How much income you require and the level of risk you're willing to accept are the most important considerations for your RRIF. If your current investment portfolio isn't throwing off enough cash to meet the minimum withdrawal requirements, you have two choices: Deplete your capital or add some higher-yielding securities, like royalty trusts. Our recommendation is to add some royalty trusts, but only those that are carefully selected and are most likely to have stable income. A financial advisor can be helpful in the selection process.

There's no doubt that you can add juice to your RRSP/RRIF returns by using these trusts, providing you can buy in at a fair price. However, don't overload your plan with them because of the higher risks involved in many cases. If you want to try adding a few, limit yourself to between 10 percent and 15 percent of your holdings. Remember, royalty trusts can be added only to self-directed plans. And be sure to check the foreign-content status of any RIT before you buy it for a RRIF.

Globalizing Your RRIF

In the spirit of diversification, it makes sense to invest at least a part of your asset mix in foreign-content mutual funds. You are allowed to hold up to 30 percent of your RRIF in non-Canadian securities, and too few of us are taking advantage of this opportunity. For the slightly more adventurous, there is a legal way to increase foreign content beyond the limit: Buy Canadian funds that make maximum use of foreign content in their own portfolio—their foreign holdings do not count toward your limit. This simple strategy effectively bumps up your portfolio's foreign content to just over 50 percent.

Foreign investments offer potential for greater long-term growth and protection, both because the economies of other countries move in different cycles and because many are growing more dramatically than the Canadian economy. By participating in the extraordinary growth of some of the world's economic "hot spots," you add both geographic and currency features to your diversified asset mix. As well, you protect your investments against any future declines in the value of the Canadian dollar.

The big international players still consider Canada one of the world's safest investment areas. However, because of our resource-based economy and the poor track record of our currency, they usually demand a higher return to invest here. Although individual investors have no control over global matters, they certainly need to ask: How do I protect myself? The answer lies in foreign diversification. You don't have to go out of the country to buy foreign stocks or bonds. Nor do you need to become an expert in them. A wide range of excellent international mutual funds are sold by many companies operating in Canada.

Indeed, for most investors, particularly those holding RRIFs, the best way to take advantage of proper asset allocation and global diversification is through reputable mutual funds whose expert money managers keep track of market, economic, and political swings around the world.

You need not be put off by the fear that international investing is too risky. We have seen many studies on the subject, and they all come to one conclusion: You actually reduce risk by investing at least some of your money outside Canada. It is more risky to leave all your money in any one country. That would be comparable to buying one stock instead of spreading an investment out over a number of good ones.

So, keeping all of your money in Canada just does not make sense in the long term. This statement may sound unpatriotic, but you cannot afford to be patriotic at the expense of protecting your family and your financial future. From the global perspective, Canada represents only 2 percent of the world's markets, it has a small economy that still is weighted towards the resource sector, and its currency is vulnerable.

In the long run (and despite some severe bouts of volatility), U.S. and international stock, bond, and money market funds—again, sold here in Canada—have dramatically outperformed the average Canadian fund. The potential profit of this RRIF opportunity is far too great to ignore.

If you are still not convinced, the table "Canada vs. the World" shows what $100 in Canadian funds invested in 1985 was worth 15 years later in various investments.

CANADA VS. THE WORLD

What $100 in Canadian funds invested December 31, 1985, was worth 15 years later.

INVESTMENT	VALUE DECEMBER 31, 2000
Canadian T-bills	$291.12
Canadian stocks (TSE 300)	$307.99
U.S. stocks (S&P 500)	$670.43
International stocks (MSCI World)	$700.34
Canadian bonds (SCM Universe Bond)	$425.91
International bonds (Salomon World Gov't Bond)	$374.62

The best way to globalize your RRIF portfolio is by using mutual funds. This gives you good diversification, and the funds can be used to generate income through a systematic withdrawal plan.

A Model Portfolio

Even a balanced, middle-of-the-road RRIF portfolio should have an equity component. The table that follows shows a model RRIF portfolio–but please remember that, as with every other example in this book, this is just a general guideline intended to make a point. You should have your own personal investment mix, in which the appropriate percentage for each investment category is based on your risk tolerance. Rely on your independent professional advisor to help you build your plan, review it at least once a year, and adjust it if circumstances warrant.

Keep interest-bearing securities in your mix. Despite the fact that rates are low and are likely to stay that way for some time, GICs and bonds should represent a core part of your RRIF. They provide income and relative safety.

The fixed-income portion of a RRIF portfolio might range all the way from 30 percent to 60 percent. The portion varies depending on your age, your risk tolerance, income needs, and market conditions. An investor's expected returns will be higher over the years with a solid bond component. When equity markets fall, bonds will cushion the blow.

Never go too far seeking growth. A portfolio made up strictly of equity holdings is potential trouble. You have absolutely no control over what market conditions will be when you retire. For instance, if everything you owned was invested in equities and you retired in the past two years, you would have been in a difficult situation. Again, diversification and balance produce both performance and protection.

If you are unsure of how to set up your asset mix, a "balanced" mutual fund can be a good place to start. These "one-stop shopping" funds are good for mutual fund beginners or for those who want a mix but haven't the time or the ability to set it up themselves. Such funds typically invest in a combination of blue-chip stocks, bonds, and cash. The professional manager decides what proportion of each will make up the fund by considering economic conditions.

The equity segment of your portfolio should hold core mutual funds that are well managed and have consistent performance. As we have said, value-oriented funds usually carry the lowest risk. For the fixed-income portion, a "laddered" portfolio of individual bonds that you build yourself should be considered because it avoids the bite that fund management fees take out of current interest rates. Fees for bond funds have averaged about 1.7 percent, a big chunk out of your portfolio's returns. You can eliminate them by putting your own bond portfolio together with the help of professional advice.

Laddering, or staggering, maturities is a concept that also makes sense with GICs in a low-interest-rate environment. It works this way: Simply buy your

GICs (or bonds) so that 20 percent of the total matures every year, over the next five years. Then reinvest the maturing principal each year for a new five-year term. In this way, you benefit from any future increase in interest rates, and you always have money rolling over into the best interest rate available at the time. This is the best way to reduce the interest-rate risk of having all your GIC money mature when interest rates are low. Investors who began using this approach five years ago would be sitting on 30 percent of their portfolio invested at rates considerably higher than those available today.

You will notice that the cash/equivalent portion of the sample portfolio can go as high as 20 percent. This is in part because the money in your RRIF must be invested so that it will generate the necessary cash flow for withdrawals—another good reason for using the laddered approach.

Note that the high-yield funds in the equity component may include funds that invest in royalty income trusts. These involve higher risk, so you may wish to talk to your financial advisor before adding them to your portfolio.

You will also see that we recommend currency diversification in your RRIF. This is especially important if you plan to spend part of each year in the U.S. Sunbelt or will have some other ongoing need for American currency.

MODEL RRIF PORTFOLIO

ASSET	RANGE
Canadian money market funds	5%–10%
U.S. money market funds	5%–10%
Short-term bonds/mortgage funds	10%–20%
Mid-term bonds/regular bond funds	10%–20%
U.S.$ bonds/foreign bond funds	10%–20%
Dividend income funds (Type B)	10%–15%
Royalty trusts/Income trusts funds	5%–15%
Blue-chip Canadian stocks/value-oriented funds	10%–15%
U.S. blue-chip stocks/value-oriented funds	10%–15%
International value-oriented funds	5%–10%

9

How Can You Reduce Your Tax Bill?

Saving money can be as important as making it, so it has become crucial these days to consider all investments from the after-tax point of view. A buck is usually a buck, but not when it comes to investment income. Our convoluted tax system treats every type of investment income differently, resulting in tremendous variations in after-tax return.

Although our tax rates have come down in recent years, tax efficiency is still an important criterion in selecting investments to be held in a non-registered portfolio. It's not something you need to be concerned about within your RRIF, because all withdrawals are taxed at the same rate. But you need to be sure your RRIF portfolio dovetails with your non-registered investments, or you could end up paying a lot more to the government than would otherwise be the case. Here's a brief rundown of the tax implications of the basic types of investment income:

Interest Although it is the most common source in Canada today, interest income from bonds, GICs, CSBs, deposit accounts, and other interest-bearing investments receives no tax advantage at all. You pay at your marginal rate, meaning at the rate you pay on the last dollar you earn.

Dividends These are payments made to holders of common or preferred shares of corporations or mutual funds. These payments are eligible for the dividend tax credit if held outside a registered plan such as a RRIF and are one of the more tax-efficient ways to receive investment income in this country.

The dividend tax credit is based on the reasoning that this income has already been taxed in the hands of the company at the time that it was earned, before being paid out to investors. So taxing the investor fully would amount to double taxation. To calculate the dividend tax credit, you must first "gross up," or increase, the amount of the dividend payment by 25 percent. You then claim a tax credit for two-thirds of the grossed-up amount. The result is that you effectively pay tax on a smaller amount.

Because dividends received inside a RRIF are ineligible for the tax break–the government won't allow you to have your cake and eat it, too–they're best held outside a registered plan (if you have a choice).

However, pensioners should watch out for a couple of potential drawbacks of this tax break. The grossed-up income that works to your advantage in calculating the dividend tax credit can work against you in other ways. The reason is that this artificially inflated income could also put you over the income threshold that qualifies for the age tax credit, and, if you're in a higher income bracket, it could also push you to a level where you would be subjected to a clawback of Old Age Security benefits.

Still, dividends do offer tax efficiency outside your RRIF, and you can switch from interest to dividends without a lot of risk. Dividend-paying investments include high-quality preferred and common shares–banks and utility companies are especially attractive–or dividend income mutual funds.

Capital Gains Only one half of your profit from the sale of shares or distributions from equity mutual funds is included in your income for tax purposes. The other half is effectively tax-free, making capital gains an attractive income option.

Rental Income Revenue received from income properties or from distributions made by real estate investments (REITs) can be tax-sheltered in part through the use of capital cost allowance (depreciation) and the deduction of other related expenses. If you have a rental property, consult the CCRA guide on the subject for specific information. Investors who hold REIT units outside their RRIF will receive a slip each year from the trust that indicates how much of the income received is taxable.

Return on Capital Some royalty trusts and mutual funds distribute a portion of their income on a tax-deferred basis each year. This is as a result of special allowances, particularly in the energy and mining industries, that are passed on to investors. This tax break applies only to income received outside your RRIF.

Asset Distribution We must stress the importance of distributing assets carefully between registered and non-registered plans and setting up your portfolios in such a way as to minimize tax payable. Generally, this means keeping interest-bearing securities such as bonds, GICs, and the like inside RRIFs, and those earning dividends and capital gains outside your RRIF.

If, however, your RRIF represents your only investment portfolio, as is the case with many people, then you should hold high-quality stocks and/or equity mutual funds in your RRIF. The growth factor should outweigh any tax disadvantages.

There are other ways to reduce your "contribution" to the Canada Customs and Revenue Agency each year. By planning ahead and implementing even a few of these investment and financial planning suggestions, you can reap significant rewards when you file your next tax return.

Tips for Those Nearing Retirement

First, we will discuss strategies that will be of greatest interest to people at or nearing retirement age. These will be followed by a list aimed at those who are already retired.

Invest in Tax-Deferred Securities That Can Grow

Capital gains from stocks are not taxed until you sell them. In other words, as long as you hold on to stocks that have gained in value, you do not have to pay anything to the Canada Customs and Revenue Agency. So, investing in such shares outside your RRIF becomes, in fact, a form of tax deferral. In addition, you have control over the timing of the realization of the gain. It makes sense to avoid selling stocks that have appreciated in value before you have to, thereby dodging the trap of realizing capital gains sooner than necessary. When the tax on a non-registered investment gain becomes due, a large chunk of your savings has to be shipped off to Ottawa, gone forever and no longer working for you. For maximum effect, choose stocks you can hold for a long time, such as dividend-paying blue chips (common stocks only) of companies that disperse dividends regularly.

The Lower-Earning Spouse Should Invest

If the lower-earning spouse is the registered investor, any investment income will be taxed at his or her rate, or not at all if his or her income is low enough.

Split Income with Your Spouse

If your spouse is in a lower income bracket, you can lower your tax bill if you transfer some of your taxable income to him or her. "Income splitting" simply means transferring money or property from a higher-income spouse to a spouse who is in a lower tax bracket. This has to be done carefully because the government's "attribution rules" prevent some forms of income splitting. For example, if you transfer or lend property or money to your spouse, any income or loss from the property will be attributed back to you for tax purposes.

However, there is an exception to this rule. If you sell assets to your spouse for fair market value and report the gain, the attribution rules do not apply. You can also lend money or property to your spouse, but you must charge interest on the loan and report that income in order to avoid the attribution rules. The interest rate must be at least equal to the Canada Customs and Revenue Agency's "prescribed interest rate"–the rate it sets as being fair according to the market–at the time. Make sure your spouse pays the interest by January 30 of the following year. If the January 30 deadline passes without your spouse paying the interest, that year's income and all future income from the loaned property will be attributed back to you.

Another way to increase the lower-income spouse's investment capabilities is to make sure that groceries, mortgage and rent payments, property taxes, credit card bills, and all other daily living expenses are paid by the higher-income spouse. This leaves the lower-income spouse with more money to invest to earn future income that will be taxed at a lower rate. If you use this strategy, you and your spouse should deposit your income into separate bank accounts. This allows you to keep records to show that the earnings of the higher-income spouse were used to pay the expenses.

A third way to effectively transfer funds is for the higher-income spouse to pay the lower-income spouse's tax bill. If you do this, make sure the cheque used to pay your spouse's tax is drawn on your own account. Any funds your spouse would otherwise use to pay taxes can be invested without the income being attributed back to you.

Transfer Income to Your Children

You can also reduce your taxes by transferring part of your taxable income to children who are earning little or no taxable income. Beware: If you give investments to a child under 18, all interest and dividends will be attributed back to you and taxed accordingly. This attribution rule does not apply to capital gains or to the child's earned income. Income from loans to adult children will be attributed back to the lender under the attribution rules. If interest is charged and paid as discussed above, the attribution rules will not apply.

Consider Registered Education Savings Plans (RESPs)

Contributions to an RESP are not tax deductible. However, the income in the plan grows tax-free, so RESPs do enjoy the effect of tax-free compounding interest. When your child or grandchild goes to college or university, the RESP provides money to help cover tuition and living expenses. This will be taxable to the child, but students usually do not have much other income and, therefore, will pay little or no tax.

The 1998 federal budget introduced a new program called the Canadian Education Savings Grant. Any contributions made to an RESP for a child 17 or under now result in a grant from the government of up to $400 per child per year. The cash from the grant will be deposited directly into your savings plan, helping it grow that much faster.

This comes on top of two improvements made in the 1997 budget. First, the limit on annual contributions per beneficiary was doubled from $2,000 to $4,000. The overall lifetime limit remains at $42,000, so this change will be most helpful for those who start saving when their children are older.

Second, if the child does not go on to university, the income from the plan can now be rolled over into your RRSP, provided you have available contribution room. Previously, such income was lost, with the interest staying in the pool for the benefit of other students.

RESPs are certainly more attractive now, but many parents and grandparents still find them narrow and restrictive. For example, it's nice that you can now transfer unused RESP earnings into your RRSP, but it probably won't help many parents, and it will be of even less use to grandparents. Few people are likely to have anywhere near the $50,000 of RRSP room they'll need in their late 40s or 50s, when this situation is likely to arise. And once you've moved from an RRSP to a RRIF, this option isn't available at all.

You can also now withdraw RESP earnings if your child does not go to university, but only at tremendous cost. The money is treated as income in the year received and taxed at your marginal rate plus a 20 percent penalty. You could end up paying between 70 percent and 75 percent on money taken out this way.

The maximum period over which income generated in an RESP may be sheltered from tax is 26 years. Family plans are subject to the same contribution limits per beneficiary, but if one of your children decides against post-secondary education, the funds contributed for this child, and the income earned, can be redirected to benefit any other children who do pursue post-secondary education.

An interesting alternative, or addition, to an RESP is to save through an investment plan that's set up as an informal trust. Here's why: The money in such a trust can be used by the child in any way, including non-educational purposes, should he or she decide not to go to university. And you can take out all or part at any time, for example, for a financial emergency.

Although earned interest or dividends would be attributed to you for income tax purposes, capital gains are deemed to belong to the child. So this sort of education savings program should focus on mutual funds that target long-term capital appreciation—which is what most equity funds are all about in any case.

Lower and Defer Taxes with an RRSP

If you are still eligible for an RRSP, you should take maximum advantage of the tax break it provides. Specifically, you should top up your contribution in the year you convert to a RRIF, as this will be your last opportunity to do so.

By contributing to an RRSP, even in the final year, you lower the amount of taxes owing and create a larger tax-sheltered capital fund within the RRIF.

You may have both a RRIF and an RRSP at the same time, as long as you are younger than 69. So you may have already set up a small RRIF, which would allow you to take advantage of the pension tax credit, while continuing to make RRSP contributions to get the benefit of the resulting tax deduction.

Here are some basic tips:

Maximize RRSP Contributions You can put up to 18 percent of your previous year's earned income into an RRSP, to a maximum of $13,500. This amount will be lower if you already contribute to a pension or profit-sharing plan. You can tell how much you can contribute for the current year by checking the Notice of Assessment you receive after filing your tax return. If you are making your final RRSP contribution, be sure to use up any carry-forward room still available.

Consider Borrowing to Reach Your Maximum Contribution Many financial institutions offer loans at prime or slightly higher to enable you to make your maximum RRSP contribution. Generally, if you can repay the borrowed funds within a year or so, or your income for the current year falls into a higher tax bracket than usual, borrowing funds for your RRSP contribution makes sense.

Save Extra with a Spousal RRSP If one spouse is the main breadwinner, it pays to place a portion of his or her annual allowable contribution into an RRSP for the other spouse. This will lower the higher earner's taxable income and, more importantly, will allow the spousal RRSP money to be taxed at a lower rate when it is withdrawn. But you have to have patience. If your spouse withdraws the funds from the RRSP within three years after the latest contribution, the amount will attribute back to you and be taxed in your hands.

Tax-Saving Tips for Those Already Retired

The following tips will be of most interest to those who are already retired.

Split CPP/QPP Benefits with Your Spouse

You may direct up to 50 percent of your Canada Pension Plan (CPP) benefits to your spouse, provided that both of you are over 60. If either of you chooses this option, a portion of the other spouse's CPP is automatically assigned back to the first spouse. If both of you are eligible for maximum CPP benefits, assignment will not change anything, since each of you will assign half of the maximum to the other. But if, for example, you have high CPP benefits and are in a high tax bracket, and your spouse has low benefits or none, the assignment can effectively transfer up to half of the CPP income. The attribution rules do not apply to such an assignment.

"Freeze" Your Estate's Value

If you have substantial assets, and particularly if you have a business that may increase in value, you may wish to obtain professional advice as to the appropriateness of "freezing" your estate. *Estate freezing* is the term used to describe steps taken to fix the value of your estate (or a particular asset) so that future growth will go to your children or other beneficiaries and not be taxed at your death. Although this field of estate planning is quite complex, an estate freeze may substantially reduce the tax payable on death without seriously impairing your access to income or assets during your lifetime.

Reduce Probate Fees by Naming Beneficiaries of Your Estate

Taxes are really just fees owed to the government for services it provides, and probate fees are no different. If you name a beneficiary to your RRSP, RRIF, proceeds from life insurance, and, in most provinces, joint real estate tenancies, you can bypass probate fees on these items. However, be sure to consult a tax advisor first. In some cases, such strategies can have other, unintended, tax consequences for your estate.

Transfer Pension Credit to Your Spouse

If your retirement income is too low to take advantage of the $1,000 pension income tax credit, it can be transferred to your higher-earning spouse. The age credit is also transferable.

10

How Can Estate Planning Protect You and Your Family?

One of the most crucial aspects of financial planning—especially for older Canadians—is estate planning. Estate planning means arranging your affairs to ensure that whatever remains of your carefully accumulated retirement savings after you die passes to your heirs according to your wishes and in the proportion you desire, without delays and unnecessary tax payments.

Many people think that estate planning is a process necessary only for the rich, but in today's complex, ever-changing tax and legal climate, it is critical even for those of us with modest assets.

Estate planning is an uncomfortable topic for many, which is probably why an astonishing 50 percent of all Canadians have failed to execute even a simple will. But for such a relatively elementary and inexpensive document (in its basic form), the consequences of not having one can be dire indeed. Dying without a will, or even with one that is out of date, can result in personal and financial tragedy for those left behind. In the absence of a will, the rules for "intestate" (legalese for without a will) take effect and the estate is distributed according to provincial formulas. The results rarely resemble what the person wanted.

If you are without a will, put aside any personal fears or superstitions about considering or discussing your death and put one in place today. The reality is that a retirement plan will become an estate plan the moment you die, and, as no one knows when that will happen, your retirement plan must include a sound estate-planning component. An estate plan will ensure that everything is arranged so that funds are available for your spouse, family, or other beneficiaries on death; that your property is disposed of according to your wishes; and that your assets are transferred in a timely, orderly, and tax-effective manner.

Most lawyers will draft a simple will for under $300. And keeping your will up to date is as important as drawing up the original. If there are any significant changes in your lifestyle—such as births, deaths, a move to another province or country, new business arrangements, marriage, re-marriage, or even new tax legislation—a new or amended will should be drawn up immediately.

Estate and retirement planning should also work together when it comes to designating beneficiaries for RRSPs, RRIFs, life insurance policies, and pension plans. In such cases, you should name a beneficiary. The benefit then passes directly to that person, avoiding probate and executor fees. But make sure this is consistent with your personal plans (see how to avoid potential pitfalls under "The Successor Annuitant Solution," which follows). On the other hand, if your will sets up a spousal trust or a trust for a child, you will then want to make sure that most of your assets do flow into your estate.

Taxes Paid by the Estate

Your will can avoid needless taxation. If you leave everything to your spouse, that transfer takes place tax-free, whereas dying intestate can trigger needless and unwanted tax consequences.

Estate planning must also go beyond the death of your surviving spouse. At that stage, the Canada Customs and Revenue Agency's "deemed disposition" rules deem all the assets as having, in effect, been sold, and tax must be paid in that year on RRSPs and RRIFs (unless, of course, you have taken advantage of newer rules that allow such assets to be passed on to financially dependent children or grandchildren) and on capital gains in stocks, a business, or even a cottage. It is important to be aware that such taxes are paid by the estate, not the heirs, a distinction that, if misunderstood, could ruin an otherwise good plan. For example, if you were to leave a cottage to one child, with everything else to be split equally among other children, the estate would be liable for the capital gains tax on the cottage. After paying those taxes, the value of the remaining estate might be reduced substantially.

Another example of an unintended repercussion occurs when someone has other assets in addition to a RRIF. Assume you have $100,000 remaining in your RRIF and another $100,000 in other assets. If you have two children, you might think the easiest and most fair settlement would be to name one child the beneficiary of the RRIF and the other the beneficiary of your estate. But things are never that simple. In this case, the $100,000 RRIF would, in effect, pass to the one child tax-free, because the estate is required to pay all fees and taxes, leaving the second child with substantially less, even though your original intent was to split the assets equally.

If you expect your estate will be relatively substantial, review the tax implications of succession with a qualified expert.

Life Insurance Can Help

Too few people realize that the government will be there, sooner or later, to scoop up its share of an estate. In fact, RRIFs containing substantial assets will ultimately trigger a tax liability amounting to 50 percent or more in most provinces. However, if you consider your RRIF monies to be estate assets in addition to a source of retirement income, you may be able to use life insurance to keep your legacy intact.

A sad but legal fact of life is that, as pointed out above, your capital assets are deemed by the Canada Customs and Revenue Agency to have been sold when you die, and any capital gains resulting are folded into your taxable income and reported on your final tax return. Your RRIFs are brought into taxable income as well.

As mentioned above, this is not the case when your estate is left to your spouse or if your RRSP or RRIF assets pass directly to dependent children or grandchildren. In these cases, the assets roll over to them tax-free. But this is merely a deferral. The Canada Customs and Revenue Agency, as you know, is relentless! In general, the tax liability is triggered when the assets are passed to the next generation. So, although it is true that you are not subject to estate tax or death duty in Canada, your heirs may end up facing a huge income tax bill that could catapult even those of modest means into the highest tax bracket.

Buying life insurance is a sound way to reduce the financial impact of the Canada Customs and Revenue Agency becoming one of your beneficiaries. The inevitable taxes will still be paid, of course, but the insurance policy generates the money needed and preserves your estate.

The basic concept is to buy enough life insurance to take care of the taxes when you (or you and your spouse) die. Providing you are in good or reasonable health, the money you pay out in annual premiums could easily be offset by future tax savings.

Some companies offer policies specifically designed to preserve estate assets. Other insurance plans are designed to pay out a lump sum when the surviving spouse dies. Life insurance can also be useful in equalizing estates, such as in the two-child beneficiary example we referred to, where assets outside a registered plan are not easily liquidated or there is no desire to sell them.

And here is a suggestion: If your children are old enough and can afford it, ask them to pick up the tab for the insurance premiums—after all, they are the ones who will benefit down the road, and they will never find an investment with as good a return.

We've noted that if you have dependent children or grandchildren, you should be aware that the 1999 federal budget made a dramatic change regarding how RRSP and RRIF assets can be passed on at the time of your death.

Dependent children or grandchildren may now inherit assets from your RRSPs and RRIFs, even if you have a surviving spouse. This new rule applies in cases of deaths that occurred after 1998, but may also be applied retroactively to 1995, if the deceased's estate and beneficiaries wish to do so. In instances where a spouse is not in need of the monies, this could represent an effective estate planning strategy for reducing taxes.

As well, the transfer options that are available to your dependent vary according to circumstances. In the case of a child or grandchild who is financially dependent because of a physical or mental infirmity, the benefits may be transferred to a registered plan (RRSP or RRIF) or be used to purchase an annuity. For a child who isn't dependent because of a physical or mental infirmity, an annuity is the only option; the term of the annuity is limited to not more than 18 years minus the child's or grandchild's age at the time the annuity was purchased, and payments must begin no later than one year after the purchase.

The Successor Annuitant Solution

If you have a spouse and want the proceeds of your RRIF to go to him or her if you die first, naming your spouse as the fund's beneficiary, either within the RRIF itself or in a will, can accomplish that goal. But, as we have said so many times in this book, things are never straightforward when you're dealing with government regulations and legalese.

Be aware that taking the beneficiary route, which is what most people do, can cause a variety of problems for your spouse at a stressful time. Why? Because, in such a case, the remaining funds in your RRIF will pass to your spouse tax-free when you die, but the RRIF itself may come to an end. In such a case, the assets will be cashed in and the proceeds rolled over into your spouse's RRIF. Tax forms must be filed, and investments must be made all over again.

Not only does this generate a lot of unnecessary paperwork, it can also result in lost revenue. This would be the case, for example, if your RRIF were holding a GIC at an interest rate higher than that currently available. Your spouse would have to buy a GIC at the lower, current rate.

A simple, legalistic change you can make on your own, however, can make all the difference in the world. Instead of naming your spouse the beneficiary of your RRIF, designate him or her as the "successor annuitant," either in the fund itself or in your will. Voilà! Now the RRIF will remain exactly the same, except that the name of the payee will change to your spouse's name.

You have nothing to lose by going the successor annuitant route and there are no additional costs. So remember the term and make sure you choose this option. All you have to do is fill in your RRIF form where indicated or make the proper designation in your will. It's best to make the designation in the RRIF rather than in your will, unless you have a particular reason for putting the fund into your estate, because the plan's assets will then pass to your spouse without probate fees.

In recent years, many financial institutions have changed their RRIF forms so that a beneficiary automatically becomes successor annuitant. Check to see where you stand. Better yet, get written confirmation.

Choosing an Executor

A will is the only document that allows you to name your executor/executrix. This is the person who will be entrusted with settling your estate according to your wishes and administering any trust you may have set up. Choosing your executor is an extremely important decision, particularly if your estate is sizeable or complicated.

There are two types of executors: corporate executors, such as trust companies, and individuals, such as family members or close friends. Please don't saddle a relative or friend with what can be an extremely complex and time-consuming job, certainly not without his or her consent. If you want to appoint someone close, make him or her a co-executor with a professional advisor or trust company.

By naming someone co-executor, you allow the friend or relative to retain the executor's powers and duties, including the right to review the work of the professional, but someone with the expertise and time takes care of the long list of details. To give you an idea of how much work is involved, here is a list of some of the basic duties required in settling an estate.

- Reading, and interpreting, the will;
- Locating all beneficiaries (not always an easy job);
- Ensuring the continuation of a private business;
- Reviewing insurance policies;
- Completing claims for life insurance and pensions;
- Notifying bankers, brokers, business associates;
- Closing accounts;
- Managing and evaluating investments and collecting income;
- Arranging for the sale of real estate;
- Evaluating real estate, cars, household and personal effects;
- Assembling a full inventory of assets to obtain probate from court;
- Distributing household and personal effects to beneficiaries (potentially a major headache if you don't know them well or if they do not get along);
- Paying legacies and bequests, submitting a full accounting to beneficiaries, and obtaining release;
- Converting assets to cash to pay debts and taxes;
- Obtaining tax clearance from the Canada Customs and Revenue Agency;
- Handling and answering correspondence.

On top of all this, an executor can be held personally liable for any mistakes. Still want the job? The duties, decisions, and knowledge required to administer an estate demand skills that few individuals possess, not to mention a great deal of time. If a friend or relative asks you to be an executor, think about it long and hard.

Your responsibilities begin almost at the moment of their death. You may, however, hire an agent, preferably a trust company, to help with any or all of the details. An executor has the right to hire such an agent without applying to a court or asking the beneficiaries. Costs are then paid out of the estate's assets.

The Team Approach

If your estate is of a substantial size, you will likely need several types of expertise. Beyond a lawyer to draft the will and an executor, you may require someone to manage your assets under a continuing Power of Attorney should you become incapable or incapacitated.

In addition, if you set up one or more trusts in your will, you will have to name a trustee, which can be the same person or organization designated executor. As more assets are involved, and as your personal situation becomes more complicated, your estate "team" should be expanded for the best results.

You definitely need a talented, professional team if you own a business. As mentioned above, income tax liabilities will be due upon the death of the majority shareholder, and the decisions you make now will have an important tax impact on your estate.

A useful strategy in such cases is a sophisticated planning technique known as an "estate freeze," through which wealth is transferred from one generation to the next in the most tax-effective fashion. We referred to this in Chapter 9. An estate freeze determines a point at which future gains in an asset begin being realized by the next generation. In this way, you can transfer shares in your company to your children without tax problems—for example, where you are the majority shareholder but your adult child is actually operating the company. You can also use an estate freeze to transfer a recreational property to your children while you are still alive; this is a good financial strategy unless you think they will start to tell you when you can and cannot use the cottage!

You will also need specialized help if you have a large portfolio, or more than one vacation property, or if you plan to name more beneficiaries than usual. Again, a major trust company is probably the best choice. You should also call on a trust company and a specialized lawyer when setting up a charitable trust, which is one of the best ways to leave money to a charity. Through this mechanism, you can make the donation and take advantage of the tax deduction before you die.

11

WHAT ARE ANNUITIES?

An annuity is, in essence, a contract between you and a financial institution, usually an insurance company, under which you give the institution an amount of money in return for a promise to provide you with a fixed income for a defined period of time, often in the form of monthly payments. Annuities come in a wide variety of types, and are normally irrevocable. You can buy an annuity at any age.

Annuity income, which is fully taxable in the year received if bought with money from a registered plan, is determined by various factors, the most important being interest rates at the time of purchase. Others include your life expectancy, your age, your gender (women get paid less in general because they live longer on average), and the amount you invest. Options such as guaranteed terms or indexing against inflation cost more, in that your payments will be lower.

Why an Annuity May Be the Right Choice for You

Although conversion to a RRIF is the best retirement income choice for most people, there is also a lot to be said about the value of annuities and how you may use them now or in the future. And while RRIFs are becoming increasingly popular, annuities may be a more appropriate choice for some people.

Properly handled, a RRIF can be your most valuable source of retirement income. But everything has its price, and along with the flexibility and the estate benefits, RRIFs come with certain risks. With control comes responsibility, and poor investment decisions and bad financial planning–

such as taking too much money out too soon—can have major negative impacts on your income and capital. Factors such as low interest rates (particularly worrisome if your RRIF investments are primarily interest-bearing securities), unfavourable market conditions, poor investment choices, unsatisfactory income planning, and lump-sum withdrawals all come into play with a RRIF.

If, for example, interest-bearing securities (GICs, term deposits, bonds) were your investments of choice in the 1980s, it made sense to choose a RRIF and to delay the purchase of an annuity. The lower minimum payout schedule in effect at that time (the rules were changed to increase minimum payout requirements in 1993), combined with the higher interest rates then available, allowed RRIF capital to grow, even as income was paid out every year.

However, interest rates have been substantially lower since the 1990s, often providing less income than the new requirements for higher minimum payouts. This means that RRIF capital (again, depending on your investment choices) could start to shrink immediately. The combination of longer life expectancy, earlier retirement, and lower interest rates leads to the risk that investors will outlive their capital.

For example, before 1993, the minimum withdrawal required of a 71-year-old was 5.26 percent of the assets in a RRIF, a sum easily covered by the interest rates being paid at that time. Now, however, that minimum has been increased to 7.38 percent, which means that the value of your plan will begin to decrease after you reach 71 unless your RRIF investments earn more than that.

Therefore, if conservative investments, security, and maximum income for life sum up your key objectives, you should take a serious look at annuities. On the other hand, if you have sizeable RRSP and non-registered assets, and your investment knowledge and approach can tolerate even the most moderate degree of risk, a RRIF is a much better fit. It will allow you to further grow your capital and maintain flexibility for estate and other planning purposes.

An important part of RRIF flexibility is that, unlike an annuity, you don't have to keep it forever. At some point, even with the balanced, diversified investment portfolio we recommend, the payments from your RRIF will begin to decline. Exactly when that will happen depends on several factors, including the amount of money you take out each year and the growth rate of the assets in the plan. Typically, however, the decline in payments will happen sometime in your late 70s or your 80s. Before it does, it might make sense to use some or all the money in the RRIF to buy a life annuity. Because of your advanced age, the annuity payments will be much higher. And they will be locked in for life, so you will not have to worry about the cash ever running out.

To sum up, annuities may be preferable to RRIFs because they are simple, predictable, and secure. Once you buy an annuity, no further money management is required on your part. You do not have to worry about GICs, bonds, stocks, or mutual funds. Nor do you have to be concerned about where the market or interest rates are going. Dramatic downward spirals in the economy will not affect your annuity nest egg. You receive a guaranteed income either for life, which ensures that you will not outlive your capital, or for a specific term, and the payments can be issued for the extent of your life alone, or can be directed to be paid to your spouse, should you die first.

You should consider an annuity if any of the following is true for you:

- You feel uncomfortable with the thought of making your own investment decisions, or you don't have the time;

- You are unable to find someone you trust to make these decisions for you;

- You feel you absolutely need a guaranteed monthly income to cover your basic needs;

- You believe that cost-of-living increases will have little impact on the expenses you will need to pay;

- You are in good health and your family has a history of long life expectancy;

- You have no dependents or heirs;

- You have only a small amount of retirement savings; or

- Interest rates are unusually high.

Two Basic Types

Annuities come in two basic types, life and term-certain annuities, which in turn are composed of a variety of forms that have appeal in specific situations.

Life Annuity

Life annuities are sold only by life insurance companies, which also sell RRIFs, LIFs, and other forms of annuities. A life annuity is described exactly by its name—the monthly payments, which are the highest of all annuities, keep coming as long as you live. But they stop on the day you die, whether that date is a few months after you take it out or if you live well past your 100th birthday.

Few people opt for a pure life annuity these days. In fact, because of the relinquishment clause, which provides the possibility of losing all your money in the event of an early death, most insurance companies actually require you to sign a waiver stating that you understand and accept that payments cease when you die. However, a life annuity of this variety would be suitable for people who do not want to manage their investments, who do not have families or charities they wish to favour with a bequest, and who want to receive the largest monthly cheque possible.

Life annuities that have one or more options are much more common and popular. The following are common types of life annuities that offer various additional features:

Joint-and-Last-Survivor Annuity This variation pays less per month, usually between 10 percent and 15 percent less, but continues payments as long as you or your spouse lives. The payments stop when the surviving spouse dies. This annuity has clear appeal to married couples. An additional feature even allows you to choose to provide the survivor with either the full amount at once or payments over a defined length of time.

Guaranteed-Term Annuity Either type of life annuity can be purchased with a minimum number of payments guaranteed. This ensures that any payments remaining or their "commuted value," meaning the equivalent lump sum of future payments under the guarantee period, are paid to your spouse or other beneficiary upon your death. Payments do not cease at the end of the guaranteed period if you are still alive. They continue until your death or until the death of your spouse in the case of a joint-and-last-survivor annuity.

Most life annuities include guarantee periods. The longest is to age 90, and they commonly range between five and twenty years. You must decide on a guarantee period at the time you buy the annuity. Again, there is a cost involved. The length of the guarantee period reduces your monthly payments. In most cases, however, the difference can be relatively minor. As in the case of RRIFs, wouldn't you prefer to see at least some money go to your family rather than to that huge, anonymous life insurance company?

Insured Annuity If you want to buy an annuity with the additional goal of preserving capital for your estate, this option is worth considering. In effect, it combines two insurance products: a life annuity with no guarantee period and a term-to-100 life insurance policy.

First, however, you must be in good enough health to qualify for the life insurance, and that means being able to pass a medical examination. Older people without serious ailments are often approved, so it's worth a try, but buy the insurance first. Insured annuities work well for non-smokers in good health, 65 or older, with at least $50,000 in non-registered investments.

The annuity guarantees income for life, and the insurance policy protects your capital, providing a probate-free and creditor-protected estate for your beneficiaries. The Supreme Court of Canada recently ruled that annuities issued as insurance contracts cannot be seized by creditors in the case of bankruptcy. This insurance does not apply to term-certain annuities issued by other financial institutions.

Here's an example: You buy $100,000 in term-to-100 life insurance with a guaranteed, fixed annual premium to age 100. Shop around. Some insurance companies continue the coverage past age 100 until death, with no further premiums. Next, buy a life annuity for a lump sum of $100,000, in return for a monthly income for life. The policy and the annuity do not have to be purchased from the same firm; in fact, you'll almost always get better deals on each product from separate companies. Insurance companies typically offer their best bargains on one product only.

The annuity provides you with income and the insurance restores the original $100,000 after your death. If you pursue this technique, choose your agent carefully. Annuity prices, the availability of such policies, and the premiums vary widely among insurance companies. You need an independent agent who will shop the entire market for you, and who will also pick a financially sound company. The last thing you need is for your insurer to expire before you do.

Term-Certain Annuity

A term-certain annuity differs from a life annuity in that it provides a fixed monthly income until the age of 90, rather than for your life. If you die earlier, payments continue to your surviving spouse until what would have been your 90th birthday. If your spouse is younger than you are, you can base this form of annuity on his or her age, thereby extending the payment schedule. If your spouse does not survive you, the remaining payments are cashed out according to the insurance company's commuted value formula and paid to your estate.

It is important to note that, although a term-certain annuity to age 90 does provide higher monthly payments than a life annuity with a guarantee to age 90, the difference in the amount of the payout is small. The advantage of a life annuity is that it provides you with the security of knowing that you will have income if you live longer, so it would be a better choice in many cases.

Term-certain annuities are sold by life insurance companies but, unlike life annuities, they are also offered by banks, trust companies, and investment dealers (which also sell RRIFs and LIFs). Mutual fund dealers and credit unions are limited to selling only RRIFs and LIFs.

Additional Options

As we mentioned at the beginning of this chapter, annuities come in many varieties. Here are six additional options that have appeal in specific situations:

Indexed Annuity Annuities can be structured to provide protection from inflation, but you must accept a lower level of payments, initially anywhere from 30 percent to 45 percent less. Four payment formulas are available, although rarely will you find them all available from any one company. Again, careful shopping is crucial. Payments increase every year, based on one of the following formulas:

- Indexing guaranteed at 4 percent, compounded annually on the date you received your first payment;

- Annual indexing at a rate set 3 percent less than the average yield on Government of Canada 90-day Treasury bills;

- Annual indexing at 60 percent of the increase in the Consumer Price Index, the generally accepted measure of inflation in Canada, in the previous calendar year; and

- Annual indexing at 100 percent of the increase in the Consumer Price Index.

An indexed annuity may be purchased in combination with a RRIF, as we'll explain in more detail shortly.

Prescribed Annuity A prescribed annuity can be purchased only with non-registered funds; the money may not come from an RRSP. The payments are made up of principal and interest, and you are taxed on only the interest portion of each payment received during a calendar year. This effectively spreads the tax impact out over the life of the contract by keeping the taxable portion—the interest—at the same level throughout the life of the annuity. A prescribed annuity may also be combined with a RRIF.

Cashable Annuity Although most annuity decisions are irrevocable, legislation has allowed cashable annuities since 1986. Few companies offer this option, but most will at least consider giving you the commuted value of a term-certain annuity because it can be easily calculated at any time (the process is far more difficult regarding a life annuity). Usually, a penalty is involved. You should consider cashing in if you've developed a serious medical condition, if interest rates are substantially higher than when you bought the annuity, or if you really need the cash. Cashed-in money can be moved into a RRIF.

Income-Reducing Annuity This form of joint-and-last-survivor life annuity provides higher monthly payments until the death of one spouse. Payments to the surviving spouse are then reduced. The rationale for this reduction, which certainly makes sense, is that one person will require less income than two people would.

Impaired Annuity If you have a medical condition that could result in a reduction of your life expectancy and you can produce a doctor's report to prove it, you may qualify for a life annuity that will pay out as if you were older. This type of annuity translates into higher payments because the actuarial tables used by life insurance companies will project a shorter-than-normal lifespan over which payments must be made.

You have nothing to lose by applying, and you don't have to be at death's door to do so. Conditions such as hypertension (high blood pressure), heart disease, stroke, diabetes, Alzheimer's disease, or cancer make you eligible for this type of annuity.

If you are married, you can still choose various options within an impaired annuity to protect your spouse in the future. The options you choose should depend on what other income-producing assets you have.

Deferred Annuity Although few reasons to opt for this choice exist in a low-interest-rate environment, it may well be important at some later date to know that you can buy an annuity now to provide income in the future, rather than starting payments at the time of purchase.

These deferred payments may not begin any later than the month of January of the year in which you turn 70, but can be put in place as much as 10 years in advance. Your eventual income will be correspondingly higher as the time frame over which you defer payments lengthens, simply because your money will be generating interest during that time. Generally, this technique makes sense only if interest rates are high and you want to lock them in, or if you feel the rates will further decline between now and the time you retire.

Combinations of RRIFs and Annuities

Depending on your investment personality and financial circumstances, a mixture of RRIFs and annuities may be the best way to balance your retirement income plan. Keep in mind that RRIF funds can be moved into an annuity in the future.

Annuities provide guaranteed income, and RRIFs provide flexibility and the opportunity for growth. A well-thought-out combination of the two could meet all your retirement needs. For example, if you do not have a company pension, and if RRSPs represent a major portion of your retirement income-producing assets, an indexed annuity alone might be the best way to cover basic living expenses. However, if you have RRSP funds above the cost of an adequate indexed annuity but still want to have that basic protection, you may wish to buy an indexed annuity and switch the remaining money into a RRIF, investing in conservative equities or growth-oriented mutual funds to help meet your future needs.

Those with substantial registered and non-registered portfolios who are attracted to annuities might consider buying a prescribed annuity with the non-registered funds and using the registered funds to invest in a RRIF. This strategy provides a blend of tax benefits, investment flexibility, and a degree of tax sheltering.

RRIF/Annuity Checklist—Which Is Best for You?

As discussed earlier, there are many factors to take into account when deciding between RRIFs and annuities–or, in some cases, a combination of both.

Do any of the following situations or goals apply to you? If so, you can see at a glance which option best meets your needs.

Remember, as well, that you can always switch from a RRIF to an annuity at a later date–but you cannot do the reverse. This checklist is intended as a general guideline. Consult your financial advisor to determine which option or combination of options is best for you and your family.

RRIF/ANNUITY CHECKLIST

SITUATION	PREFERRED MATURITY OPTION
In addition to significant registered assets, I have sizeable non-registered investment assets.	RRIF
I must have guaranteed income to meet my basic living needs.	Annuity
I feel confident that I can manage my investment assets to ensure the lifetime income I require.	RRIF
I do not feel confident that I can manage my investment assets to ensure the lifetime income I require.	Annuity
I am worried about inflation and particularly concerned about outliving my capital.	Annuity
Personal control over my assets is very important to me.	RRIF
My main objective is to get the maximum income possible for the rest of my life.	Annuity
Estate preservation is my primary objective.	RRIF
Income flexibility would be advantageous to me for tax planning purposes.	RRIF
I am in good health, and there is a history of long life expectancy in my family.	Annuity
Investment growth for my future income needs is a primary objective.	RRIF
I have no dependents or heirs.	Annuity
Income flexibility is important because I anticipate irregular or increasing income requirements.	RRIF
My RRSPs represent my main source of retirement income.	Annuity
My retirement income from all sources will be in excess of my projected needs.	RRIF
I have minimal retirement savings.	Annuity

Other Retirement Income Planning Considerations

If an annuity is your preferred maturity option, you should also consider such features as guarantee period, indexing, or backing up the annuity with insurance. If you are married, a joint-and-last-survivor annuity should be considered.

If a RRIF is your preferred maturity option, you should also give careful thought to whether your RRIF investments will be primarily fixed-income or growth-oriented, and whether your account should be self-directed or managed. The income you can derive from your RRIF will depend on the investment performance of your RRIF assets and the overall management of your plan.

Above all, remember that the earlier you begin planning your conversion strategies, the better choice or combination of choices you will be able to make.

Take Care in Choosing Your Life Insurance/Annuity Provider

You may have noticed that we chose our words very carefully when referring to life insurance companies. When describing life annuities, we said you give your money to an insurance company in return for a "promise" to provide you with a fixed income for a defined period. When discussing insured annuities, we suggested finding an independent agent who, among other things, would pick a company or combination of companies that are financially sound.

Life insurance company products–in particular, annuities and life insurance policies to protect your estate–can be of great importance and benefit to older investors. However, what was once the unthinkable is happening in Canada: Life insurance companies can no longer be considered rock solid, and some are facing financial difficulties.

A few, the most shocking example being giant Confederation Life, have even folded. Although an industry protection fund exists, it covers only specific amounts and, even if you are fully covered, the failure of your insurer would result in endless inconvenience and hassle, not to mention uncertainty and anxiety (see Chapter 6 for more details.) Those of you who were caught up in the Confederation Life crisis can certainly attest to this. Therefore, you should do everything in your power, even if it means paying more in premiums or accepting a slightly lower annuity rate, to ensure that the company you deal with is going to be around to make the payments in the future.

As far back as June 1994, the Federal Superintendent of Insurance issued a public statement telling consumers to be careful about which life insurance companies they dealt with because of the possibility of financial trouble.

Unfortunately, he did not warn people specifically about Confederation Life, which went under later that year. The sad truth is that Confederation Life was not the first Canadian life insurance company to go out of business, and it will not be the last. In 2001, there were 127 insurance companies operating in Canada. Industry experts expect this number to steadily decline because of financial failure, mergers, or acquisitions; an estimate of 50 in a decade or so, they say, is reasonable.

The consumer protection program for the life insurance industry, known as Canadian Life and Health Insurance Compensation Corporation (CompCorp), was introduced in 1990, but it also covers policies or products sold previously. This program protects customers of member companies in the event of a company's failure.

The first step, then, in dealing with any insurance firm is to make sure it is a member of CompCorp. The following are CompCorp's RRIF, life annuity, and life insurance limits:

- RRIFs: either a lump sum of up to $60,000 or a life annuity for up to $2,000 per month;

- Life annuities: up to $2,000 per month;

- Life insurance: up to $200,000 in total.

If the policy you buy involves more than $200,000 worth of life insurance, make sure you buy from only the biggest companies with the best credit ratings. Again, as shown in the shocking Confederation Life saga, the foremost principle of the marketplace is still *caveat emptor* (buyer beware).

Here is one last tip: A surefire way to protect yourself is to spread your coverage around by buying different policies from several companies, each for $200,000 or less. You can spread annuities around in this way, as well. It's a lot more bother, but as a result you are covered no matter what happens. It's called purchasing peace of mind.

12

How to Find a Financial Planner You Can Trust

Although younger people tend to believe that those of us over 50 have been completely organized for years when it comes to finances, the surprising and dismaying truth is that one of every seven people over the age of 50 has not even begun to save consistently for retirement. Only 8 percent of those over 50 have paid for a written retirement plan, and, when asked to select their primary source of financial advice from 15 options, 50 percent astonishingly listed themselves. Second key source? Their spouse or a relative!

These statistics are downright scary, and if you fall into any of these categories, we urge you to seek professional financial help. With countless investment options, including more than 3,000 mutual funds available to Canadian investors and a complexity of strategies for RRSP conversion, professional financial planning advice is a must.

Still, it's painfully obvious that financial planners are not yet widely employed by those over 50. Why are so many in this age group wary of dealing with such professionals? The answer does not lie in the products themselves; a recent survey showed that only 1 percent expressed dissatisfaction in this area.

The study showed that, while fees were a potential deterrent to getting professional financial advice, the crucial factor was the relationship between client and planner—in particular, the degree of trust the client did or did not feel for potential advisors. Confidentiality is also crucial to the mature investor. The planner may know that all your financial affairs, and even your name, address, and phone number, will be kept confidential. But how do you know if you're not told? What assurances do you have, for example, that an investment your planner makes for you will not result in unsolicited and unwanted sales pitches from outside parties?

Other reasons for not using professional financial planners were that people felt they received unreliable advice and that their investments performed poorly. But, interestingly enough, these two reasons rated last on the list of objections. Still, judging from the mail and phone calls we receive, there's little doubt that many older people are dissatisfied or uneasy with the advice or the level of respect and attention they receive from their financial planners.

There is no question that we all need solid financial planning and advice. And since there are as yet no government regulations setting standards for the planning business, it's up to you to find a planner you can trust. So, how do you find a financial planner who will satisfy your needs for trust, confidentiality, and sound advice? For starters, interview several planners before you make up your mind. You must be comfortable with the person who will be reviewing your finances and discussing your future plans. Second only to your spouse, this is likely the only person who will know every detail of your personal financial affairs.

Look first for someone who will be honest about what he or she can and cannot do for you. As stated earlier, a good two-thirds of the people in the business are commission sales people, and the rest are independents. But what does the word *independent* mean? Many people who use that term to describe themselves are not independent at all, since they, like many insurance agents, can sell only the products of one company or group of companies. If you are considering a particular advisor, find out if he or she is bonded. What regulatory bodies does the company he or she works for belong to? Is this advisor duly licensed to sell investments and/or insurance?

As well, find a financial planner who is prepared to help you in areas beyond his or her expertise, such as by referring you to a trusted insurance agent, a mortgage broker, or a specialist in reverse mortgages.

Look for someone who will provide you with at least a reasonable level of hands-on, personal service. This kind of attention is rare in today's marketplace, but it alone can make a huge difference when you are making important decisions about your future.

Most institutions have qualified financial advisors who will be happy to help you out in the hopes of getting your business. Some banks and brokerage firms have also recently been hiring and training advisors who specialize in retirement income planning. Fortunately, most of them are thorough and talented professionals. But make sure you deal only with an advisor who can help you buy the products that are right for you. You may find those products at one provider, but more often, you will not want to be restricted to a professional who is selling only the investments of one company. Remember that the world of financial institutions has changed. Where once a bank, for example, provided only its own products, now, especially through subsidiaries, a wide range of products is available.

Believe it or not, recommendations from friends and relatives concerning advisors they like and trust count for a lot. If you find a financial advisor you feel good about, start working with him or her right away. You cannot afford to be without professional help at this stage of your life, and first-rate advisors will be in increasing demand in the coming years.

What an Advisor Can Do for You

Most people are confused by today's complex financial decisions, and no wonder, given the myriad choices available. The help of a knowledgeable advisor can make an important difference. This difference has actually been measured. For example, a research survey by Dalbar Financial Services, a respected U.S. assessment firm, showed that in a period of almost 12 years, mutual fund investors with a financial advisor held their funds longer and earned almost 17 percent more in total cumulative return than those who bought funds on their own. This sort of performance can make a huge difference in your retirement lifestyle and is worth the expenditure of some time and effort on your part.

How can a good financial advisor increase the returns on your portfolio? Here are some questions to ask and the services you should expect from your advisor:

Where do I stand? Your advisor should provide you with a clear picture of where you stand right now in terms of income, assets, debt, and taxes, and should evaluate your situation and tell you what you can do to improve it.

What are my goals? Your advisor should help you clarify your goals in terms of what you want and when you want it and, most importantly, should tell you whether or not you are being realistic. Don't be put off by very frank comments. You don't want someone who will simply tell you your goals are terrific. You need someone who will be honest about what is achievable in your situation and what is not.

What are the problems? It is part of your advisor's job to identify specific current or potential problems or pitfalls that could prevent you from achieving your objectives.

What are the alternatives? Your planner should provide you, without being asked, with a written report outlining recommendations and a suggested step-by-step process for organizing your financial affairs now and in the future.

How do I do it? Once you have decided on the financial plan that is right for you, your planner must be able to help carry it out and also find other professionals to fill in areas beyond his or her expertise.

When do I review and revise? Your advisor should revisit and, if necessary, adjust your financial plan, goals, investment portfolio, asset mix, and returns at least once a year to make sure you are up to date. A review should also take place when major changes occur. Examples would include divorce, marriage, receipt of an inheritance, sale of your home, etc.

Should You Manage Your RRIF?

Many people find they don't have the time, inclination, or ability to manage the assets in their RRIFs. Yet, especially if a RRIF is worth more than $200,000, this is no reason to let it languish in a low-return account or switch to an annuity. The larger a RRIF, the more important expert preparation and implementation of an investment plan tends to be. The variety and complexity of today's investment opportunities, combined with the explosion in information technology, require expertise and specialized knowledge. Even the most keenly interested person will find it impossible to keep current with all investment events and options.

Most financial institutions provide an excellent service that takes the task of managing your RRIF off your shoulders and shifts it to a professional money manager. This process, known as "discretionary investment management," can be most useful. Unfortunately, this concept is not widely recognized or understood, and even those investors who are intrigued by the idea hesitate to act because of concerns about costs and loss of control. However, these fears are groundless for the most part, and they should not prevent you from investigating this option further.

Think of it this way: Discretionary investment management is exactly the opposite of a self-directed RRIF, in which you are entirely on your own in making investment decisions. Under a discretionary management arrangement, those responsibilities are taken over by a professional who adjusts your account as circumstances warrant, based on overall objectives you set in advance during one or more planning sessions. These sessions are intended to explore in depth such factors as time frame, your tolerance for risk, and your need for income.

The portfolio manager will also be available for further discussion at any time, ready to change your investment strategy whenever you or circumstances dictate. In fact, if you enrol in such a service, you should certainly keep in touch on a regular basis to make sure the manager knows about pertinent changes in your life or needs.

Most institutions offering this service provide a high level of personal attention, as well as access to the expertise of their international team should you wish your portfolio to be invested in global securities. All investments are guided by the agreed-upon terms set out during the planning sessions. Your advisor will not consult (or bother) you about every transaction because you have given blanket approval for investment decisions within the specific parameters set out in advance.

A mutual fund RRIF, for example, is a form of managed portfolio that lies between a self-directed and a fully managed RRIF. The mutual fund managers run the fund, setting the asset mix and making all the investment decisions within the fund's portfolio. Still, you or your investment advisor must pick the fund or funds for your portfolio.

With a fully managed RRIF, your personal money manager builds a custom-tailored portfolio that fits with your goals and circumstances. The portfolio is usually administered daily, and you receive quarterly reports showing your current asset mix and the market value of your holdings.

You will need to ask about costs, of course, but they are generally comparable to the administration fees charged by mutual fund companies and have the added advantage of being tax-deductible. (The fees on such managed accounts are considered by the CCRA to be carrying charges and thus are deductible for tax purposes. In contrast, administration fees on self-directed RRIFs are not included in this definition.) The fees are structured as a percentage of your portfolio's market value, rather than per transaction, so the manager shares your interest in increasing your assets.

The amount of money you need to have in your RRIF (or, for that matter, in non-registered portfolios) in order to qualify for discretionary management varies among institutions. However, a minimum of $100,000 will often entitle you to receive at least a simplified version of management. Portfolios consisting of $200,000 or more usually entitle you to a full discretionary management account.

Should Someone Else Administer Your Financial Affairs?

Whether or not you are comfortable managing your portfolio, you may not have the interest or ability to take care of all the paperwork associated with your investments or with other mundane financial matters. In addition to the services described above, most banks, trust companies, and investment dealers provide administrative services that take care of all the necessary record keeping and reporting–for a fee, of course. You need a minimum of between $100,000 and $200,000 in assets, depending on the institution and how much business you do with it.

These services will often include paying household bills and managing other aspects of your personal finances, which is particularly useful for those who spend a lot of time out of the country. Some examples of the day-to-day details they will take off your hands are:

- Filling out income tax returns or other tax forms and making any necessary payments;

- Safekeeping your securities and collecting investment income such as interest or dividends and reinvesting the income as directed or depositing it into your designated account;

- Reporting regularly on where your investments stand and providing evaluations as needed; and

- Executing any investment transactions you require.

13

How to Deal with Your Bank

It can be intimidating dealing with the bank, but we consumers have a lot more clout than we think—we just don't know how to use it.

In fact, you don't have to be wealthy to get first-class attention, good service, and reasonable rates from your bank branch. If you add up all your assets that have anything to do with that particular bank, you may well find that you represent enough business to be important to them. And, though it may be an unfortunate truth, how much you're worth to a bank does make a difference in the service you get. All bank customers are not treated alike. Consider the following business you may be giving your bank: mortgages, personal belongings, RRSPs, RRIFs, savings and chequing accounts, credit cards, and car and other loans. The trick is to use your combined leverage as a customer to get the very best deals available.

The number one rule in dealing with a bank is to remember that every transaction, every single fee for service, is negotiable. And some people get better deals just because they know that.

We all like to be treated with respect when we deal with retailers, and banks should be no exception, no matter what your net worth. You can get the service you deserve by creating a long-term relationship with one institution and, even better, with one manager or account representative. If your savings are with one bank, your RRIF/RRSP with another, and your mortgage somewhere else, you are diluting your negotiating power. Consolidate everything you have with the bank you know best. When you consolidate your business in this way, you can gain not only recognition as being more important, but also a lot more clout when it comes time to negotiate services or loan rates.

Most people think bank fees are carved in stone. But there's always a bit of room built in. Never hesitate to remind your bank that hungry competitors are after your business. Believe us, they are. In fact, do some comparison shopping first.

Bank Charges and Your RRIF

There are a number of ways you can use your clout with your bank to save money on your RRIF. These include:

Higher Interest Rates If you plan to use some GICs in your RRIF, negotiate for the best possible rate. Posted GIC rates used to be carved in stone, but no longer. Managers have the discretion to improve on them and often will—you may get up to half a point more. The amount of money you are investing and your total business with the bank will be influential in determining how good a deal you can make. But you have to ask!

Reduced Administration Fees If the bank charges an administration fee for RRIFs, ask that it be waived—not just for one year, but forever.

Reimbursement for Transfer Fees Your bank wants your RRIF business, especially if the amount is sizeable. If you have RRSPs at other institutions, there may be transfer fees payable to switch the assets into a centralized plan. Ask your bank to pick up those costs.

Reduced Counselling Fees If your bank offers investment counselling services for a fee and you're interested in setting up a managed account, ask for a reduced rate.

Reduced Brokerage Fees If you plan to trade securities within your RRIF, ask for a break on commissions from the bank's subsidiary brokerage firm.

Be Cautious about Investing Advice

You can obtain top-level wealth management advice through the banks, for a fee. These people are well qualified and knowledgeable. However, be wary of free advice from someone in your branch who may not know a great deal about investing strategy in general and RRIFs in particular. Although bank staff are better trained these days, turnover tends to be high and our experience has been that some personnel who are supposed to be qualified to discuss mutual funds, for example, are poorly informed. In one case we encountered recently, a bank mutual fund "expert" didn't even know what a labour-sponsored venture capital fund was. After the client explained the concept, the employee remarked, "Sounds interesting. I must look into that." Not exactly confidence-inspiring!

If you do get bad advice that goes sour, either in your RRIF or with other investments, don't be afraid to seek redress. Here's an example: A woman living in a small Canadian city was managing her 91-year-old mother's money. When the investments came due, she met with her bank and asked whether or not she could improve upon the low rate of return. The bank's representative scanned the list of their funds and said, "The best-performing fund last year was our emerging markets fund. Let's put your mother's money into that!" Not being aware of the risks involved, the daughter agreed. Eight months later, when her mother had lost $1,500, the daughter consulted independent experts and complained to the bank's head office. After reviewing the situation, the bank's compliance department ruled that, while the advice was inappropriate, the client had to accept some responsibility as well. Its recommendation to the local branch manager was to refund half the loss. However, the local manager decided to go one better, and refunded the entire $1,500! So it does, in fact, pay to speak up.

Getting More Bang for Your Banking Buck

Moving away from RRIFs for a moment, there are two keys to getting the biggest bang out of your banking buck. First, keep things simple by sticking with a single chequing account and a daily interest savings account–that's all you really need. Make sure you maintain the minimum balance, usually around a thousand dollars, that magically makes all your basic transactions free or, at worst, low cost.

Second, avoid as many service charges as possible. Make no mistake, there are service charges on everything from withdrawals to bill payments to money orders–and they quickly add up. Be vigilant; be prepared to question every single charge. If you don't think a service fee is fair, question it. You'll be surprised how often the bank will compromise.

Here are some further banking tips:

- Try to avoid writing cheques in foreign currency–that can cost up to $15 per cheque on top of the currency exchange. Use money orders instead.

- It pays to buy overdraft protection (if you're a good client, you may be able to get it free). If things get tight, you'll face charges of $20 or more for every NSF cheque you write.

- Use the Internet. If your bank or financial institution provides online account service, sign on. You'll be able to access your account balance and detailed transactions at any time (some banks now charge just to tell you how much money you have if a teller has to do it). You'll also be able to perform a number of transactions from your computer, such as paying bills, at a reduced cost or free.

- Use automated teller machines whenever possible. They're no longer a luxury or status symbol. They've become a necessity in today's financial world. They're fast, easy to use, and cheaper. Paying bills through the machines often means a lower service fee. And many financial institutions have already begun charging extra for dealing face-to-face with a real live person. Isn't it interesting how the banks keep finding ways to reduce their costs, while at the same time increasing ours?

  But keep this in mind: Using an automated teller machine can be great once you get the hang of it, but you have to be careful. There's no physical danger, but studies show they can be hazardous to your financial health. In the same way that credit cards or casino chips don't seem real to some people, machine withdrawals are so easy and remote they can get out of hand. Don't visit too often and don't take out more cash than you really need.

Don't Treat Joint Bank Accounts Lightly

Most of us rely on the service and convenience of a local bank or trust company branch. While we often complain about their level of service and insistence on charging fees for every transaction under the sun, one of the things they do best is make it easy for us to transact day-to-day business with a minimum of fuss and bother.

A good example is the joint bank account, most useful because it allows two people to have exactly the same cheque-writing and withdrawal privileges on the same account.

Joint bank accounts, therefore, are good for any two people who pay day-to-day expenses together—spouses, parents and children, close friends, even roommates. But don't get involved in such an account without careful thought. Teaming up with anyone on a joint account is certainly convenient, but potential danger lurks.

In the end, whether you should have a joint bank account boils down to a single question: How much trust is there between the two people involved? When you give someone else the legal right to sign cheques on an account, you also give the right to withdraw every cent in that account at any time.

The courts are full of lawsuits involving cases in which a husband or wife cleaned out entire joint bank accounts at the first sign of marital trouble. Trying to collect in such cases is almost impossible. In many other instances, one of the parties simply took off with all the funds, never to be seen or heard from again.

Banks are useful, but they're not in the business of protecting your financial security. That's up to you. And joint bank accounts provide an excellent example of why you have to watch out for yourself.

If you still feel such a two-way account fits your circumstances, you should be aware that there are two kinds of joint bank accounts, with practical and legal differences between them.

The first is called "joint tenants with right of survivorship." That technical language simply means that if one party dies, the other gets problem-free ownership of the account even before the deceased's will is probated. This is the usual type of joint account, where either person can sign cheques.

The second is called "tenants in common." In this case, if one person dies, the account is frozen and no money can be released until probate. That might be exactly what you want, or it could place unnecessary financial hardship on your family. This is the type of joint account where every cheque must have both signatures.

If you choose the first type, a survivorship account, your partner in the arrangement will have immediate access to the funds if you should die, without legal hassle. While this might seem to be the appropriate choice in every case, you have to think about potential problems for your estate.

Suppose your joint account is set up with an adult child. If you give him or her right of survivorship, the money in the account will become the property of that child long before your estate is settled.

That situation could create problems if your will stipulates that the entire estate, which would include the money in the account, is to be divided equally among all heirs. It could easily be "family feud" time, because the child who is the partner in the joint account has legal ownership of all the money within it.

In fact, you probably shouldn't use a joint account in this way. A power of attorney document works best. It gives your adult child the ability to access the account should you become incapable, but no future ownership. When you die, your will governs what happens to your money.

It's important to choose the type of joint account that best suits you and your family. However, if you feel even the slightest lack of trust or have even small reservations, it's best to steer clear of these types of arrangements.

14

WOMEN AND MONEY

Money may have sex appeal, but it recognizes no gender. A stock, for example, doesn't know or care who its owner is—man or woman—but there are tremendous differences between the sexes when it comes to earning and dealing with money.

It's a sobering but proven fact that government and industry discriminate against women. Females are paid less in the workplace than their male counterparts; they are often at the top of a corporate downsizing hit list; and they receive a fraction of their mates' pensions as a spousal allowance. These injustices are being fought by such organizations as Canada's Association for the Fifty-Plus (CARP) and the National Action Committee on the Status of Women, and some progress is being made.

In addition to such sociological and financial inequities, another handicap faces many 50-plus women. Kept busy juggling career, home, and family (often children and aging parents), far too many women don't even try to toss the ball labelled "money matters" into the air. They leave financial decisions to their spouses and learn little about personal investment planning.

As a result, far too many women (whether single, married, or widowed) remain at a disadvantage when it comes to looking after their own financial future. This is usually a serious mistake. Consider the following:

- Women's life expectancy is approximately six years longer than men's, and 90 percent of women will be entirely responsible for their own financial affairs at some point in their lives—most often through divorce or the death of a partner.

- On average, women earn less than 70 cents for every dollar a man makes. This means women have to live longer on less money, often with the end result that one out of three women subsists at or below the poverty line.

- Having children often reduces a woman's earnings and retirement savings. If, for example, a woman takes a year off to have a child, her contributions to an RRSP may be delayed because of a lack of earned income. Absence from the workforce may even affect her private pension plan.

- Studies show that female workers over 50 looking for employment have significantly lower chances than men of finding work and virtually no chance of finding or keeping employment after the mandatory retirement age of 65.

But even with these tough constraints, every woman should do as much as possible to implement proper investment strategies with an eye to a comfortable retirement. Here are some practical tips:

1. Make it an absolute priority to know what's happening with the family finances. At the very least, find out where everything is–bank accounts, power of attorney, wills/living wills, insurance policies, debts, and assets.

2. Always keep a portion of capital completely liquid. While everyone should have a readily accessible emergency fund equal to three months of living expenses, it is especially crucial for women to do so in the event of sudden death or separation from a spouse.

3. Don't wait to learn about finances. Often women wait until disaster strikes before they're motivated into investment planning. Learn about your financial situation today, and you'll be prepared to take over and control your finances down the road.

4. Have an investment plan separate from your spouse's. While spouses should coordinate their finances, women should have separate investment plans, bank accounts, and RRSPs. Joint or spousal assets can be tied up or frozen, pending court settlement due to death or divorce proceedings.

5. Establish your own credit rating. Start by opening your own line of credit and having at least one credit card in your own name. Remember, it wasn't that long ago when women were often turned down for credit on the basis of their gender. Today, while it's illegal to discriminate because of gender, marital status, race, religion, or age, you may find some isolated holdouts who can make your life miserable.

6. Consider more aggressive investments, such as mutual funds, that are compatible with your own risk tolerance. Because women live longer, they have to make their money work harder. While women have traditionally shied away from making investments they perceive to be risky, the irony is that they need the growth potential of equities. Historically, far more women than men spend their later years in poverty.

7. Go to "school." Read as many of the excellent personal finance and retirement planning books that are on the market as you can. Attend seminars, financial trade shows, and exhibitions and get referrals from friends about reliable financial planners.

What You Need to Know about Your Retirement Plan

Now let's address the specific issue of what women need to know about the family's retirement income plan.

Details of the RRIF If income is going to be received from a RRIF or RRIFs, find out where the plans are held, the details of the accounts, the amount of the payments, the frequency with which they are received, and a contact name and phone number for each plan. Make sure the "successor annuitant" option has been used.

Survivor Rights of an Employer Pension Plan If the husband has a pension from work, find out if it carries survivor benefits. Get the name and phone number of a contact person if anything should happen.

Annuity Information If an annuity is being considered, a woman should protect her rights and livelihood by ensuring that a joint-and-last-survivor option is taken (see Chapter 11).

Other Income Sources and Investment Accounts It's essential that a wife know all the details of retirement income sources and accounts. A heart attack can carry off a husband in minutes, leaving no time for a proper briefing. So be prepared.

If you're a woman, you owe it to yourself to become actively involved in your family's finances. Many women still do not get fair treatment in the financial world—so it's crucial to become an independent individual, a person in your own right and in the eyes of your bank or trust company. By leaving the financial decisions to someone else, you're jeopardizing your own future.

15

HAVE YOU CONSIDERED

RETIRING ABROAD?

Many Canadians decide to live out part or all of their retirement years in places where the sun shines all year round. They've had a lifetime full of our harsh winters, and that's enough for them.

If you are going to join this exodus, you need to do some advance planning. The most important decision is whether you want to cut your ties with Canada partially or totally. You can spend your winters in the warmth and still remain a Canadian resident, with all the pluses and minuses that involves. Or you can sever your connection with Canada entirely and take up full-time residency in another country.

In general, you retain your Canadian resident status for tax purposes if you maintain a home in this country and live here for more than half the year. In some cases, even if you are abroad for more than six months each year, the Canada Customs and Revenue Agency (CCRA) may take the view that you're still a Canadian resident for tax purposes if you retain ties to Canada by continuing to hold real estate, bank accounts, investments, club memberships, a Canadian driver's licence, etc.

By remaining a Canadian resident, you retain coverage under your provincial health care program, a benefit many older people are reluctant to surrender. However, "residency" for the purpose of health insurance varies from one province to another, so make certain that you understand the rules for your particular province.

Continuing to be considered a Canadian resident also ensures you will receive the social benefits to which you are entitled. Some of these may be lost under certain conditions if you leave the country–Old Age Security (OAS) benefits, for example, may be discontinued after six months if you take up residency abroad. You could also be disqualified from OAS benefits if you did not live in Canada for at least 20 years after the age of 18. But if you meet the qualifications for continued payment, you'll be able to draw OAS while sunning on the beach, and you can even arrange to have your money deposited directly to a U.S. bank if you take up residence in that country.

Unlike OAS, benefits earned under the Canada Pension Plan (CPP) are payable no matter where you live. Remember, you and your employer have paid directly into CPP, whereas OAS payments are funded from general tax revenues. Direct deposit to a U.S. account can also be arranged for CPP payments.

Of course, one drawback of retaining Canadian residency is that you'll be liable for Canadian taxes, which are much higher than those in the most popular snowbird destinations, including the United States. You'll have to weigh the economic pros and cons.

If you decide to move abroad full time, make inquiries about residency requirements at the embassy or consulate of the country you're considering. Moving to the U.S. has become easier in certain situations as a result of the Free Trade Agreement, but you'll still need to meet certain U.S. qualifications. You'll have to obtain a Green Card–which could take some time–or meet what's called a "substantial presence" test, which is based on a period of residency in that country. Later in this chapter, you'll find a summary of how and when this test applies, but check with the U.S. immigration department for full details.

You also need to consider the new Canadian departure tax. The government doesn't call it that, of course, but a departure tax is really what it comes down to, and it may make it financially difficult for you to take up residence in another country, depending on your situation.

It works like this. On the day you leave the country to take up residence elsewhere, the CCRA takes the position that you have sold all your stocks, bonds, mutual funds, and other securities. This is called a *deemed disposition.* You must declare any capital gains (or losses) that result from this fictitious sale on your final Canadian tax return. If you have a lot of invested money, the tax liability could be huge.

There are a few exceptions to the deemed disposition rule. You don't have to declare any Canadian real estate that you own, any Canadian business property (if the operation is run from a permanent Canadian address), pensions and other rights, stock options, and certain property of short-term residents.

You can, if you so choose, defer paying the tax on property subject to this rule until it is actually sold. The catch is that you have to provide the CCRA with "acceptable security" to ensure it will eventually get paid. You must also provide a list of all your worldwide assets if their fair market value totals more than $25,000.

As you can see, leaving Canada can be expensive, and it will certainly entail a lot of paperwork.

There are a number of other matters that you must address if you decide to take up residency abroad.

Income taxes are clearly a major consideration for non-residents, and the big issue to be resolved is who gets paid. Generally, the rules vary depending on where you choose to live, but we'll focus on the U.S. because it is the most common destination of Canadians.

If you spend a significant amount of time in the U.S., you may be classified as a "resident alien." To determine if this is your situation, take the "substantial presence test." It works like this:

- For the current year, count every day spent in the U.S. as one day.

- For last year, count every day as one-third of a day.

- For the year before that, count every day as one-sixth of a day.

If the total exceeds 182 days, you meet the substantial presence test. If so, you have to file a U.S. tax return and report your worldwide income.

So, for example, suppose you spent 125 days in the U.S. in each of the past three years. That's about four months a year. Here's the calculation:

This year = 125 x 1	=	125 days
Last year = 125 x 1/3	=	42 days
Prior year = 125 x 1/6	=	21 days
Total		188 days

Even though, in this case, you never spent more than about four months in the U.S. in any one year, you qualify as a resident alien of that country.

You can get around this if you meet three conditions:

1. You were in the U.S. fewer than 183 days in the current year.

2. Your tax home is in Canada, meaning you are employed in this country or live here regularly.

3. You have a "closer connection" to Canada than to the U.S. This can be determined by variety of things, from where you vote to the church you attend.

In this case, you have to advise the IRS by filing form 8840, *Closer Connection Exception Statement*. You'll find a copy in a useful pamphlet published by the CCRA titled *Canadian Residents Going Down South*. The pamphlet also outlines your obligations either as a resident alien or non-resident alien in the U.S.

If you do end up paying any U.S. income tax as a result of all this, you may be able to claim a foreign tax credit when you file your Canadian return in order to avoid double taxation on the same income.

Managing Your Plan from Outside Canada

How you look after your RRSPs and RRIFs is another issue that will inevitably come up if you take flight from Canada. Of course, if you remain a Canadian for tax purposes, nothing happens. Your retirement plans are subject to the same rules as before you took up residence elsewhere.

But if you should become a resident of another country, that all changes. Again, everything will depend on which country you choose and the tax treaty that prevails between that nation and Canada.

In the case of the U.S., the value of an RRSP when you become a U.S. resident is considered capital and is therefore not taxable. Any income earned within the plan after you become a U.S. resident may continue to compound tax-free. You become liable for U.S. taxes only once you start making withdrawals from the plan, and then only on those amounts that relate to income earned in your RRSP after you became a U.S. resident, plus any unrealized capital gains. This makes it a sound strategy to take any capital gains in your RRSP before you leave Canada, thereby reducing the U.S. tax for which you'll eventually be liable.

If you've lost money in your RRSP to the extent that the plan's value is less than your total contributions, you'll face no U.S. tax at all.

You will have to pay a withholding tax of 25 percent in Canada when you make withdrawals from your RRSP after you become a non-resident by moving to the U.S. Periodic payments from a RRIF or annuity are subject to a 15 percent withholding tax. (Withholding rates may differ if you move to another country; the standard rate on pensions, RRIFs, and annuities is 25 percent, but any tax treaty provisions take precedence.) If you become a non-resident, the CCRA will regard the withholdings as your full payment. This means you'll pay tax at a much lower rate than you would at home. Of course, some tax may be assessed in the U.S. (or wherever else you're living). But if you're in the States, such tax will be payable on only a portion of your withdrawals, as we've seen. As well, you should be able to claim a credit for your Canadian withholdings against your U.S. taxes payable.

These changes in the rules make it advantageous to keep your RRSP if you decide to move to the U.S. Your investments will continue to grow, tax-sheltered, just as if you'd stayed in Canada.

To get this tax break, you have to make a declaration to the IRS that you intend to use this provision of the tax treaty. This requires a special election, which is made with the first U.S. return you file. You'll be required to supply detailed financial information about your RRSP at that time.

The same rules apply to RRIFs.

Pension income may also receive a tax break if you move to the U.S. Employee and employer contributions made to the plan on your behalf are considered capital, in the same way as your RRSP or RRIF, and therefore won't be taxed. However, any income earned by the plan, either before or after you become a U.S. resident, will be taxable. This is a basic difference from RRSP/RRIF rules, so watch out for it.

Like withdrawals from your RRSPs and RRIFs, other pension payments originating in Canada are subject to withholding tax if you become a non-resident. Again, the standard rate is 25 percent, but what you pay will be determined in the provisions of the tax treaty between Canada and the country that is your destination.

Several other types of Canadian income may also be subject to withholding tax at source when you leave the country. These include most interest payments, dividends, rental income, CPP, and OAS.

The only other major issue surrounding your registered plans when you live outside Canada has largely been resolved by legislative changes in recent years. When the U.S. Securities and Exchange Commission (SEC) suddenly began enforcing an old rule that U.S. residents cannot do business through brokers not registered in that country, Canadians with RRIFs and RRSPs were left in a bind. (A second related rule, which required securities sold to U.S. residents to be registered with U.S. securities regulators, was also being enforced.)

The effect of this was to freeze assets in RRSPs and RRIFs, because brokers in Canada, where the accounts were domiciled, could not accept trading orders. Pressure from Canadian investment dealers and industry groups succeeded in reversing these outdated laws. In June 2000, federal securities regulators in the U.S. passed rules exempting Canadian dealers and securities from the restrictions. In short, the changes allow Canadian brokers who already have a relationship with a client to continue dealing with that client when he or she moves to the U.S. As well, securities of foreign issuers, including securities of foreign funds, can be sold to Canadian/U.S. participants without being registered under the *Securities Act*. Most states have now adopted corresponding rules. To be absolutely sure, check *before* you take any action in your RRIF.

The Currency Effect

Still, it is clear that tax and securities regulations make it crucial to carefully consider your investment strategies if you decide to leave Canada for good. However, one risk that's unrelated to government rules is the possibility that your assets will lose value because of trends in our currency. So, leaving the bulk of your assets here puts you at risk of losing purchasing power should the Canadian dollar fall in relation to the currency of your new country of residence.

The best way to lessen the impact of this possibility is to switch a large proportion of your investments into securities denominated in the currency of the country in which you'll be living. Once again, we'll use the United States as an example.

The foreign-content limitations and the rule that says you cannot hold foreign currency in a registered plan are not as restrictive as they seem at first glance. In effect, you can convert Canadian dollar securities into U.S.-denominated assets quite easily, even in registered plans such as RRIFs. Here are a few strategies for increasing your U.S. exposure.

U.S. dollar-denominated bonds from Canadian issuers such as the federal and provincial governments are considered to be 100 percent Canadian content for RRIF purposes. So are mutual funds that invest in these securities.

Some financial institutions issue U.S. dollar term deposits and GICs that are considered Canadian content for RRIFs. As well, some Canadian stocks are denominated in U.S. dollars and pay dividends in that currency. Ask your broker for a list.

In the case of your non-registered investments, there are no barriers of any kind to switching to a U.S. dollar-based portfolio. It's simply a matter of selecting the securities you want. U.S. equities, as a group, tend to outperform Canadian stocks, so that could be a plus if you want to maintain a growth component in your portfolio.

You won't be able to protect yourself from currency fluctuations when your income originates in Canadian dollars—such as payments from OAS, CPP, employer pension plans, and the like. You'll have to accept a degree of currency risk, although you may wish to convert your funds to U.S. dollars as soon as they're received to minimize this effect.

Yet another financial consideration is the cost of living. Canada is a very expensive country in a number of ways. Sunbelt living may be cheaper, even given the weakness of the Canadian dollar in recent years. Living in Florida, for example, is generally less expensive for such important budget components as food, clothing, and gasoline.

Estate Planning Considerations

Canadian retirees thinking about buying a property in the Sunbelt to escape from our long, cold winters have for years found themselves facing a complicated and potentially expensive problem—U.S. estate taxes.

Well, we have some good news for you. In most cases, you don't have to worry about it any more. There have been some major changes that make estate planning much easier for Canadian snowbirds, at least for the time being.

The problem is that if you live long enough, you could find yourself looking at exactly the same difficulties all over again! Believe it or not, the changes that the U.S. Congress introduced to the estate tax laws in that country all expire after 2010, and we'll be back to square one unless something more is done.

But before we get into all that, let's look at some background.

The U.S. approach to determining the value of an estate is quite straightforward. Essentially, they just add up the value of everything you own and apply the appropriate tax rates to it. There is no blanket exemption for spouses, although they do receive a partial tax break. Nor can you escape by giving your property away because the U.S. imposes a gift tax at the same rate as the estate tax.

Until the mid-1990s, U.S. non-residents were entitled to an exemption of only US$60,000 on the value of their estate when they died. Anything beyond that was subject to American taxes at onerous rates that could run as high as 92 percent (federal plus state), according to the Canadian chartered accounting firm of BDO Dunwoody.

And it was not just U.S.-based property that was at risk. A Canadian estate could end up being taxed on anything with a U.S. connection, including bank accounts, stocks, bonds, and other types of securities. It was a potential nightmare.

As a result of changes to the Canada–U.S. tax treaty in the mid-1990s, the exemption for Canadians was raised to US$600,000, the same as for U.S. citizens and residents. But that wasn't an absolute amount. The exemption had to be pro-rated by the total value of a Canadian's estate, which meant that it might in fact end up being worth much less once your home in Canada, your RRSP or RRIF, your Canadian investment portfolio, your cottage on the lake, and anything else you own was taken into account.

So, many Canadian snowbirds with winter homes in Florida, Arizona, California, Hawaii, or elsewhere in the U.S. were still potentially on the hook.

In 1998, the U.S. Congress approved a measure to gradually increase the exemption for calculating estate taxes, and the higher limits also extended to Canadians under the tax treaty provisions. The limits have been rising gradually, and were fixed at US$700,000 in 2002–03. After that, they were to escalate sharply, reaching US$1 million in 2006.

However, that was still not enough for the U.S. Republican Party, which historically has found its main constituency in middle- to upper-income Americans who oppose estate taxes in principle. When George W. Bush was elected, one of his priorities was to eliminate the U.S. estate tax entirely, as part of his massive tax-cutting program.

Legislation that appeared to fulfill that goal was passed by Congress in May 2001. But, as the accounting firm of Ernst & Young commented after analyzing the measure in detail, "reports of death of the estate tax have been greatly exaggerated."

Here's a summary of where things stood at the time of writing.

In 2002 and 2003, the estate tax exemption was increased to US$1 million. The federal estate tax rate was reduced to 50 percent in 2002 and to 49 percent in 2003 (it was 55 percent, with a 5 percent surtax on certain estates over US$10 million).

The exemption rises to US$1.5 million in 2004–05, with the tax rate dropping one percentage point each year.

From 2006 to 2008, the exemption moves up to US$2 million, with the tax rate dropping to 45 percent. In 2009, the exemption jumps to US$3.5 million, and in 2010, the estate tax disappears entirely.

But here's the rub. The new Act has a sunset clause that could cause all its provisions to disappear after the end of 2010. Ernst & Young notes that this is a function of the *Budget Act* of 1974, which curtails the ability of the U.S. Congress to pass any tax cut that increases the federal deficit beyond certain limits.

In other words, a future Congress will have to decide whether to leave the estate tax abolition intact by passing new legislation. If nothing happens, the situation will revert to the status of 2001.

Clearly, this throws a monkey wrench into the entire process of U.S. estate planning. Canadians do not know what rules they will be operating under in the future, any more than Americans do.

The increased spending requirements brought on by the war on terrorism and the need to substantially beef up domestic security may cause a future Congress to think twice about extending the estate tax repeal. Even if the abolition of estate tax is believed to be fiscally sound, a Democratic-controlled Congress under a future Democratic president might find the resurrection of the tax to be philosophically desirable.

So where do you stand? Here are some guidelines to help you:

1. Unless you're very wealthy, don't worry about the impact of U.S. estate taxes until 2011. If you think you still might be subject to estate tax even with the higher exemption, talk to a professional advisor.

2. Don't take a hefty mortgage on your U.S. property if the sole aim is to reduce estate tax exposure. Only non-recourse mortgages have that effect and few qualify.

3. If you own a U.S. property through a single-purpose corporation, review the situation with your lawyer/tax advisor. The recent changes in the estate tax laws may have made the need for such corporations obsolete.

4. As the years pass, pay attention to new changes in U.S. estate tax laws to see if the repeal is extended or if the tax will come back again after 2010. Plan accordingly.

In short, you probably don't have to worry now. But you may have to worry later.

Choosing your country of residence is one of the biggest decisions you'll face in your retirement years. Do the research and take the time to get it right.

16

How Can the Internet Help You?

When we think of mature Canadians and the Internet, we're reminded of the anecdote that appeared in the 1998 CARP*News* Annual Financial Guide for the 50-plus: "On the day of her 50th wedding anniversary, Queen Elizabeth recapped some of the extraordinary events that had helped shape the world during the last 50 years. The 71-year-old monarch drew a round of indulgent chuckles from a gathering of party guests when she confessed that, while she'd heard rumours that many people were surfing the Internet in recent years, she could only admit to having actually talked to a few live bodies who admitted they had entered the world of cyberspace. Perhaps a good example of how far the monarchy is out of touch!"

According to eMarketer, Inc., a firm that measures Internet use, well over 600 million people, or 14 percent of the world's adult population 14 and over, will be "surfing the Net" by 2004. In our country alone, active Internet use is closing in on 9 million, and this number has nowhere to go but up. However, some studies show an unfortunate trend: Older Canadians are among the least eager to embrace the Internet, with fewer than 13 percent of people over the age of 60 (compared to 63 percent of younger people) using the Internet in 2000, according to Statistics Canada. This reluctance hurts us in many ways. How?

The Internet empowers older Canadians in three ways. First, it gives them access to a wide range of current and historical information on the Internet's giant library called the World Wide Web. Second, it allows them to keep in touch with friends and family, thanks to the computerized postal service, "e-mail." This is particularly important for individuals living with limited mobility, sparse community resources, and limited finances. And third, it allows them to join electronic communities called "discussion groups," where they can share their views with others from all walks of life through what is, in essence, one giant party line.

While these components form a powerful communication tool that helps keep people informed and involved, they also create a world that can be quite bewildering to novices—largely because it has spawned a jargon all its own.

One of the best ways to start learning about the Net is to sit down with a friend who has all the necessary equipment or go to a local library that's equipped with a computer and give it a whirl. As well, computer and software companies everywhere who are eager for your business will give you a few basic lessons.

And if you have grandchildren, well, consider yourself doubly blessed if they'll agree to be your private tutors. The youth in this country are masters of this electronic domain and can explain it in the simplest and, often, most amusing of terms.

Surfing the Net for Fun and Profits

Even if the Internet is old news to you, you may not have explored it as a fast-track way to some of the most interesting financial planning information around. Best of all, it's usually free. Topics abound to help you manage your finances online, including: bank account management, stock investments, estate planning, tax filing, insurance planning, government programs, and additional resources. Following is a summary of some of these key categories, along with various useful Web sites for your reference.

Bank Account Management

Thanks to the Internet, you can now have quick and easy access to information about all the leading financial institutions, as well as direct access to your accounts. Many firms post current promotions or special services (such as reduced service fees) right on their Web sites, and some even offer financial calculators or electronic tutorials to assist with definitions or financial calculations.

But best of all, many now allow you to do much of your everyday banking—such as making deposits and transfers, checking account balances, and paying bills—right online. These features are particularly useful to snowbirds who want to keep in touch with their finances while out of the country.

Company Information

For the first time, regular investors can have access to company financial information at the exact time it's released to stockbrokers, securities regulators, the business press, and others in the financial community. With the help of electronic filing, companies now disclose and disseminate information—such as quarterly results or news releases, for example—as fast as the telephone and cable lines will deliver it. However, anyone using Internet-based services for investment purposes should look carefully at the source of the information, keeping in mind four important considerations: accuracy, authority, objectivity, and timeliness.

What type of investment information is available on the Internet? The list is endless: stock, bond, and futures/options quotes; investment product performance graphs and charts; regulatory filings; initial public offerings; annual reports; corporate news releases; trading services; mutual fund information; educational materials; and so on. You can buy and sell stocks and mutual funds online as well.

Some useful sites to consult are Globeinvestor.com (**www.globeinvestor. com**), Yahoo Finance (**www.yahoo.ca**), Advice for Investors (**www.advicefor investors.com**), and Quicken Finance (**www.quicken.ca**).

Mutual Funds

Gordon Pape, co-author of this book, writes a great deal about mutual funds and the financial markets in general. His site at **www.buildingwealth.ca** provides free access to a comprehensive mutual fund directory, links to all fund companies, a weekly audio mutual fund commentary, a weekly video investing tip, and a searchable Q & A database containing hundreds of finance-related questions and answers. Newsletters, books, and a complete database of all his mutual fund ratings and recommendations are available on a subscription basis. Pape's site also offers free book excerpts, transcripts of Kendrew Pape's CBC financial commentaries, and useful links to other financial sites.

Pape also hosts the Money section in the 50plus Web site (**www.50plus. com**). It includes a module specifically devoted to mutual funds that offers a wide range of information, from basic advice on fund investing to current news and tips.

For detailed fund statistics, you won't find a better source than GlobeFund (**www.globefund.com**), where you can call up performance numbers for every fund in Canada, read the latest fund news, and more.

Insurance Planning

If you want to re-examine your current and future insurance needs, many Internet Web sites can be helpful. Information about life, home, automobile, business, travel, and other types of insurance is all available online, and you can comparison shop at your leisure. To get a good idea of what's available and how your policies stack up, check out the Web sites of your insurer and its competitors. General information about insurance, including tips and help for consumers, can be found at the industry-sponsored Canadian Life and Health Insurance Association's site (**www.clhia.ca**) and at Industry Canada's government-sponsored site (**www.strategis.ic.gc.ca**).

Retirement Planning

Financial planning is a key component of retirement planning, but if you want to look at the big picture–including health, housing, and leisure-related issues–the Internet could be your guide. Three useful sites for an overview approach to retirement planning are Retire Web (**www.retireweb.com**), The Wealthy Boomer and its Wealth Discussion Forum (**www.wealthyboomer. com**), and Canada's Association for the Fifty-Plus (**www.50plus.com**). The 50plus site includes a Retirement Planning Centre, which has RRIF news, investment tips, mutual fund recommendations, and model portfolios, as well as sections on tax planning and estate planning.

While these and other useful information sources are available on the Internet 24 hours a day, it's important to remember that they are not meant to replace the relationship you have with your financial advisor, but rather to enhance it.

Government Programs

Contrary to what some people might think, governments have outperformed the private sector in providing unbiased and useful Web sites. The reason? Governments, along with small independent operations, represent the original driving force behind the Internet. Accessing government sites is a valuable, reliable way to gather information and avoid lengthy delays through more traditional avenues of contact. The Human Resources Development Canada Programs and Services page at **www.hrdc-drhc. gc.ca/isp** is the place to look for information about Old Age Security and other federal income programs. Separate "departments" within this general site also explain other programs such as the Canada Pension Plan.

For tax information, the Canada Customs and Revenue Agency Web site is first rate, although finding exactly what you want can at times be a bit daunting, as the internal search engine often lists many out-of-date documents. It's located at **www.ccra-adrc.gc.ca**.

Additional Resources

Andrew Dagys' best-selling book *The Internet for 50+: The Complete Guide for Every Canadian Over 50*, produced in co-operation with Canada's Association for the Fifty-Plus (Prentice Hall Canada, 1997), is an invaluable guide to pre-retirement and retirement financial planning on the Net.

Despite all this information being available–literally, at our fingertips–some older Canadians still believe the Internet is just for kids, and this misconception may rob them of years of pleasure and valuable service. The Net is an essential financial tool–as revolutionary and astounding as the telephone once was.

17

THE EXECUTIVE SUMMARY

Here's a quick summary of the most important points we've covered so far in this book.

1. RRSP Conversion You must make plans to convert your RRSP to an income fund. If you are willing and able, you can continue saving for the rest of your life, but not within an RRSP. The goal of an RRSP—and the reason the government allows you to make tax-deductible contributions and to earn money on your RRSP investments tax-free over the years—is to provide you with a future source of retirement income. In return, the government requires you to begin withdrawing income, which is taxable as you take it out, when you reach the age limit.

2. Age Limit You must convert your RRSP savings to a vehicle that pays out a stream of retirement income by December 31 of the year in which you turn 69. This age limit was reduced from 71 in the 1996 federal budget. It is best, if you can, to wait until the last minute before converting. But that does not mean midnight on December 31. You should take advantage of the full benefit of RRSP contributions and tax sheltering as long as possible, but you should avoid getting caught up in the year-end rush. Not only will the process be much more difficult, but financial advisors may not have the time to provide you with proper advice. In addition, you may not have enough time to transfer securities from one financial institution to another. If you are moving your account in the process of conversion, you should allow three months to be on the safe side.

3. Conversion Options You have three options for converting your RRSP:

- *Take the cash.* The government will happily allow you to take out all the money in your RRSP at conversion time. We say "happily" because every cent would then be considered taxable income in the one year and you would hand over a big chunk of it to Ottawa, basically defeating the whole point of your RRSP. This option makes sense only if you have a small RRSP.

- *Buy an annuity.* The rules allow you to buy an annuity from a life insurance company or investment dealer. Annuities come in many varieties, but, in essence, you relinquish your RRSP in return for a cheque every month for the rest of your life or for a guaranteed period. Annuity payments are based on a number of factors, including your age, but the most important is interest rates at the time of purchase.

- *Switch to a Registered Retirement Income Fund (RRIF).* A RRIF is essentially an RRSP in reverse. You can hold the same investments, it provides you with the same tax sheltering of earnings, but instead of contributing each year, you must make an annual minimum withdrawal based on your age. However, you can take out more if you want or need to.

4. RRIF or Annuity? In most cases, choose a RRIF over an annuity, certainly for the first 10 years or more after conversion. Here's why:

- *Control.* With an annuity, you give your money to an insurance company and lose control of it forever. Payments are based on current interest rates, and if they go up in the future, you cannot change your mind and switch to some other investment. With a RRIF, you retain control and have the option of purchasing an annuity later, should interest rates go up or should you decide that you want that regular monthly cheque in later life.

- *Estate benefit.* An annuity has little or no estate value. You can purchase an annuity with guarantees that provide something for your heirs, but you will pay for it with noticeably lower monthly payments. If estate preservation is important to you, this is not the way to accomplish it. With a RRIF, any money remaining in the fund on your death passes to your spouse tax-free or becomes the property of your estate.

- *Protection against inflation.* Annuity payments almost always remain level throughout your life or for the guaranteed period. You can buy an annuity that's indexed against inflation, but, again, you will be penalized with reduced monthly payments. Even with inflation at low rates, your buying power will be eroded in time. The greatest advantage of a RRIF is that your investments keep working for you, tax-sheltered, allowing your capital to grow and provide a safety net for the inevitable cost-of-living increases to come.

Despite the above, some people prefer annuities because they like the idea of receiving a set amount every month. They don't want to worry about managing their money, they have neither dependents nor heirs, or they have a genetic history of long life. Bear in mind as well that, in some cases, it makes sense to combine RRIFs and annuities.

5. Work with a Financial Advisor Most people get lost trying to make today's complex financial decisions, and no wonder, given the myriad choices available. For example, over 3,000 mutual funds are being sold in Canada alone. There is no question that the help of a professional financial advisor you trust can make a significant difference. This difference has actually been measured in dollars and cents. A research survey by Dalbar Financial Services, a respected U.S. firm, showed that over a period of about 12 years, mutual fund investors with a financial advisor earned almost 17 percent more in total cumulative return than those who bought and managed funds on their own. That sort of performance can make a huge difference in your retirement lifestyle, so it is worth spending time and effort shopping for an investment advisor who is right for your needs.

6. Start Planning in Advance In your early-to-mid 60s, and certainly before you reach 65, you should be revising your financial plan to reflect retirement realities, consolidating your RRSPs, and reorganizing your portfolio.

Over the years, you may have set up RRSPs with a broad range of institutions as you saved for retirement. As you approach conversion time, however, you would be wise to consolidate them into one—or at most two—plans. The reason for doing so is that each RRIF must issue the minimum annual payment, and the foreign-content limit must be calculated separately for each. This can become a major headache if you have too many plans.

You should also be adjusting your portfolio to ensure you have the right mix of income and growth when you switch to a RRIF, perhaps reducing holdings in more volatile mutual funds, for example, and replacing them with solid balanced or blue-chip funds.

If you are in your final year before conversion, you are moving from the savings phase to the income phase of retirement planning. Your goals now are to keep taxes at a minimum, to preserve capital, and to ensure that the income from your RRIF fits your spending needs.

Make your last, maximum RRSP contribution, use up any unused contribution room you may have, and remember that in this final year only, your deadline is December 31, not March 1 of the next year. By then you will no longer have an RRSP to contribute to! Pick the right RRIF plan from the four types. Make sure your withdrawal formula will provide you with enough to cover your needs, but not overly diminish your RRIF.

7. Plan for Your Heirs Few people realize that the government will be there, sooner or later, to "scoop up" its share of an estate. In fact, RRIFs containing substantial assets will ultimately trigger a tax liability amounting to 50 percent or more in many provinces. However, if you consider your RRIF monies to be estate assets as well as a source of retirement income, you may be able to use life insurance to keep your legacy intact.

A sad legal fact of life is that your capital assets are deemed by the Canada Customs and Revenue Agency to have been sold (referred to as "deemed disposition") when you die, and any resultant capital gains are folded into your taxable income and reported on your final tax return. Your RRIFs are brought into this taxable income, as well. This is not the case when your estate is left to your spouse or to your dependent children or grandchildren—a condition introduced with the 1999 federal budget—as it rolls over tax-free in these cases.

Remember, though, that this rollover is merely a way to defer taxes. The tax liability will be triggered when the assets are passed to anyone other than your spouse or dependent children or grandchildren.

So, although you are not subject to estate tax or death duty in Canada, your heirs may end up facing a huge income tax bill, which may shift those of modest means into the highest tax bracket. Buying life insurance is a sound way to reduce the impact of the Canada Customs and Revenue Agency becoming one of your beneficiaries. The inevitable taxes will still be due, of course, but the insurance policy will generate the necessary funds and preserve your estate.

8. Use an Appropriate Investment Approach Canadian investors, especially those who are retired, are often too conservative for their own financial good. You should certainly keep interest-bearing securities in your asset mix. Even though interest rates are low and are likely to stay that way for some time, GICs and bonds should always play a core role in your RRIF for their ability to provide income and relative safety.

But no matter how conservative you are and no matter what your age, always keep some growth investments—best held in a variety of solid, reputable mutual funds—in your portfolio. Remember that diversification and balance produce both performance and protection.

Even a balanced, middle-of-the-road RRIF portfolio should have a solid equity component, relatively equal to the fixed-income portion.

On the other hand, never go too far seeking growth. A portfolio made up entirely of equity holdings can be hazardous. Remember that you have absolutely no control over what market conditions will be in the future.

The bond portion of a RRIF portfolio might range all the way from 30 percent to 60 percent, depending on your age, your risk tolerance, and market conditions. Portfolio returns can be expected to be higher over the years with a solid bond fund component, and the diversification benefits make this approach worthwhile. If equity markets crash, bonds will likely bail you out.

If you are unsure how to set up your asset mix, a balanced mutual fund can be a good place to start. These mutual funds are good for beginners, or for those who want a mix but do not wish to make the asset-mix decisions themselves. Such funds typically invest in a mix of blue-chip stocks, bonds, and cash. The professional manager decides what proportion of each will make up the fund by taking into account economic conditions.

9. Look for Alternatives to Low-Interest-Rate Securities When interest rates began to drop early in the 1990s, millions of conservative North Americans were taken by surprise. Rates had been high for so long that people who had money to invest, especially retired people, simply became accustomed to making an easy 10 percent or so a year. No one realized that there was an inherent risk in interest-bearing securities in terms of interest rates. Most investors thought this easy ride would never end, but now we are facing a whole new world, one of low interest rates that are likely to remain low for a long time.

Here are five recommendations for improving returns:

- Diversify your holdings, both in your RRIF and in your non-registered portfolios.

- Become somewhat more aggressive in your investment strategy. Include at least some growth securities in your portfolio.

- Never attempt to time the market.

- Take advantage of global investment opportunities.

- Think about returns in after-tax dollars.

10. Consider Professional Management If you don't have the time, inclination, or ability to manage the assets in your RRIF, you still should not let your RRIF languish in a low-return account or switch to an annuity, especially if your assets are more than $200,000. Most financial institutions provide an excellent service that takes this task off your shoulders and shifts it to a professional money manager. This service is known as "discretionary investment management," and can be most useful. Unfortunately, this concept is little understood, and even investors who are intrigued by the idea hesitate to act because of concerns about costs and loss of control. However, these fears are groundless and should not deter you from seeking such services.

In addition to this service, most banks, trust companies, and investment dealers provide administrative services for a fee, which take care of all the necessary record keeping and reporting. You should have a minimum of between $100,000 and $200,000 in assets, depending on the institution and how much business you do with it. The company may also pay your household bills and manage other aspects of your personal finances, which could be particularly useful for people who spend a lot of time out of the country.

18

Your RRIF Questions

Answered

The Retirement Planning Centre at the 50plus.com Web site (**www. 50plus.com**) contains a great deal of information about RRIFs, LIFs, and LRIFs. It's become a popular source of guidance for people wanting answers to their specific retirement-income questions. Here is a selection of the questions we have dealt with. If you have a retirement question you would like answered, just visit the site and complete the e-mail question form you'll find there.

Which Pays More—LRIF or LIF?

QUESTION I am trying to determine which vehicle would provide the greater payout (based on the maximum allowed) to age 80–a LIF or an LRIF. I am 62 and my spouse is 65. Our goal is to receive the maximum amount of money while we are here to use it.

I have been told, "A LIF pays more." "An LRIF pays more." "There is no significant difference." "We cannot provide advice–we follow your instructions." "Talk to your financial advisor."

Our financial advisor gets his quotes from the trustee based on our instructions. In order to provide instructions, I need to know the facts. Only when I know the facts can I make a decision and provide instructions. Yet the financial institutions want me to make decisions without providing all the facts. They are quick to provide the legislation involved, but this does not tell me the payout I might receive from one or the other of a LIF or LRIF based on the same rate of growth.

My concern is that I have received every possible answer. The consumer apparently has no way of making an educated decision.

– J.C.

ANSWER There isn't a straightforward answer to your question, which is why you are getting such different input. It boils down to "it depends."

You didn't state your province of residence, so we will use Ontario as the example.

For an LRIF (locked-in retirement income fund), the maximum amount that can be withdrawn each year is "the greater of the minimum required by the *Income Tax Act* or the previous year's actual investment return." In other words, if the return on the fund does not exceed the minimum legal withdrawal (which is the same for a RRIF, LIF, or LRIF), then that minimum becomes your maximum for the year as well.

For a LIF (life income fund), the maximum withdrawal is a specific percentage of the fund's value on January 1. That percentage rises each year.

Here's a simple way to look at it. Starting at age 63 and ending at age 80, the average annual maximum withdrawal rate for a LIF in Ontario works out to 8.84 percent. In order to be able to withdraw more from an LRIF, your average annual return on the plan over that period would have to be more than that. The older you are when you start withdrawing, the higher the average rate to age 80 will be.

Since most LIFs and LRIFs are conservatively invested, it might be difficult to achieve an 8.84 percent average annual return. However, if you are prepared to accept a higher degree of risk (e.g., more equities, royalty trusts, etc.), you may be able to average 10 percent annually or even a bit more. It would be unrealistic to assume anything higher.

It all comes down to how you plan to invest the money, which is why no one can provide a definitive answer to your question.

How to Draw Retirement Income

QUESTION My wife and I are in our early 50s and we plan to retire in about two years. We have RRSPs and a non-registered portfolio, each of which will be worth about $400,000 when we retire (both are roughly 60 percent equity mutual funds and 40 percent cash/income funds). I know that the conventional wisdom says to live on the non-registered investments first, then on the RRSPs (RRIFs). However, I'm wondering if perhaps this line of reasoning may no longer be true, considering the recent reduction in capital gains tax. What would be your advice?

– *A.P.P.*

ANSWER As a first step, we suggest rationalizing your plans to make them more tax-efficient. You are holding significant equity fund assets in a registered plan, where you will not get any advantage from the lower capital gains rate. At the same time, you have large income-producing assets outside the RRSPs, where the income is taxed at your full marginal rate.

Step one would be to engineer a swap, exchanging equity funds within the RRSPs for cash and income funds held outside the plans. There are no tax consequences for doing this since, presumably, the cash/income assets do not have any unrealized capital gains attached to them. (If they did, such a swap would be a deemed disposition for tax purposes and you would have to pay tax on the gains.)

Once that is done, your RRSPs should be almost entirely in fixed-income securities and your non-registered portfolios in mutual funds. Now the decision becomes more clear-cut.

Since there is little or no gains potential inside the RRSPs, you draw out the income generated within the plans each year, leaving the capital intact. This will ensure an ongoing source of steady income for your retirement years.

If that isn't enough to live on with whatever sources of other revenue you may have (e.g., pension plans), you should talk with a financial advisor about setting up a systematic withdrawal plan and/or shifting some of the non-registered assets into tax-advantaged, income-producing securities such as preferred shares, income trust funds, and royalty income trusts. This will enable you to generate income from your non-registered portfolio that will be taxed at a lower rate.

The bottom line is that, before you sell anything inside or outside the RRSPs, you should maximize the after-tax cash flow and the capital gains potential of both the registered and the non-registered assets.

Should I Make Big RRIF Withdrawals?

QUESTION I have to start a RRIF at the end of this year. Since I am not in a high-income bracket, would it be advisable to withdraw more than the minimum requirement, so that if I should die within (say) the next ten years, my children will not lose half of my RRIF to the government in the form of income tax?

– *G.M.*

ANSWER It's not a strategy we would recommend. Look at the other side of your question. Suppose you live for 30 years. If you start drawing down your capital now, your RRIF may run out of money well before you pass on.

Our advice is to take out what you need, invest the RRIF assets wisely, and let events take their course. Don't try to outguess death or the tax department. It's a loser's game.

RRSP or RRIF?

QUESTION A co-worker has just retired. He received an early retirement supplement as a lump sum of $37,000 instead of monthly payments of $375 up to age 65 (total of $45,000). The $37,000 he deposited into his RRSP and then immediately changed it to a RRIF. He is 56. Should he have just received the monthly payments of $375 instead of taking the lump sum? Since he has a RRIF now, I do not believe that he is any further ahead, because he has to take a certain amount from his RRIF each year. Should he have just kept his RRSP until he is 69? Is there still compound interest from a RRIF? When it is my turn, I think I will take the lump sum, deposit it into my RRSP, and let it grow for 10 years without making any withdrawals. What do you think?
–C.D.

ANSWER Let's do a little math here. If he had put the $37,000 into an RRSP and left it to compound at a modest 6 percent, it would be worth $62,510 at age 65 (nine years). At 6 percent, that would yield $3,750 per year, or $312 a month plus change. At a 7 percent growth rate, the original amount would increase to $68,023, yielding $4,761 a year, or $397 a month. Such is the power of a percentage point.

It would certainly appear that your friend would have been better off keeping the RRSP and allowing the capital to compound. However, perhaps he needed the income. The $37,000 in the RRIF will produce $2,220 a year ($185 a month) at 6 percent until he has to encroach on the capital. That won't be until age 71–until then the minimum annual withdrawal does not exceed 5 percent.

He did not have to make the RRIF conversion, of course. He could have kept the RRSP until age 69. As for compound interest in a RRIF, certainly you can earn it. A self-directed RRIF can invest in just about everything an RRSP can.

That said, it's hard to judge whether he did the right thing without knowing his complete financial picture. We all have to make our own decisions on that basis.

Retiring Soon—Which Strategy Is Best?

QUESTION I am 58 years old and have $700,000 in assets–$200,000 is in RRSP GICs, $350,000 in regular GICs, $100,000 in government bonds, and $50,000 in gas shares. All are coming due shortly. I intend to retire at 60. How would you suggest I invest the $700,000 at my retirement? I own my own home clear of title and have no other income.
– *M.L.*

ANSWER You will want to employ different strategies for the RRSP/RRIF portion and for the non-registered securities. In both cases, however, you should adopt a conservative approach, since this is the only source of retirement income you will have, apart from CPP and OAS.

For the RRSP, you do not need to convert the assets into a RRIF immediately, even though you will be retiring. You can retain the RRSP until age 69, and we recommend you do that. Once you convert to a RRIF, you must make regular annual withdrawals. This is not necessary in an RRSP, but the money is there for you if required. So you have more flexibility.

We suggest that you invest part of the RRSP, say 50 percent, in securities with modest growth potential and low risk. These could include your gas company shares and units in conservatively managed mutual funds. See a financial advisor for specific recommendations. The balance of the portfolio can be held in government bonds and/or GICs.

The non-registered investment portfolio should be structured so as to provide tax-advantaged cash flow with minimal risk. GICs are not recommended here because the interest income they pay is taxed at your regular rate. Consider moving to a portfolio that includes preferred shares and dividend income funds to get the benefit of the dividend tax credit. You may also want to consider some low-risk royalty income trusts and/or REITs, which can also provide tax-advantaged cash flow. Again, ask a financial advisor for specific recommendations.

Retirement Dilemma

QUESTION I am in a dilemma. I have used many different brokers, since I have lived in different parts of Canada and overseas over the years. Many have been totally useless and some have been far too inexperienced. The result is that my wife and I have ended up with poor returns and bad advice in the past.

We took early retirement in 1998 and, since building a permanent home by the lake north of Muskoka, I have transferred our investment accounts to a discount broker and have paid close attention to financial news and advice in the newspapers, on the Internet, and through publications such as *Gordon Pape's Internet Wealth Builder.*

I am happy with my asset mix and think that I have a good quality portfolio, but my dilemma is that I am spending far too much time tracking what is going on and I feel too stressed and concerned regarding major changes affecting individual stocks that I hold. I am coming to the conclusion that I don't get enough time to do other things I want to do because I am thinking too much of market swings and whether I should move out of this or move into that. Perhaps it would be better for my peace of mind to change direction.

Inside and outside of RRSP/RRIF accounts, my wife and I have enough money invested to last us past 90 years of age based on our current budget escalated by a 3 percent annual inflation rate, providing that our investments show a minimum combined annual return of 7.5 percent. As I still want to have some involvement in our financial affairs, I am facing three options:

1. Move the bulk of our investments to mutual funds and only keep tabs on the choice and appropriate blend of funds over the years to come, and leave the balance in blue-chip stocks only. This would be easier and less stressful than being concerned with the performance of individual securities. The downside is that I have to be prepared to pay approximately 2 percent annual MER on the bulk of our investments.

2. Seek the financial advice of a professional who could make recommendations and who would act as a sounding board to investment opportunities that I come across. The downside is that sometimes trades are seemingly recommended for purposes of generating commission income. The alternative is a flat 1 percent annual fee on the total investment value, but that would be in addition to MERs on any mutual funds held and I am not sure it is worth the cost.

3. Continue with my discount broker and act on advice provided by publications such as yours backed up with my own research before executing orders, while maintaining a more conservative approach.

Any comments you may have would be appreciated.
– D.G.

ANSWER You have a dilemma. You're doing quite well with your investments, but you don't want to devote as much time to the process.

The logical answer is to simplify your financial life. This is not a time to be fretting about the cost—a couple of percentage points is worth it if it buys you peace of mind and more time to do the things you enjoy. Therefore, we would suggest the following approach:

1. Move primarily to a mutual funds portfolio, using core funds only. Avoid sector funds, which have to be treated like stocks and require constant monitoring. Use a conservative asset mix so you won't have to worry about stock market gyrations.

2. Find yourself a good financial advisor in whom you have confidence and who will build your portfolio, keep watch over it, and contact you if a change is indicated.

3. Stay informed about current developments in the market so that you'll be in a position to ask intelligent questions and to bring a critical assessment to the advice you are offered.

Two RRIFs Not Better Than One

QUESTION Recently, I went to my bank to convert my RRSP to a RRIF. There, I was advised, for the first time, that since my RRSP comprised GICs and mutual funds, I had in fact two RRSPs, one for GICs and one for mutual funds, and therefore I would have two RRIFs. As well, the relevant annual percentage withdrawal would apply to each fund within the mutual fund RRIF. Since many mutual funds are now languishing, it seems grossly unfair that one should be forced to withdraw from them, especially since the common advice of most so-called experts is to hold on to mutual funds because they will recover over the long term.

Is this anomaly attributable to federal government regulations or is it unique to my bank?

– J.M.

ANSWER It has nothing to do with the government regulations, nor is it unique to your bank. Financial institutions offer different types of RRSPs. They have plans for GICs, plans for in-house mutual funds, plans that can hold third-party funds, plans for CSBs, etc.

Although you obviously don't recall it (as it was probably many years ago), you would have been required to sign separate documents to open two plans. Perhaps the implications of what you were doing weren't explained at the time.

However, there should be an easy solution to your dilemma. Simply instruct the bank to set up a self-directed RRIF and to roll both RRSPs into it. We're surprised that this hasn't already been recommended. You'll have to pay an annual fee for the self-directed plan of $100 or so, but it will give you the flexibility to decide which securities you wish to cash in.

We suggest you also give instructions to ensure you have some of your GIC money coming due every year to provide the necessary cash flow (staggered maturities) or use monthly-pay GICs.

Preferred Shares or Bonds?

QUESTION I have read most of your books, as well as those of several other personal finance and investment writers; however, I don't recall coming across a comprehensive yet understandable discussion of the relative merits of preferred stock shares versus corporate bonds, particularly for a RRIF.

Specifically, what criteria should be used in deciding between, for example, a Royal Bank bond yielding 6.5 percent and Royal Bank preferred shares also yielding 6.5 percent? Does the bond's coupon rate matter, or is the current yield all that's important? The fact that either issue will likely be purchased in the "secondary market" also muddies things in my mind. Is it preferable to buy "new issues"? Is this even possible?

– R.L.

ANSWER If you're investing outside a registered plan, the preferred shares have the edge because the dividend they pay is eligible for the dividend tax credit. That means your income will be taxed at a lower rate than if it comes from a bond, which pays interest.

Inside a RRIF, it's a different story, however. The dividend tax credit has no bearing since all money taken out of a RRIF is taxed at your marginal rate, whatever the original source. So you need to apply some different criteria. These include:

1. *Term to maturity or next call date.* All bonds and most preferreds have a maturity date. Many preferreds can also be called at the option of the issuer, which is usually done if the coupon rate is higher than the market rate at the call date. Before you invest in any security of this type, find out how long you can hold it for. The call date may be just months away.

2. *Yield to maturity.* The coupon rate means little if you are buying a bond or a preferred in the secondary market (yes, you can buy new issues—check with your broker). Even the current yield may not mean a lot if the bond or preferred is priced at a significant premium or discount to par. For example, a preferred with a current yield of 8 percent may look very attractive—until you probe further and see that it is trading at $26.50 but can be called at $25 in 12 months. That means you would suffer a capital loss of $1.50, which would

significantly reduce the yield to maturity, which takes into account both the interest/dividends and any capital gain/loss.

3. *Credit standing.* Bonds take precedence over preferreds in the pecking order if the issuing company runs into financial difficulty.

4. *Payment method.* There are two main types of preferred shares: fixed rate and floating rate. The fixed-rate preferreds pay the same dividend at all times. The floating-rate preferreds pay a variable dividend that is based on a standard measure such as the Bank of Canada rate. Most bonds pay a fixed interest rate, except real return bonds—their rate is adjusted to reflect changes in the cost-of-living index.

5. *Capital gain/loss potential.* Fixed-rate securities have greater potential for capital gains or losses than those with a floating rate.

Generally, when all the variables are sorted out, bonds from comparable issuers will be found to produce better returns for purposes of a RRIF.

RRIF Foreign-Content Limit

QUESTION When I change my RRSP to a RRIF when I am 69 years old, will the RRIF still have a 30 percent foreign-content limit? Also, I heard that if I withdraw the minimum 5 percent, there is no withholding tax.
– L.M.

ANSWER The foreign-content limit for a RRIF is the same as for an RRSP. That means it is 30 percent from 2001 forward. However, some RRIF administrators discourage clients from operating too close to the limit because regular withdrawals from the plan will constantly change the book value, on which the foreign-content allowance is based. This creates the risk of going over the limit and incurring penalties. As a result, you may be advised to stay 5 percent below the allowable maximum.

All RRIF withdrawals are subject to tax at your marginal rate, no matter how large or small they are. In the event that tax is withheld at source, a credit can be claimed when you file your return.

Calculating Minimum Withdrawals

QUESTION What is the formula for calculating the minimum withdrawal from a RRIF? Has it changed recently?
– D.F.

ANSWER There has been no change in the minimum withdrawal formula for RRIFs. Up to and including age 70, it is the value of the fund on January 1, divided by 90 minus your age on that date. So if you were 69 on January 1, 2002, and the market value of the RRIF was $300,000, the minimum withdrawal for that year would be $14,285.71 ($300,000 divided by 21). From age 71 on, a government formula is applied that increases the withdrawal percentage annually.

Are U.S. Money Funds Foreign Content?

QUESTION If I open a U.S.-dollar money market fund in my RRIF, is it subject to the foreign-content regulations?
– *M.T.*

ANSWER It depends on the fund. About half of the U.S.–dollar money market funds currently available are 100 percent eligible for registered plans, without restriction. The manager achieves this by investing in Canadian short-term securities that are denominated in U.S. currency. It may be hard to believe, but the fact that a note or a bond is in U.S. dollars (or any other currency) does not automatically make it foreign for purposes of registered plans. The key is the issuer. If it's a Canadian government, Crown corporation, or company, then the security is fully eligible.

U.S.-dollar money funds that meet this test include those offered by CIBC, CI, Guardian, HSBC, Investors Group, National Bank, PH&N, Scotiabank, and TD Bank.

As a general rule, we suggest you choose a no-load fund, since it doesn't make sense to pay a sales commission to acquire a money market fund.

How Much of a RRIF in One Fund?

QUESTION I am 69 this year and will be changing my RRSPs into RRIFs by the end of this year. The RRSPs currently comprise 70 percent in GICs and 30 percent in Canadian equity. You mention the importance of a low-risk, diversified portfolio with income and also some growth potential. I am considering the Ivy Growth and Income fund for the 30 percent of my portfolio. Would this one fund provide sufficient diversification (with the GICs), or should I also choose another fund?
– *E.K.*

ANSWER Ivy Growth and Income is a fine fund, offering good diversification. However, it is a balanced fund, not an equity fund. If your goal is to hold 30 percent of your assets in Canadian equities, this fund on its own won't achieve that for you because it also has fixed-income securities in its portfolio. Also, solid a performer as this fund has been, we would question the wisdom of holding 30 percent of a RRIF in any single mutual fund. That's a major commitment of your assets. As an alternative, you may wish to consider putting some of this money into a conservatively managed dividend income fund with another organization.

You may also want to reconsider the idea of holding 70 percent of your assets in GICs, which pay a very low rate of return. As an option, consider some Government of Canada or senior provincial bonds, which would offer a better yield. Mortgage-backed securities are another low-risk choice. You may wish to discuss the possibilities with a financial advisor who specializes in RRIFs.

One Broker or Two?

QUESTION In the near future I will have to transfer my government pension plan funds into an annuity, LRIF, or LIF. Should I set up a diversified portfolio with one brokerage firm, or would it be wiser to split the money and set up diversified portfolios with two separate brokerage firms?
 – *R.H.*

ANSWER If you use the money to buy an annuity, the question is moot because there will be no portfolio to administer. Assuming you choose the LRIF or LIF, then our usual advice is to consolidate the money in one place. There are four main reasons for this:

1. *Cost savings.* Each plan will attract administrative fees.

2. *Withdrawals.* All your payments will come from a single plan, which makes the cash flow easy to track. Also, you don't have to worry about different minimum and maximum withdrawal requirements between accounts.

3. *Foreign content.* Each separate plan would have to conform to the 30 percent foreign-content limit.

4. *Portfolio balancing.* It is easier to construct one single portfolio to meet your asset-allocation requirements.

Converting Spousal RRSP to RRIF

QUESTION My wife will convert a spousal RRSP to a RRIF this year. Next year, my wife will make a minimum withdrawal from the RRIF. She will be 62 in November 2002. I made a $1000 contribution for the 2001 tax year. I am retired as well.

1. If my wife makes a minimum withdrawal from the RRIF next year, will the income tax be paid by my wife or me?

2. At age 62, what is the minimum withdrawal allowed for my wife?

3. Can I start a new spousal RRSP and make contributions to the spousal RRSP? This would mean my wife had a RRIF and a spousal RRSP at the same time. Would the new spousal RRSP have any taxation effect on the RRIF withdrawals?

– D.C.

ANSWER The answers to the first two questions are straightforward.

1. The rules state that if a spousal RRSP is converted to a RRIF, there is no attribution of any withdrawals made in the first three years unless they exceed the minimum withdrawal amount. So, if your spouse takes out only the minimum, the RRIF payments will be taxed in her hands, not yours.

2. The formula for calculating a minimum RRIF withdrawal for someone under age 71 is 90 minus the person's age on January 1, divided into the value of the plan on January 1. Your spouse will be 62 on January 1, 2003, so the factor for that year is 90 – 62 = 28. If the RRIF were valued at, say, $50,000, the minimum withdrawal in 2003 would be $1,785.71.

Question 3 isn't quite as clear-cut. While we can find nothing in the Interpretation Bulletin IT307R3 that specifically rules out your idea of starting a new spousal RRSP while your wife is receiving payments from the RRIF, the concept appears to be in conflict with the spirit of the rule, which is intended to prevent short-term income splitting. In effect, you would be receiving a tax deduction for a new spousal RRSP contribution while your wife is taking money out of the RRIF at a presumably lower tax rate.

I suggest you get a copy of form T2205, *Calculating Amounts from a Spousal RRSP or RRIF to Include in Income* and work it through, plugging in your actual numbers. You can download it from the Web site of the Canada Customs and Revenue Agency: **www.ccra-adrc.gc.ca**.

Work through it and see how the numbers tumble out. That's the best way to find out if you will have any tax liability.

Also, you say that you are retired. Remember, only earned income is eligible for an RRSP contribution.

Royalty Trusts and RRIFs

QUESTION I am particularly interested in royalty trusts for RRIFs. Can you tell me more about this idea?
– D.L.

ANSWER Royalty income trusts can be used in RRIFs to improve cash flow–some are currently generating yields of upwards of 10 percent. During periods of low interest rates, these trusts can be used to enhance the low returns produced by traditional fixed-income securities such as bonds and GICs.

However, the risks associated with royalty trusts are quite high and the income is not guaranteed, unlike a bond. Therefore, you have to be careful with your selection. We recommend choosing lower-risk royalty trusts for a RRIF (for example, those involved with such industries as hydro generation) even though the yields are less than those available from energy trusts.

For more information on royalty trusts and RRIFs, see Chapter 8.

Preparing Portfolio to Retire

QUESTION I am 59 and hope to retire at 60. My RRSP portfolio amounts to just over $300,000, plus I own investment rental property, which produces a net of $18,000 per year. Living costs are about $35,000 after tax and I'm worried about the fall in value of my portfolio. Since the beginning of last year, it has dropped about 3 to 4 percent. I'm going to need about 5 to 7 percent growth each year. Should I be moving to GICs?
– K.R.

ANSWER You're retiring early, so you need to plan your cash flow very carefully. You say you need $35,000 after tax, which probably means somewhere around $40,000 to $45,000 before tax, depending on the tax credits available to you. We'll use $42,000 for purposes of this discussion.

You say that $18,000 will come from the rental property. That leaves a cash requirement of around $24,000 a year to meet your needs. Five-year GICs are currently paying less than 5 percent, which means if you move all your RRSP investments there you will only generate around $15,000 a year. If you withdraw that amount from the plan (or a RRIF), you'll be short $9,000 annually. You don't mention any other income sources, but presumably you will apply for a reduced CPP benefit at age 60. If you qualify for full CPP payments, they would be worth about $6,500 a year at the reduced rate you would receive at 60 (70 percent of the rate at age 65). That cuts your shortfall to about $2,500.

In other words, you're almost there even if your registered plan returns only 5 percent annually. You should easily be able to increase the return to 6–7 percent by using a combination of GICs, bonds, high-yielding common stocks, and conservative royalty trusts or REITs. We suggest you review the portfolio with your financial advisor with this goal in mind.

Should I Open a RRIF at Age 55?

QUESTION I am 55 and am unemployed with not many prospects. My advisor suggests that I place my RRSPs (approximately $100,000) into a RRIF plan in GICs in order to have a monthly income. I have mutual funds and some bonds. Would I be better off with another plan—perhaps a withdrawal plan from my mutual funds?
– W.D.R.

ANSWER The main problem with converting RRSP assets to a RRIF at your age is that there is no mechanism for reversing the decision later. If circumstances should change and you get another job, you'd still have to withdraw income from the RRIF. That would increase your tax burden and deplete the RRIF's capital.

If you keep the RRSP, you leave your options open. You can make withdrawals from the plan if you need the money. These will be taxed as income, exactly the same as if they had come from a RRIF. The difference is that you retain the option to stop making withdrawals if your situation changes. So there is flexibility in this approach that the RRIF does not provide.

We suggest you discuss the situation with your advisor in this context and see what he or she has to say.

Wants to Split RRIF Income with Wife

QUESTION When I transfer my RRSP content to a RRIF, I am allowed to specify my wife's age—she's nine years younger than I—which means I benefit from a lower amount of mandatory withdrawal from the RRIF, over time. Given this set of circumstances, am I allowed to split the withdrawal amount with her so that it will be taxed in her hands rather than the full amount in mine?
– H.M.

ANSWER You're correct about using the age of the younger spouse, but splitting income between the two of you to reduce taxes is absolutely not allowed. This is where a spousal RRSP would have worked to your advantage had you created one years ago. Some of the money that is in your RRIF would instead have ended up in your spouse's plan and she would have been able to convert that into her own RRIF at the appropriate time. That would have allowed for the income-splitting you're looking for, but we're afraid it's too late.

The only way in which you would be able to split RRIF income with your spouse would be under a settlement arrangement if the two of you should separate. It seems like a rather extreme way to save a few tax dollars!

Wants to Invest in Bonds

QUESTION I am interested in investing in one or two high-quality bond funds for the fixed income part of my portfolios, one in a RRIF and one in a non-registered account. Do the same principles hold true when investing in bond funds as in individual bonds? If so, is this a sensible time to invest, or should I wait until I think interest rates have peaked? If now is not a good time, what alternative is there for fixed income other than GICs?

– *D.S.*

ANSWER For starters, the tax implications of your bond investments are very different inside and outside the RRIF. In the non-registered portfolio, the interest income will be taxed at your marginal rate, which means you may not have a lot left at the end of the day. For example, if the bond yields 6 percent and your marginal tax rate is 40 percent, your net after-tax return will be only 3.6 percent. Inside the RRIF, of course, the full amount of the interest will be received and taxed only when you make withdrawals from the plan.

So, for your non-registered portfolio, you may want to consider investments that are more tax-efficient. High-quality preferred shares, such as those offered by the major banks, are one option since their payments are eligible for the dividend tax credit.

As far as timing is concerned, how will you know when interest rates have peaked? Even professional bond traders are never sure. For the ordinary investor, attempting to time bond or stock markets is a losing game. If you want to invest in bond funds in the RRIF, choose a couple of good ones with low MERs and let the managers worry about the timing.

How to Choose a Self-Directed Plan

QUESTION I am currently looking into self-directed RRSPs for both my wife and myself. We have to convert to RRIFs within two years, so we will want a plan that can carry on into a self-directed RRIF as well. There is currently a little over $100,000 invested in each plan. Each plan is invested primarily in mutual funds, divided among two or three companies with mixed asset allocations, and a bank term deposit. It is becoming increasingly difficult to balance my desired asset allocation and to maximize foreign content.

While I feel quite certain that self-directed plans are the way to go, I am having a little difficulty deciding which company would be the best for me. I am comparing several companies with respect to administration costs, costs to buy/sell securities, online research, and client assistance. Could you please give me some advice on selecting a firm and list some of the questions I should be asking them.

– *I.G.*

ANSWER You're on the right track. Cost is a factor, of course, but it should not be the sole criterion in making this decision. Here are some of the questions we would pose:

1. What kind of advice can you expect? Will you have to make all the decisions yourself, or can you count on help from a professional advisor? If the latter, who is the advisor, what are his or her qualifications, how long has the advisor been at this job, and how well do you relate to the person? This is a critical issue because, while the cost of an advisor-assisted plan may be a little more, the help you receive in making your decisions may be well worth it.

2. What restrictions are there on the plan? Every company has its own rules and some of them may cause problems. For example, some companies set an arbitrary foreign-content limit on RRIFs that is lower than the maximum allowed by the government.

3. What do the statements look like? Some companies issue excellent portfolio statements that clearly show the assets, the original purchase price, the current market value, the foreign-content position, the account activity in the past month, and a lot more. Other companies are still in the Dark Ages in this regard.

4. Are there special charges that may affect you? For example, do you want to set up a systematic withdrawal plan? If so, is there a special fee attached, and how much is it?

Combining answers to these questions with the research you are already doing should help you select a company that will be right for the job.

LIF Maximum Limit a Problem

QUESTION My employer has a locked-in money purchase retirement plan. The choices at retirement will be a LIF, LRIF, or annuity. The LRIF seems like the best choice, but the maximum withdrawal percentage set by legislation will not provide an adequate income. Because of this, would it be better to purchase an annuity?

– B.B.

ANSWER You have encountered one of the main problems with life income funds (LIFs) and locked-in retirement income funds (LRIFs): provincial governments (under whose jurisdiction these plans fall) limit the amount that can be withdrawn each year.

The purpose of the limit is to make sure the money lasts and that the plan is not depleted too quickly. But the maximum withdrawal requirement can create the kind of problem you describe.

In Ontario, for example, the maximum annual withdrawal at age 71 is 8.6 percent of the plan's market value on January 1 of that year. Compare this to the federally mandated minimum withdrawal of 7.38 percent for a 71-year-old, and you can see there is not a lot of leeway.

If the maximum withdrawal formula does not generate adequate income, take a look at an annuity to see how much money it would generate. However, you may be disappointed, because low interest rates mean low annuity payments.

Good Pensions—How Should We Manage Our RRIF?

QUESTION My wife and I are going through a review of our portfolio, which includes both registered and non-registered accounts, as we are about five years from retirement. You and others recommend a disciplined asset allocation approach, which of course makes good sense. I have a question, though, about fixed-income allocations. In our case, we will both retire with secure, inflation-protected pensions. It could be argued that our pension income will equate to a large fixed-income instrument, and that therefore we do not need a significant fixed-income component to our portfolio. On the other hand, it can be argued that our investment portfolio should be managed as an entity of its own, ignoring the future pension income. I have not seen this issue discussed in any of the literature I have read and would appreciate your views.

  – C.D.

ANSWER As a general rule, a RRIF (which is where you will end up with your registered assets) should be managed conservatively, with the twin goals of generating cash flow and preserving capital. The fact that you have secure pension income might change your approach somewhat, however.

Some people in your situation prefer to be more aggressive in managing their registered assets. Since they know that their retirement income is guaranteed, they use the RRSP/RRIF money for luxuries–an expensive holiday, buying a boat or a new car, etc. In an effort to maximize their returns, they will assume a higher degree of risk than would normally be found in a RRIF portfolio. This does not mean being silly and investing in penny stocks. But in circumstances when markets have slumped badly, such an aggressive approach might involve adding inexpensive blue-chip stocks to a self-directed plan in an effort to maximize capital gains in the future. Of course, you must be very sure that your pension income will be adequate before you do this.

The other point to keep in mind is tax-efficiency. If you have considerable assets invested outside your registered plan, concentrate your equity investments there and look for higher-yielding fixed-income securities (which attract a higher tax rate) within the RRSP or RRIF.

Setting Up an LRIF

QUESTION My question concerns my $130,000 LRIF and how to structure it so as to provide about $20,000 annual income. I would appreciate your advice on this.

  – R.S.

ANSWER The problem is the same whether it's an LRIF, LIF, or RRIF. You want to achieve an annual return of more than 15 percent, and this at a time of low interest rates!

Frankly, the likelihood of being able to create a plan that would generate that kind of income on an ongoing basis is almost nil. You have set an unrealistic goal.

If you are prepared to take a lot of risk, you could invest the money into a portfolio of stocks with high growth potential plus some high-yield royalty trusts and hope that the markets turn around. But this is not the kind of strategy we would counsel for a retirement income plan.

Unless you're prepared to dip into capital to get your $20,000 a year (not a good idea), you need to scale back to a more achievable target–$8,000 to $10,000 a year, for example. This is an amount that can be sustained over time with a reasonable level of risk.

As far as the precise securities are concerned, you should sit down with a financial advisor and work through the details.

Trapped in a LIF

QUESTION My husband is 78 and the pension portion of his money is now in a life income fund (LIF). We were told when his money was transferred into the LIF that when he turned 80 the money would have to go into an annuity. This makes us very unhappy because, as we understand it, the money is in effect no longer ours, but the life insurance company's in exchange for a life income.

We have recently been told by our broker that we do not have to transfer our money to an annuity but can put it in a "Locked-in Retirement Income Fund" or "Life Retirement Fund" (I'm not exactly sure of the term), which would allow us to keep control of our money, albeit with the minimum and maximum withdrawal restrictions that we now have with the LIF.

I am completely confused and am hoping you can clarify this situation for me.

– K.G.

ANSWER The correct term is life retirement income fund, or LRIF for short. Several provinces now offer this option to people with locked-in accounts, as well as the traditional LIF.

You are correct–if you have an LRIF, you do not have to convert the assets to an annuity at age 80. The plan keeps going. The minimum annual withdrawal requirements are the same as for a RRIF or LIF. However, the maximum amount you may take out in any given year is determined by a different formula. This can vary from province to province, but it is typically based on the previous year's investment return. So if an LRIF earns, say, $20,000 in 2002, that would be the maximum withdrawal allowed in 2003.

Not all provinces have approved LRIFs, so you need to check the status and the rules where you live. Contact the company that administers the existing LIF and ask if arrangements can be made to transfer the assets to an LRIF.

Pengrowth for a RRIF?

QUESTION Last year, I purchased units in Pengrowth Energy Trust after reading about it in Gordon Pape's *Internet Wealth Builder* newsletter. I am very pleased that I purchased this. I was wondering if you could tell me if this trust would be advisable to purchase in a RRIF account. The retiree has about $35,000 to invest and takes approximately $300 pension monthly. She is 71 and has another RRIF that she also draws a pension from that is in GICs.
– B.S.

ANSWER Pengrowth is a royalty income trust that is involved in the oil and gas sector. That makes it problematic for a RRIF for three reasons:

1. The cash flow is not predictable. It will vary in accordance with gas and oil prices.

2. The market price of the shares can be quite volatile.

3. Some of the income is received on a tax-deferred basis. That advantage is lost inside a RRIF.

However, we are aware that some people buy royalty trusts like this for RRIFs during low-interest-rate times to boost returns. It's the old trade-off of risk/return. You don't say what percentage of the RRIF the $35,000 represents, but we certainly wouldn't overload the plan with this type of security. We recommend your friend talk to a professional financial advisor about structuring a plan that will meet her income needs while not unduly risking her capital.

19

How to Use Mutual Funds in Your RRIF

We believe that you should seriously consider using mutual funds as the base of your RRIF, LIF, and LRIF portfolios. But what are they? Despite the fact that interest in them has exploded in recent years, many investors have questions about what they are, how they work, and most importantly, how to pick the winners.

At the back of this book is a section containing reviews and ratings of our selections for the top mutual funds for RRIF investors. But before you plunge into that, here are some mutual fund basics that we suggest you review if you have any questions about this type of investing.

A mutual fund represents a large pool of money contributed by a considerable number of investors. This allows for much greater diversification than any individual could achieve on his or her own. A mutual fund can easily hold 40 to 50 securities, and often many more.

And this diversity can be broader if you invest in a portfolio of funds in different asset classes (cash, stocks, bonds), industrial sectors, and various parts of the world. Diversity also provides risk protection in that it is most unusual for all markets to move in the same direction at once.

Many mutual funds have excellent long-term growth records because their investment choices are made by money management experts. The pool has another advantage. You share expenses with everyone else, reducing your own costs.

You own a share in a mutual fund, somewhat like a stock in a corporation. Your share is called a "unit," and the price of each unit, known as the "net asset value" (NAV), is calculated by dividing the fund's market value, less expenses, by the number of units sold.

Unit values fluctuate, of course, along with the rise and fall of the market value of a fund's investments. Some funds are more active than others, as a result of both their holdings and their announced objectives. When the goal is greater returns, such as in certain equity funds, it is almost always accompanied by higher risk and increased volatility.

No Guarantees

Remember that mutual funds are securities, not deposits, and are not insured by the Canada Deposit Insurance Corporation (CDIC). This holds true even if you purchase them and hold them with a bank or other deposit-taking institution, and even when it comes to interest-bearing money market funds, which act like deposits in many ways.

In 2001, however, the newly formed Mutual Fund Dealers Association was recognized as the self-regulatory body responsible for the thousands of fund sales people who did not already belong to a self-regulatory organization. One aspect of the MFDA is a contingency fund for fund investors. Generally, this puts your mutual fund investments on equal footing with your bank deposits when it comes to losses that might result from insolvency of your fund company. However, you are not protected in any way against market-related losses within a fund's portfolio.

Ultimately, the performance of your own portfolio will depend on the types of funds you choose (an energy fund, which focuses on one sector, would involve more risk than a balanced fund, which aims to diversify its investments), the risk level, market movements, and the fund manager's expertise.

It may seem like dull reading, but mutual fund companies must provide prospective investors with a current copy of their simplified prospectus. Try looking through one–it will disclose everything you need to know about the fund's investment objectives, degree of potential risk, policies, fees, and expenses. You'll find the honesty in this document refreshing–the disclosures are required by law and are a far cry from the marketing hype you see in advertising. This information can actually help you pick a fund whose investment objectives and risk levels are similar to yours.

You can shelter any form of mutual fund income from taxes by holding your funds in a registered plan such as an RRSP or RRIF. However, you should ensure that your registered and non-registered portfolios are structured in such a way as to pay the smallest amount of tax possible. Generally, this means keeping interest-bearing funds (fixed income, money market) inside a registered plan—interest income is taxed at the highest rate. Equity and dividend funds should be kept in your non-registered portfolio because you get a better tax deal.

A Matter of Style

Even within the same mutual fund company, different funds are managed by individual professionals who decide where and when the assets will be invested, and for how long.

The fund managers' job is to adjust investments according to political, economic, and corporate conditions. They try to make changes before these conditions have a negative impact on their funds' holdings.

Managers operate not only under defined mandates but also according to specific styles. In fact, a manager's style is the key factor in your fund's performance, especially when comparing it to similar funds. Here are the major style categories:

Growth Searching out companies, often small or medium-sized, with a track record of increasing sales and profits, and potential for dramatic growth in the future.

Value Combing a sector for undervalued assets, such as a company or industry on the verge of a turnaround or a corporation with unrecognized assets.

Sector Rotation Deciding which sectors of the economy are likely to outperform and over-weighting the portfolio towards those areas.

Momentum Searching out the hottest stocks, in the hottest sectors. When the markets are riding high this style will pay off big, but these funds will get clobbered in major market downturns, such as those we experienced in 2000 and 2001.

Index Tracking the performance of a specific index, such as the TSE 300 or the S&P 500. There are index funds for both bond and stock markets.

Interest Rate Anticipation Applies to bond fund management. The manager attempts to forecast interest rate fluctuations. If rates are set to increase, fund managers will shorten the duration of a bond portfolio; if rates are dropping, managers will lengthen it. Timing is crucial here.

The Fund Basket

Most professional money managers agree that, as we commented earlier, investing in the right blend of assets is a much more likely route to success than picking individual securities or funds.

The most effective method of implementing this asset allocation strategy is to work with your financial advisor to put together a basket of mutual funds representing different management styles and investment objectives.

Many investors think that any mutual fund is automatically risky. In fact, mutual funds range from the ultra-conservative to the heart-stoppingly aggressive. Here, for example, are the major types of mutual funds and the kinds of investments they hold, ranked in order of potential risk and return, from lowest risk to highest:

Money Market Funds The most conservative and safest, these funds invest in government securities (such as Treasury bills) and usually generate a return two or three percentage points more than savings accounts.

Income Funds The objective of these funds is to provide investors with regular income payments, with the possibility of long-term growth through capital gains. Investments include combinations of Treasury bills, bonds, and mortgages.

Balanced Funds These funds combine income and growth through a mixture of investments in stocks, bonds, and money market instruments. As mentioned elsewhere, such funds are best for investors new to mutual funds, or for people who want to handle their asset allocation decisions in a single fund.

Growth Funds (Canadian) Geared to investors looking for long-term growth through capital gains, these funds offer a wide array of choices, ranging in focus from blue-chip companies to specific industries (for example, mining, manufacturing) to small and medium-sized firms with potential for growth. Your time horizon here should be at least five years.

Growth Funds (U.S and International) These funds invest in various stock markets around the world. They provide the opportunity for additional diversification, as well as participation in economic growth taking place globally.

And Now for the Fees

All mutual funds charge management fees to cover such things as administrative costs, salaries, and profits. These costs are summarized in a fund's management expense ratio (MER). The MER is the management fee and all other expenses, expressed as a percentage of the fund's total assets. This usually ranges between 1 percent and 3 percent, with the industry average running at about 2.2 percent. On top of this, some mutual funds charge a "load," their term for sales commission, either front-end (when you buy) or back-end (when you sell).

These costs are important factors in any decision to buy a fund. You can find MERs, track performance, compare sales commissions, and review a wide range of useful information in the second half of this book, as well as in special mutual fund tables found in newspapers such as the *National Post* and *The Globe and Mail*. The tables may seem intimidating at first, but they come with self-explanatory notes.

We're in no way suggesting that you make decisions in this way, without the help of your professional financial advisor, but the better informed you make yourself, the better your advisor will be able to do his or her job.

The Dual Purpose of Income Funds

It's true, as indicated in the list of mutual fund types above, that income funds represent the conservative side of the investment world. But they have a dual purpose.

They are certainly the investment of choice for conservative retirees who require income and the opportunity for moderate capital appreciation, but they can also reduce the risk of your overall investment exposure.

You know by now that we believe anyone with a long-term view should have a well-balanced, diversified portfolio. And while a key part of that mix should be made up of equity mutual funds, an important portion should also be composed of one or more of the types of fixed-income funds.

Here's why: Income funds can, at times, produce better returns than equities, and they offer protection in that equities and bonds rarely move in the same direction at the same time. Adding fixed-income funds to your asset mix can lead to better returns at lower risk in the long run.

There are worlds within worlds. Even at this conservative end of investments, you have different categories of risk. Money market funds, for example, are low-risk, a step above savings accounts–unlikely to drop, but generating very low returns. They make no sense as a long-term investment, but can work if you're being defensive or "parking" funds while waiting for an investment opportunity.

The next stepping stone is a mortgage fund. This is still a savings instrument, but is a step up from GICs. Your return over the longer term will be better, and unlike with GICs, your money is not locked in for a specific term.

When you move up again to a bond fund, you're shifting from savings to an actual investment vehicle. The yield on bonds tends to be higher, and over the years, bond funds will outperform both money market and mortgage funds. There is a bit more risk involved, but along with that comes the potential benefit of protection from a decrease in interest rates.

For more details and information on other types of fixed-income funds, see Chapter 8.

Bond Prices vs. Interest Rates

Bond prices fall when interest rates rise (and vice versa) because bonds trade in open markets. If an investor buys a 30-year bond with an 8 percent coupon at a price of $100, the yield-to-maturity of that bond will be 8 percent. If interest rates for 30-year bonds drop to 7 percent, new bonds will be issued at $100 with a 7 percent coupon. For the 8 percent coupon bond to be competitive with the new 7 percent coupon bond, the price of the older bond must move up, to $110, or to whatever point necessary so that the two bonds will have the same rate of return.

But be aware that this will have no effect on you if, as is usually the case with mature investors, you're buying for long-term income. There are two very different sides to bonds—investing and trading. When you buy a bond, it will pay the annual coupon and the face value upon maturity no matter what day-to-day fluctuations it may go through as a tradable item on the market.

What portion of a portfolio should be dedicated to fixed income? That depends on where you are in your life cycle, your objectives, and how much risk you can tolerate.

Still, Canadians in general are far too cautious for their own good, and this caution extends even to this conservative sector of investments. Most reputable, middle-of-the-road, balanced income funds end up with an average mix of about 60 percent equities, 40 percent fixed income. Too much fixed income translates into not enough growth to sustain you over time and to protect you against inflation.

The fixed-income part of your portfolio is certainly safer, but more importantly, it provides you with the opportunity to take more risk in other areas. By offsetting, or balancing, risk, you can feel more comfortable about buying a growth fund with your other investment capital.

The overall goal should be to have a balanced, diversified portfolio reflecting your investment personality. A middle-of-the-road approach would be to put everything into a balanced fund; more aggressive investors might hold 50 percent in a balanced fund, 50 percent in equity funds; and conservative investors might hold 50 percent in a balanced fund and 50 percent in a bond or mortgage fund.

However, we believe you can do much better than that by carefully selecting a blend of mutual funds to meet your needs. Chapter 22, "The Top RRIF Funds," provides recommendations that you may find helpful.

20

How to Use the Investment Ratings

The ratings on the pages that follow are designed to help you determine the suitability of specific investments that you may be considering for your RRIF, LIF, or LRIF. They should not be interpreted as buy or sell recommendations! You should consult an investment advisor before making any final decisions. Obtain a copy of the simplified prospectus (the document that provides all the information about the fund and its management) and study it carefully before going ahead.

For ongoing mutual funds information, try our monthly newsletter, *Mutual Funds Update*, which is available in both print and electronic formats. You can obtain full information and view a sample copy by going to **www. buildingwealth.ca**.

Key Ratings Considerations

The ratings that follow take into account a number of factors. These include:

Risk Level A higher-risk fund, even one that has a good performance record, will generally receive a lower rating than one that may not promise as good a return but that is less risk-prone. The degree of risk is an especially important consideration in a RRIF context, where capital preservation should be a top priority. Risk levels are relative within each fund category. Equity funds, for example, are generally higher risk than fixed-income funds.

So a medium-risk equity fund will have a higher degree of risk than a medium-risk fixed-income fund.

Performance Record Previous performance is no guarantee of future success. A lot can happen over time: Economic conditions may change, a mutual fund manager may depart, interest rates may move, a foreign government may be overthrown—all these factors and more can have an impact on returns. But to ignore history is foolish. In the case of mutual funds, we can discern patterns in managerial style, risk levels, and consistency of performance that help us make an educated guess about the probability of where the fund is heading. Because we regard performance records as being particularly important in judging the suitability of mutual funds, in this book we mainly include funds that have been in existence for at least three years in this book.

Our information sources include data compiled by the *National Post, The Globe and Mail Report on Business, The Fund Library*, Southam's *Mutual Fund SourceBook, PalTrak*, plus the mutual fund companies themselves.

Trend Pattern As well as past performance, we take the trend pattern of each fund into account. We give more emphasis here to relatively recent performance, which means that a fund with a strong record over the past five years would rank higher than one that did well five to ten years ago but has tailed off recently.

Economic Conditions Certain funds may be more suitable under specific economic conditions. If so, we will specify this in the reviews.

Style The style used by a fund manager is increasingly recognized as an important element in judging risk and reward characteristics. For example, in the late 1990s, value investing, in which managers seek out stocks that are trading at bargain prices, was out of favour. As a result, the funds that use this style tended to underperform during that period. By contrast, funds that employed growth and momentum styles, which focus on fast-growing companies with less regard for price, flourished. However, during the bear market of 2000–01, value-oriented funds came back into favour and many performed extremely well. We recommend that a RRIF portfolio place more emphasis on a value approach because it is inherently lower risk. You will find a style definition for each fund in the listings.

RRIF Eligibility We show which funds are fully eligible for registered plans by the RIF designation in the summary line. Funds that have a £ symbol are eligible for registered plans as foreign content only; however, some of these funds may have fully RRSP/RRIF-eligible clones. If so, we mention it in the text.

Costs High costs will have a negative impact on the rating of a fund. A low-cost fund (one with a low management expense ratio, or MER) earns Brownie points. In cases where a front-end load (commission) is charged, assume the fee is negotiable unless the entry specifically states otherwise. Regardless of the posted commission scale, you should not pay more than 4 percent when purchasing a fund with a negotiable fee, even if the amount you're investing is small.

Management Where management is a factor in performance, as it is in all actively managed mutual funds (as opposed to index funds), this has been taken into account in the ratings. We've included in each rating the name of the fund manager and the year he or she took over, if it could be obtained. Note that in some cases, companies refuse to give the name of a lead manager, claiming the decisions are made by a team. You will also find some cases in which a corporation is shown as manager, rather than an individual. We've complied with these designations in the reviews, since we don't have much choice. But it has been our experience that, in business, every team has a leader. Hopefully, these firms will acknowledge this in future.

Personal Experience Over the years, we've found that some funds have done better in our portfolios than others. These personal experiences are an important consideration in the mix because they tell a lot more than raw numbers.

Now for some other important points to note.

Exclusions With a few exceptions, you will not find any funds in this book with a performance record of less than three years. We also exclude funds that are open only to a specific group of people (e.g., doctors, teachers, public servants).

Rates of Return Reference in the ratings to "compound average annual rates of return" refers to the amount by which a fund would have grown each year over the period, assuming all dividends, interest, and capital gains were reinvested. Thus, a fund that is said to have an average annual compound rate of return of 15 percent over 10 years is one in which $1,000 invested a decade ago would have grown at an average annual rate of 15 percent. Rates of return of one year or less are simple rates of return—how much your money would have increased in value since you made the investment.

Load Charges and MERs Load charges are not taken into account in any of these calculations since they will vary from one investor to another.

The reference to MER in the ratings means management expense ratio. This is the percentage of the fund's assets that is deducted each year to pay for management fees and other costs associated with the business. Investors don't pay this fee directly; in most cases it's deducted before the net asset value of the fund is calculated. However, the net result will be to reduce your return. For example, if a fund earns a gross return of 10 percent and has an MER of 1.5 percent, the return you'll actually receive will be 8.5 percent. MERs are especially important in assessing the potential return from money market and fixed-income funds at a time of low interest rates. The lower the MER, the greater the likely return.

Wherever possible, we've used the MERs published in the fund company's latest annual report or in the prospectus.

Availability Note that not all mutual funds are sold in every province. Consult a sales representative in your area to determine whether any fund in which you're interested is available.

Fund Categories In 1999, the industry agreed on a reclassification of fund categories, to attempt to get a better apples-and-apples comparison of funds of the same type. These have been updated since to stay abreast of new developments. For example, Far East funds are now divided into three separate groups: Asia/Pacific Rim Equity (the fund can invest anywhere in Asia and Australia/New Zealand), Asia Ex-Japan Equity (the Japanese market is off-limits for the manager), and Japanese Equity.

The system is still being refined and we don't agree with all the fund designations, but we use the new categories in this book. You'll find a list of the symbols under Mutual Fund Types, following.

Each entry is introduced with a series of symbols. Here's how to interpret them.

Overall Suitability

$$	Average. Returns will likely be about average for the category, or the fund may have a higher cost or risk level. If it is included here, it is because it offers some special benefit for RRIF purposes.
$$$	Above average. Should be seriously considered for your RRIF.
$$$$	Superior. Should consistently perform in the top quartile of its category. Funds with this rating should be at the top of your priority list.

Risk Level

↑	High. Suitable only for investors willing to accept above-average risk for a fund of its type.
→	Medium. Some degree of risk involved.
↓	Low. Minimal risk for a fund of its type.

Asset Type

C	Cash or cash equivalent.
FI	Fixed income.
G	Growth.
FI/G	Balanced.
G/FI	Balanced, with a growth bias.

Characteristics

#	Front-end load.
*	Back-end load.
#/*	Optional front- or back-end load.
#/*/No	Front-end, back-end, and no-load options.
#&*	Front- and back-end loads applicable.
No	No load.
S	Segregated fund of an insurance company.
RIF	Fully eligible for RRIFs, without restriction.
£	Foreign property. Limits apply.
MER	Management expense ratio. The costs charged against the assets of a fund before units are valued. The lower the MER, the better.
Style	The investing approach used by the fund's manager.

Mutual Fund Types

CE	Canadian equity. Invests in a broadly diversified portfolio of Canadian stocks.
CLC	Canadian large-cap equity. Specializes in stocks of large Canadian firms.
CSC	Canadian small capitalization. Invests primarily in stocks of small and mid-size Canadian firms.

DIV	Dividend. Invests in high-yield common stocks, preferred shares, and other income securities, with the goal of maximizing tax-advantaged cash flow.
USE	U.S. equity. Specializes in stocks of larger American companies.
USSC	U.S. small-to-mid-cap equity. Specializes in small to medium-size American corporations.
NAE	North American equity. Focus is on U.S. and Canadian stocks. May contain some Mexican content.
IE	International equity. Invests in international stocks from countries outside North America.
GE	Global equity. Invests in stocks from around the world, including North America.
PRE	Asia/Pacific Rim equity. Invests in stocks from throughout Asia and the Pacific Rim.
JE	Japanese equity. Specializes in Japanese stocks.
AXJ	Asia ex-Japan equity. Invests in stocks from all Asian countries except Japan.
LAE	Latin American equity. Invests primarily in stocks from Mexico, Central America, and South America.
EE	European equity. Invests in European stocks.
EME	Emerging markets equity. Invests in stocks from developing countries.
SPE	Specialty/miscellaneous. Emphasis is on a specific sector or theme.
ST	Science and technology. Invests in science and technology issues.
HC	Health care. Focus is on companies involved in pharmaceuticals, biotechnology, manufacture of health-related products, health service companies, etc.
FS	Financial services. Invests in banks, mutual fund companies, brokerages, etc.
NR	Natural resources. Specializes in natural resource stocks.
PM	Precious metals. Invests in gold, precious metals, and shares in mining companies.
RE	Real estate. Invests primarily in commercial real estate.
AS	Alternative strategies. Mainly hedge funds and market neutral funds.
CB	Canadian bond. Invests primarily in Canadian-dollar bonds and debentures with maturities of more than one year.
FB	Foreign bond. Invests in bonds and debentures denominated in foreign currencies.
HYB	High-yield bond. Invests in bonds that pay higher yields (sometimes called "junk bonds").

STB	Canadian short-term bond. Specializes in bonds with short maturities, to reduce risk.
M	Canadian mortgage. Invests mainly in residential first mortgages.
CBAL	Canadian balanced. Invests in a blend of Canadian equities and debt securities.
CTAA	Canadian tactical asset allocation. Invests in a blend of Canadian equities, bonds, and cash using tactical asset allocation strategies.
CIT	Canadian income trusts. Invests in a variety of income-generating securities including equities, royalty trusts, REITs, and bonds.
GBAL	Global balanced and asset allocation. Invests in a blend of foreign equities and debt securities. May use tactical asset allocation.
CMM	Canadian money market. Invests in Canadian short-term debt securities such as Treasury bills.
USMM	U.S. money market. Invests in short-term securities denominated in foreign currencies, usually U.S. dollars.

21

What Should You Hold in Your RRIF?

General

This chapter offers some broad investment strategies you should consider when making your RRIF/LIF investment decisions. This guidance is based on the premise that the two top priorities of RRIF/LIF investors are safety and income. That means it is important to adopt a long-term strategy for your retirement income plan and stick to it, regardless of the economic climate at any given time. Making major strategic shifts in response to short-term developments is not appropriate action for a plan like this. If you have a financial advisor, we recommend consulting with him or her on how best to structure your RRIF portfolio before selecting the specific securities that will be used.

As we have stated earlier in this book, a portion of your plan should be in growth securities, either stocks or equity mutual funds. But the selection process should be quite different from the one you may have used when you were younger. Stock markets, as we have seen in recent years, can be extremely volatile. Since you do not want to expose your RRIF to significant market losses, you need to select very carefully.

If you choose to invest in stocks directly, we recommend focusing on stable companies with a proven track record and what is known as a low "beta." This is a measure of the volatility, and hence the risk, inherent in any stock. A beta of 1.00 means the stock moves exactly in concert with its benchmark index (say the TSE 300). A beta of more than 1.00 signals a stock whose movements, up and down, are more volatile than those of the index— the higher the beta, the more volatile the stock. Conversely, a beta of less than 1.00 denotes a stock that has low volatility. The lower the beta, the better from that perspective. While a low beta does not mean a stock cannot experience a loss, it indicates that the chances of that happening are reduced.

As well as focusing on a low beta, we advise concentrating on stocks that pay decent dividends and that have a historically strong record in this regard. Dividend-paying stocks will provide some cash flow for your RRIF, even though the benefit of the dividend tax credit will be lost inside the plan. Also, such stocks tend to be more stable in terms of market value.

If the growth component of your RRIF is in equity mutual funds, you can reduce risk by selecting funds with a value orientation. These are funds in which the manager uses the principles of value investing to choose stocks. He or she will concentrate on companies that are relatively cheap compared to the overall market and have low price/earnings ratios, a good balance sheet (which effectively means low debt), sound management, a dividend stream, and reasonable growth potential. Some value managers go beyond these parameters to add other criteria, such as buying only stocks that trade below their book value.

Value funds tend to underperform in bull markets. However, they usually stand up much better when stocks are tumbling, as we saw during the bear market of 2000–01.

Another option for protecting RRIF growth assets is to use segregated funds, sponsored by life insurance companies. These provide guarantees that limit losses, shielding at least 75 percent of your investment at death or maturity (10 years) and in some cases provide 100 percent protection. You'll find more information about segregated funds in Chapter 8.

The mainstay of any RRIF should be fixed-income assets. These will generate the cash flow needed to fund the periodic withdrawals you will be making from the plan. At times of low interest rates, it becomes a challenge to put together a fixed-income portfolio that will do the job for you, without incurring undue risk. However, it can be done—review the various options we set out in Chapter 8, as well as the model asset mix you will find there.

As you plan your RRIF investment strategy, here are some of the things to watch for.

Inflationary Trends Inflation has been kept under control in recent years, but that doesn't mean it can't resurface in the future. Even a modest infla- tion rate of 2 percent annually can gradually erode the purchasing power of your RRIF income over time. If it starts to go beyond that, it should sound some alarm bells, and you want to ensure that your plan is protected against the effects. This can be done by increasing the growth component and by adding some real return bonds, or mutual funds that specialize in them. These are bonds issued by the Government of Canada that guarantee a basic return and are indexed to increases in the Consumer Price Index for both principal and interest.

Interest-Rate Movements You need to be very conscious of interest-rate trends on a continuing basis if you are going to manage your RRIF to maximum effect. Never buy long-term bonds or lock in to three- or five-year GICs when interest rates are low. When they seem to be nearing a cyclical high is the time to make such commitments. Also, don't purchase an annuity when interest rates are low—you'll be locking in those low rates for the rest of your life!

Stock Market Trends Short-term stock market movements should not be a concern in RRIF management or in your investment choices. A retirement income fund should never be treated as a trading account. The days for that are long past. However, you should stay aware of broad market movements, since the growth component of your plan will be affected by them. For example, if the stock market rises sharply, the overall value of your RRIF may increase significantly, requiring you to make a larger minimum withdrawal in the subsequent year than you were anticipating. A declining market could have the reverse effect.

Economic Conditions You shouldn't need to be as concerned about the impact of changes in the economic climate as you were earlier in life. If your RRIF portfolio is set up properly, the effect of such changes should be minimal and manageable. As with the stock markets, however, you should keep an eye on developments and review your plan at least quarterly to make sure that no adjustments are needed.

Currency Movements This is an area that does need to be monitored, especially if you spend any time outside Canada (e.g., snowbirds). The Canadian dollar showed a steady decline against U.S. currency throughout the 1990s and into the early part of this century. There is no way of knowing if that will continue, but it certainly represents a risk to the purchasing power of your RRIF income if you need to convert some of the money to U.S. dollars. We recommend keeping a portion of your RRIF in U.S.-dollar-based assets, such as U.S. money market funds and foreign bond funds. The exact percentage will depend on how much of your RRIF income is earmarked for spending outside Canada, but as you will see by referring to our model portfolio in Chapter 8, we suggest that the U.S. asset component of your plan be at least 25 percent. Even if you never plan to set foot outside our borders, you should include some U.S. dollar assets as they will also protect your Canadian purchasing power.

Following are our ratings for the suitability of various types of securities within a RRIF. In these ratings, X indicates a commission is payable; NO means there is no sales charge. CDIC means the asset is covered by deposit insurance. See Chapter 22 for specific mutual fund recommendations.

RRIF Suitability Ratings—General

BONDS (CORPORATE) $$$ → FI X

Corporate bonds normally offer a better rate of return than government issues, but for RRIF purposes stick with companies with high safety ratings. For direct RRIF bond investing, we recommend that only corporate bonds with an "A" or better safety rating be considered. A broker can advise you of the rating of any bond you're looking at, or you can check out the Web sites of Canada's two bond rating services, Dominion Bond Rating Service (**www.dbrs.com**) or Canadian Bond Rating Service (**www.cbrs.com**). Be wary of any bonds with unusually high yields. The risk of default (which means the issuing company can't pay the interest or perhaps even the principal) may be relatively high. We've indicated that a commission will be payable on the purchase of any bonds. You won't see it on a transaction statement, however. It will be incorporated into the price you pay. You will also be required to pay any accrued interest when purchasing a bond. For self-directed RRIFs only.

BONDS (FOREIGN CURRENCY DENOMINATED) $$ ↑ FI X

Bonds issued by Canadian governments and corporations in foreign currencies are fully RRIF-eligible. They work best when two conditions exist: a weak Canadian dollar and falling interest rates internationally. There are many domestic issues available, both government and corporate, that are denominated in major international currencies, including U.S. dollars, euros, and Swiss francs. Don't expect big returns, however. Basically, these bonds should be treated as currency insurance. If you spend a lot of time in the U.S., you can protect your purchasing power there by holding U.S.-dollar bonds in your plan. For self-directed RRIFs only.

BONDS (GOVERNMENT) $$$ → FI X

Bonds issued or guaranteed by the federal government or the provinces will offer a somewhat lower return than those of corporations. However, their safety rating is generally higher. The price of bonds is affected by interest rate movements, so if it appears that rates are on the rise, reduce risk by staying short term. That means keeping your maturities to no longer than five years.

BONDS AND COUPONS (STRIPPED) $ ↑ FI X

At the time you convert to a RRIF, you may find you are holding some stripped bonds or coupons. These were popular RRSP investments when interest rates were high, and you may be holding some that have not yet matured. Strips are government or government-guaranteed bond issues from which the interest coupons have been separated (stripped). The coupons and the bond itself are then sold at a discounted price. No interest is paid, but at maturity the coupon or bond is cashed in for full face value. The attraction for RRSPs is that strips offer a guaranteed rate of return over many years (up to 20 or more) with maturities that can be timed to coincide with retirement. However, new purchases of strips are generally not recommended for RRIFs, for several reasons. First, your money is locked up until maturity at a time when cash flow is important. Second, the long time horizon of strips makes them unsuitable for RRIF purposes. Finally, they are more volatile than normal bonds, making them highly vulnerable in a rising interest rate environment. If you decide to sell prior to maturity, you risk a loss if interest rates have gone up since your purchase.

CANADA PREMIUM BONDS (CPBS) $$$ ↓ FI NO

The Government of Canada has made a determined move to muscle in on the RRSP/RRIF market. Reason: to reduce its dependence on foreign lenders by placing more of its debt securities in the hands of Canadians. Premium Bonds (formerly called Canada RRSP Bonds) were first offered for the 1997 RRSP season for a 10-year term. They did not meet with great success at the outset because of the skimpy rate of return they carried. The new Premium Bonds are a better idea. They offer a three-year rate guarantee and can be cashed in on the anniversary date each year, and for 30 days thereafter. The safety aspect is first rate, a very important consideration in a RRIF context. However, the yield will likely be less than you would receive on a regular government bond or a corporate bond with a three-year maturity.

CANADA SAVINGS BONDS (CSBS) $ ↓ C NO

You won't find anything safer than CSBs to tuck away in a RRIF from a guaranteed repayment point of view. No matter what happens, short of a total economic collapse, the Government of Canada will repay its CSB obligations. Ottawa has made CSBs more attractive in recent years, and they're easier to hold in retirement plans through the use of no-fee government accounts. However, the Premium Bonds are a better choice for RRIFs because of their higher returns. That explains the disparity in the ratings between the two.

CASH $ ↓ C NO CDIC

Cash is safe, but unless you're careful, the return on your money will be extremely low. Most bank deposit accounts pay very low interest rates. Your money isn't going to grow very fast there. If you must hold large amounts of cash in your RRIF, make it work harder by switching into T-bills, term deposits, money market funds, or high-interest accounts offered by some foreign banks, credit unions, and trust companies.

GUARANTEED INVESTMENT
CERTIFICATES (GICS) $$$ ↓ FI NO CDIC

GICs are one of the most common investments held in RRIFs. There's a good reason for that–GICs are simple to understand, easy to purchase, and protected by deposit insurance within the usual limits. Their defects are vulnerability to inflation, lack of growth potential, and, as many people have discovered in recent years, interest rate risk. When rates are high, GICs look more attractive. But remember the guidelines when buying. Longer-term GICs (three to five years) should be purchased when interest rates are near their cyclical peak. When interest rates are relatively low, shorter-term GICs (one to two years) should be given preference, with the idea of reinvesting the money for a longer term when interest rates are higher.

MORTGAGES $ → FI X

Holding individual mortgages in a RRIF can be tricky and expensive, which is why the rating is low. If the mortgage is on your home or a family member's, set-up costs will be high. If it's a third-party mortgage obtained through a mortgage broker, there may be fees to pay. Also, some mortgage brokers have run into financial difficulties, resulting in large losses for investors, so you have to be careful. They also don't provide much in the way of return when interest rates are down, although the rate of return on a mortgage will usually be higher than from a GIC. But you have to decide whether the cost, the risk, and the hassle are worth the effort.

MUTUAL FUNDS—SEE CHAPTER 22

MUTUAL FUND LIMITED PARTNERSHIP UNITS $ → FI £ X

Limited partnership units that are traded on a stock exchange can now be held in a RRIF, but some are classified as foreign content, so be sure to check before you invest. An example of a limited partnership is the Mackenzie Master Limited Partnership that started trading on the Toronto Stock Exchange in mid-1995. This is an amalgamation of several Mackenzie Financial mutual fund partnerships. It generates ongoing income for unit holders, but there is no growth potential. There are certain circumstances in which putting these into a RRIF makes sense because of the cash flow they generate. But remember, you may be limiting your foreign-content allowance.

OPTIONS (CALL) $$$ ↓ C X

Call options are RRIF-eligible. However, the only type we recommend for retirement plans are covered calls. These can be used only in conjunction with stocks held in a self-directed plan, but not all financial institutions will permit them. Where they are allowed, they're a useful way to generate additional cash flow from stock holdings. They don't represent any risk to you, as the seller, beyond the fact that you may have your stock called away if the share price rises above the option strike price. This is one way to generate extra cash flow in a RRIF, which can be important during times of low interest rates. However, covered calls are most suitable for knowledgeable investors who have their own RRIF stock portfolio and who understand the complexities of these trades. If you're in that group, by all means consider them. Otherwise, forget they even exist.

PREFERRED SHARES $$$ → FI X

The major attraction of preferred shares is a high dividend that benefits from the dividend tax credit. This tax advantage is lost inside a RRIF. However, if you don't have the option of holding these securities outside a registered plan, high-yielding preferreds may be considered for an RRIF for their good cash flow and relatively low risk. True dividend income funds (those that hold a high percentage of preferreds) may also be considered for the same reasons.

RIGHTS AND WARRANTS $\uparrow$ G X

Revenue Canada allows you to hold rights and warrants in a RRIF, but it's not a practice we recommend. These investments are highly speculative—you might win big but you can also lose big. And you'll have to pay commission charges on all transactions. Gambling with your retirement funds is not our idea of wise RRIF management.

SAVINGS ACCOUNTS $\downarrow$ C NO CDIC

Some RRIFs offered by financial institutions are nothing more than savings accounts in disguise. These are poor places for your money, as they offer a very low rate of return. Safety is their only virtue—but you can find equally safe investments with much more generous returns.

SAVINGS CERTIFICATES $\$$ $\downarrow$ C NO CDIC

Savings certificates (also called cashable or redeemable GICs) are offered in one form or another by a number of institutions, mainly smaller trust companies. They're similar to CSBs in that they can be cashed any time for full face value. However, they don't come with the multi-year rate guarantee of the CPBs, although these certificates may pay a slightly higher one-year rate of interest. Since they're covered by deposit insurance, they're a safe way to hold cash reserves in your RRIF while earning a higher rate of return than a savings account would pay. Savings certificates are especially useful at times when interest rates are moving up, because you can roll them over at a higher rate of return any time.

STOCKS (CANADIAN) $\$\$\$ \rightarrow$ G X

Holding units of equity mutual funds in a RRIF to add some growth potential is a good idea in many cases. Developing your personal stock portfolio is something else again. For an inexperienced investor, the stock market can be an expensive, high-risk minefield. Unless you have the necessary expertise, we suggest you avoid trying to become a stock market player through your retirement plan. Use equity mutual funds instead, which also offer the advantage of a systematic withdrawal plan so that you can generate some cash flow. However, that said, if you have the knowledge and experience to invest directly in stocks, by all means do so. We recommend concentrating on low-risk, blue-chip stocks that pay dividends, so as to add to cash flow.

STOCKS (FOREIGN) $ ↑ G £ X

Building a portfolio of foreign stocks in your RRIF is trickier than trying to set up a Canadian stock portfolio. You'll keep bumping up against the foreign-content rule, and it's difficult to get information about foreign companies, except those that trade in New York. For that reason, most of the foreign stocks you're likely to include in a RRIF will be American or ADRs (American Depository Receipts), which trade on U.S. exchanges but represent shares in foreign companies. In the past, the U.S. government required that 15 percent be held back from any dividends remitted to foreign residents, including Canadian RRIFs. However, that changed with the implementation of amendments to the Canada-U.S. Tax Treaty at the beginning of 1996, so it's no longer a problem. If you want to hold foreign stocks in your retirement plan, we recommend going the mutual fund route. However, if you prefer to build your own portfolio in a self-directed plan, we suggest you stick to shares of U.S. companies, which are easy to acquire and to monitor.

TERM DEPOSITS $$ ↓ C NO CDIC

Although *term deposit* and *GIC* are often used interchangeably, a term deposit generally refers to a certificate that can be cashed early if required, usually with a penalty. Most commonly, they are issued for terms of less than one year. Term deposits are useful as a temporary place to park RRIF cash. As interest rates move higher, they look more attractive. Deposit insurance applies, subject to the usual rules.

TREASURY BILLS $$$$ ↓ C X

T-bills, along with CSBs, are about the safest place for your money that you'll find in terms of guaranteed principal. And the short term (91 days to one year) means your money is constantly rolling over so you benefit from any increase in rates. On the other hand, your return will steadily decline when rates are falling. At the present time, T-bills look attractive because it appears that rates should be stable going forward. A fairly high minimum purchase is usually required for T-bills. This can be $5,000 to $10,000 if you buy through a stockbroker; more if you deal with a bank or trust company. We've indicated that a commission will be payable on T-bill purchases. As in the case of bonds, you won't see it, though; it's buried in the price you pay. However, because many brokers use T-bills as loss leaders to attract clients, the commission is usually very low and should not be a factor in your purchase decision. T-bills can be held only in self-directed RRIFs.

22

THE TOP RRIF FUNDS

The best funds for registered retirement income plans (RRIFs) are not necessarily the same as those for RRSPs. That's because the objectives of the two types of registered plans are quite different. The long-term goal of an RRSP should be steady growth with minimal risk. In the case of a RRIF, however, cash flow becomes a key consideration. Growth should remain a component of a well-balanced RRIF portfolio, but will not be as important a factor as during the RRSP years.

The 181 funds on the following pages comprise those we believe are best suited to a well-structured, diversified RRIF portfolio. You may find that a few of the funds have not been in existence for three years, and therefore do not qualify for a formal rating. This is because many new income funds based on royalty trusts, REITs, etc., have been launched within the past couple of years. They don't have a long track record, but their investment mandate makes them good candidates for RRIF consideration. Such funds are designated with an NR, for Not Rated. Don't be put off by the fact that they aren't rated; if they are included in this section, it's because we consider them appropriate candidates for a RRIF portfolio.

You will note that some dividend funds appear in the Canadian Equity section, while others are in the Income section. We have made this distinction because of the wide variance in the goals and performance of dividend funds. Some are designed mainly to provide a steady revenue stream, and these show up among the Income funds. Those that place more emphasis on common stocks and capital gains are in the Canadian Equity section.

Canadian Equity Funds

AGF CANADIAN DIVIDEND FUND $$$ → G #/* RIF CE

Managers: Gordon MacDougall, since inception (1985), and Martin Gerber (Connor, Clark & Lunn), since 1994

MER: 1.88%   **Style:** Top-down Growth/Value

Suitability: Growth investors. Not suitable for income investors.

This is officially classified as a dividend income fund, but any resemblance between this and a real dividend fund is purely coincidental. The fund throws off virtually no cash flow, which is supposed to be an integral feature of a true dividend fund. In fact, the annual study we do for the *Mutual Funds Update* newsletter consistently shows that this fund has a cash distribution so small you'd need a magnifying glass to find it. Keep that in mind if you're an income investor. AGF should consider renaming this fund to more accurately reflect its investment style, because as things stand, investors are likely to be misled. Despite that criticism, this is not a fund to ignore. Looked at as a pure equity fund, it offers a well-structured portfolio of blue-chip stocks that includes a lot of banks and big industrial companies. The fund is conservatively managed by Gordon MacDougall and Martin Gerber, who are with the investment house of Connor, Clark & Lunn. Returns have been consistently good. Especially impressive is the fact that this fund did not record a losing calendar year for a decade, until 2001. So approach this fund as a pure blue-chip entry for risk-averse RRIF investors, and make your purchase judgment on that basis. Using that criterion, it's a winner. Formerly known as the 20/20 Dividend Fund and, in the distant past, as the Sunset Convertible Preferred and Dividend Fund. All financial advisors (except those tied to a single company) can acquire units for you.

AIC DIVERSIFIED CANADA FUND $$$ → G #/* RIF CE

Manager: Jonathan Wellum (Georgian Capital Partners), since inception (1994)

MER: 2.26%   **Style:** Bottom-up Value

Suitability: Buy-and-hold value investors.

For several years, everybody loved the AIC funds because of the great returns they generated. Their performance was mainly tied to two strategies: a strong emphasis on financial service companies and a commitment to the value investing approach of Warren Buffett. When value investing took on a Dark Ages look in the go-go Nasdaq boom and bank stocks were pounded by rising interest rates and merger disappointments, AIC's funds took heavy losses and investors fled. But the new century brought a shift in attitude, and AIC's approach suddenly looked pretty sound again in a period of slowing growth, sober markets, and declining interest rates. The fund has a sizeable position in Buffett's Berkshire Hathaway Inc., so Warren Buffett and his team have a direct impact on some of your money. Long-term returns are better than average. Risk is about average for the Canadian Equity category. This is a useful holding for the growth section of a RRIF portfolio. The fund is available through most financial advisors.

BEUTEL GOODMAN CANADIAN EQUITY FUND $$$ → G #/NO RIF CE

Manager: James Lampard, since 1991
MER: 1.32%   **Style:** Value
Suitability: Low-risk investors.

The fund selects its stocks mainly from the TSE 300, which gives it a bias towards large-cap issues. However, the fund can hold small-cap stocks for added growth potential. This fund has outperformed the TSE 300 and its peer group in recent years, thanks to its value bias. The fund holds a concentrated group of about 40 stocks. It has relatively low volatility as measured by both its low standard deviation and very low beta, which means that your risk here is minimal—always an important consideration in a RRIF. The managers will hold high cash balances in slumping markets, which contributes to this defensiveness. The fund will usually outperform in bear markets, but in a bull market the conservative approach to equities will limit its upside potential. If you live in Ontario, you can purchase Beutel Goodman funds on a no-load basis by ordering directly from the company. Call 1-800-461-4551 or 416-932-6400. Elsewhere in Canada, you must go through an investment dealer and pay a sales commission of up to 4 percent. Minimum initial investment is $10,000.

CHOU RRSP FUND $$$$ ↓ G # RIF CE

Manager: Francis Chou, since inception (1986)
MER: 2.12%   **Style:** Value
Suitability: Low-risk investors who are prepared to go off the beaten track.

Manager Francis Chou holds a senior position with Fairfax Financial and runs this and the companion Chou Associates Fund more or less in his spare time. The funds grew out of an investment club and are very small. They're available only in Ontario. But those few people who own units are very glad that they do. Chou is a dedicated value manager who absolutely refuses to overpay for a stock. That means he did not participate in the tech boom, nor in the tech bust. One comment he made to unit holders sums up his views: "Paying 500 times for hot air is not an investment; it's pure speculation." This fund focuses on companies with sound fundamentals, many of which will be unfamiliar to most investors. No matter—it's the results that count, and this fund delivers them. No matter what time period you look at, this fund has outperformed the averages. Plus it has a very fine safety record. One other thing you should know about the manager: He is a unique person. When the fund was underperforming in 1994 and 1995, he waived the management fees, refusing to accept any payment for what he regarded as poor results. It was a matter of "fairness and honour" he told unit holders. And he reduced his fee in 1999, because of the weak performance. That's the kind of approach this industry needs to see more of. Too bad the fund is not more widely available. Call 416-299-6749 for more information. Minimum initial investment is $3,500.

CI HARBOUR FUND $$$ ↓ G #/* RIF CE

Manager: Gerald Coleman, since inception (1997)
MER: 2.46% **Style:** Value
Suitability: Low-risk investors.

The introduction of the Harbour family of funds was based on the arrival at CI Funds of highly regarded money manager Gerald Coleman. The name and logo of the fund family (a square-rigged sailing ship with all sails set) could not have been more appropriate for the fund's objectives and Coleman's investment style. All the Harbour funds are intended for conservative investors with a long-term perspective who want above-average returns and have a low risk tolerance. This makes the family highly suitable for RRIFs. Thus far, the mission has been accomplished. The "harbour" in question is well inside the territory we like best, the one referred to as low risk/high return. The fund will tend to underperform in strong bull markets but will hold up well when things get tough. Over time, returns have been well above average for the Canadian Equity category, and risk is low. The trick for Coleman is to select a portfolio of only 30 to 40 holdings that he can keep close watch on. Canadian enterprises in the fund are well diversified, with banks, retail, metals, oil, and manufacturing all represented. Selected companies must exhibit sound fundamentals as well as staying power and the potential for growth. Yes, more stratospheric returns may be available elsewhere. But for the conservative investor, this would be a comfortable and profitable voyage.

CI SIGNATURE SELECT CANADIAN FUND $$$ → G #/* RIF CE

Manager: Eric Bushell, since 1998
MER: 2.57% **Style:** Value
Suitability: Conservative investors.

You'll find a lot of aggressive funds in the CI organization that don't fit comfortably into a RRIF. But, like the Harbour Fund (above), this is an exception. Eric Bushell, who also manages the two Signature dividend funds, runs the show here. He concentrates on large-cap companies, and thus far he is doing a great job selecting stocks. What has been especially impressive is Bushell's ability to steer the portfolio through the rocky shoals of bear markets; this was one of the top-performing funds in its category during the 2000–01 bear market. Throw in a better-than-average safety rating and you can see why we like this fund for your RRIF.

CLARICA SUMMIT CANADIAN EQUITY FUND $$$ ↓ G */NO RIF CLC

Manager: Mackenzie Investment Corp.
MER: 3.01% **Style:** Bottom-up Value
Suitability: Conservative investors.

This fund invests primarily in large-cap Canadian equities, with a goal of providing long-term capital growth. The portfolio will generally hold no more than 75 companies at a time, making it easier for the managers to follow the investments. The portfolio is well-diversified, with about a quarter of its assets outside of Canada, primarily in the U.S. Management takes a defensive stance and will hold a large amount of the portfolio in cash when markets are falling. All this leads us to believe that the fund is run by Mackenzie's crack Ivy team. It would be nice if Clarica would say so, as it would certainly be useful knowledge for investors. Initial returns following the fund's launch in mid-1997 were weak, as value investing was out of style. But this fund looked much better after 2000 as value investing came back into vogue. This fund shows much less volatility than most Canadian equity funds (this may be partially due to its tendency to hold large amounts of cash), which means that RRIF investors should feel more comfortable with it. You can buy units only through agents of Clarica Investco. Call 1-888-864-5463 for information, or visit the Web site (**www.clarica.com**).

CLARINGTON CANADIAN EQUITY FUND $$$$ ↓ G #/* RIF CLC

Manager: Peter Marshall (Seamark), since inception (1996)
MER: 2.90%   **Style:** Value
Suitability: Low-risk investors.

This Canadian equity fund has been a steady above-average performer for most of the time since its inception in late 1996. The first year was a little weak, but since then returns have generally been solid, and the fund is frequently in the first quartile of its peer group, the Canadian Large-Cap category. As a bonus, the risk profile is one of the top in its class. The Canadian equity portion of the portfolio focuses on well-known blue-chip stocks, such as the big banks. The fund also takes advantage of its eligible foreign content by having about a quarter of its assets in U.S. and international stocks. We like the look of this one and are rewarding it with a top $$$$ rating in recognition of continued good performance. Clarington is not a well-known organization, but most financial advisors and discount brokers can acquire these funds.

CO-OPERATORS CANADIAN CONSERVATIVE
FOCUSED EQUITY FUND $$$ ↓ G #/* RIF CE

Manager: George L. Frazer (Leon Frazer, Black and Associates Ltd.), since April 1976
MER: 2.56%   **Style:** Top-Down/Blend
Suitability: Low-risk buy-and-hold investors.

This is a new name for an old fund. Mutual fund buffs will remember it as the Associate Investors Fund, and it has a history of more than half a century under the management of the same house, Leon Frazer, Black and Associates. It has always been a solid, low-risk performer and is especially well-suited to a difficult investment climate—it tends to outperform in such situations. The portfolio is very strongly blue-chip oriented, with an emphasis on Old Economy stocks. The management team targets companies with good earnings, book values, and steady dividends, such as banks and utilities. There is no foreign content. Not many people know about this one, but it's a worthwhile entry for conservative investors. Safety record is very good. This used to be a no-load fund, but it is now sold on an optional front- or back-end load basis through investment advisors. For more information call 866-866-2635, or visit the Co-operators Mutual Funds Web site (**www.cmfl.ca**).

EMPIRE ELITE EQUITY FUND $$$ ↓ G * RIF S CE

Manager: Vince Zambrano, since 1998
MER: 2.41%   **Style:** Bottom-up Value
Suitability: Investors with an Empire Life account.

This fund went through a series of managerial changes in the mid-1990s, but has been under the direction of Vince Zambrano since October 1998, which has brought much-needed stability to the portfolio. The fund has been an above-average performer under his guidance and has a safety record that is very good. One major stumbling block is the fund's MER of 2.41 percent, which is much higher than that of the companion Empire Premier Equity Fund (see below), which comes in at 1.44 percent. The portfolio is well-diversified and includes a wide mix of foreign issues. Smaller stocks are added for more growth potential, but the overall portfolio has a large-cap value bias. Note: There is a difference in the purchase option and management fee between this and the Premier Fund. The Elite funds are back-end load, while the Premier has a front-end load but a much lower MER. So to benefit from the better performance with the Premier Fund, you'll have to hold it for several years. For long-term RRIF investors, it may be the better choice. This and the Premier Fund can be purchased only through agents of Empire Life or licensed insurance brokers.

EMPIRE PREMIER EQUITY FUND $$$ ↓ G # RIF S CE

Manager: Vince Zambrano, since 1998
MER: 1.44%   **Style:** Bottom-up Value
Suitability: Investors with an Empire Life account.

This fund is similar in every aspect to the companion Elite Equity Fund, but returns are slightly better here. The reason is this fund's low MER, which more than offsets its front-end fee over time. If you hold for the long term, you should enjoy superior returns. As with the Elite fund, Vince Zambrano took over as manager in late 1998. With the lower MER, returns are above average for the category. The risk level is about the same as that of the companion Elite Equity Fund. If you're purchasing an Empire Canadian equity fund, buy this one for the long term and save on the MER.

GREAT-WEST LIFE DIVIDEND/
GROWTH FUND (M) $$$ ↓ G/FI */NO RIF S CLC

Manager: Mackenzie Financial Maxxum Team
MER: 2.48%   **Style:** Bottom-up Value
Suitability: Investors with a Great-West Life account.

The emphasis here leans to the growth side rather than to dividend income, which is why this is officially classified as a Canadian Large-Cap fund. But as long as that isn't a problem for you, this fund is worthy of inclusion in any Great-West RRIF portfolio. Emphasis is on blue-chip stocks, but the fund will also hold some real estate invest-ment trusts. Mackenzie's Maxxum team is in charge, which means the fine hand of

Bill Procter is operating unseen in the background. He has done very well with his Mackenzie funds, and this one has benefited as well. In fact, it was one of the best performers in its category in recent years. The historic risk level of this fund is very low–less than half that of its benchmark TSE/S&P 60 Index. As long as you aren't misled by the name into thinking this is a real dividend fund, it's a good RRIF choice. There are two purchase options for all Great-West funds: back-end load and no load. The no-load option carries a higher MER, so we advise choosing back-end units, as presumably you are buying this fund for the longer term. However, if you think you may need to redeem units soon to obtain cash for RRIF withdrawals, then go with the no-load choice. Available only through Great-West Life representatives and insurance brokers.

GREAT-WEST LIFE EQUITY FUND (M) $$$ ↓ G */NO RIF S CE

Manager: Mackenzie Financial Ivy Team
MER: 2.55%   **Style:** Bottom-up Value
Suitability: Investors with a Great-West Life account.

This fund's conservative approach resulted in an off-year (in relative terms) in 1999–2000. But the value style showed its merit when markets tanked in 2000–01. While the majority of Canadian stock funds were posting losses, this one came through with a decent gain. Longer-term results are comfortably above the category average. The fund is run by Mackenzie's Ivy group, and that shows in the portfolio composition (mainly blue chip), the large cash position in times of market stress (at times in excess of 15 percent), and the fund's performance history. The historic risk level of this fund is very low, which adds to its appeal in turbulent markets.

GREAT-WEST LIFE LARGER COMPANY FUND (M) $$ → G */NO RIF S CLC

Manager: Mackenzie Financial Maxxum Team
MER: 2.65%   **Style:** Bottom-up Value
Suitability: Investors with a Great-West Life account.

This fund's long-term record is undistinguished, but it has shown considerable improvement in recent years. The investment approach is similar to the companion GWL Equity Fund (M), with a lot of blue-chip stocks in the portfolio. However, in this case, the management is by Mackenzie's Maxxum team (Equity Fund is run by the Ivy folks), which has shown significant improvement in the past few years. Risk in both funds is better than average; however, Equity (M) has the edge in that regard. This fund is looking better these days, which is why we include it here.

GREAT-WEST LIFE NORTH AMERICAN
EQUITY FUND (B) $$ ↓ G */NO RIF S CE

Managers: Tor Williams and Jim Lampare (Beutel Goodman)
MER: 2.49%   **Style:** Bottom-up Value
Suitability: Investors with a Great-West Life account.

This fund's mandate is to seek long-term capital appreciation through investing mainly in medium to large Canadian and U.S. companies that may be undervalued and/or show superior growth potential. It may also hold up to 25 percent of its assets in small-cap issues for additional growth potential and diversity. Although this is called a "North American" fund, its foreign content is restricted to the prevailing limit to retain full RRIF eligibility. So we classify this as a Canadian equity fund. Like many value funds, this one struggled through the late 1990s and into 2000. But also, like many value funds, it recovered as markets generally slumped. This is not an exciting fund, but it is steady and solid with a good management team.

LEITH WHEELER CANADIAN EQUITY FUND $$$ ↓ G NO RIF CE

Manager: Leith Wheeler Investment Committee, since inception (1994)
MER: 1.40%   **Style:** Bottom-up Value
Suitability: High-net-worth, low-risk investors.

Like most value funds, this buy-and-hold entry experienced hard times in the late 1990s. However, also like most value funds, it staged a comeback after the collapse of the high-tech sector, and its long-term record is quite good. While the low-risk nature of the portfolio makes it suitable for a RRIF, if you are looking for a fund for your non-registered retirement portfolio this one may be of interest. All securities are purchased with the intention of retaining them for two to four years, so there isn't a lot of active trading. This makes for a tax-efficient portfolio, with little in the way of annual distributions to attract the attention of Canada Customs and Revenue. The portfolio consists mainly of large-cap stocks, but a few small- and mid-cap companies are mixed in. Historically, this fund has always been defensive by nature. That means it will tend to underperform in bull markets but protect your assets in bear markets. We like this fund, but you will need a substantial RRIF to invest in it as the minimum required is $50,000. There are no commission charges if you purchase units directly from the manager; call 1-888-292-1122 for details. Some brokers may also offer the units, but you may have to pay a fee to acquire them that way. Available only in Alberta, B.C., Manitoba, Ontario, and Saskatchewan.

LONDON LIFE CANADIAN EQUITY FUND $$$ → G * RIF S CLC

Manager: London Life Investment Management
MER: 2.40%   **Style:** Bottom-up Value
Suitability: Investors with a London Life account.

Since taking over from long-time manager Rohit Sehgal, who left for Dundee Capital, the in-house managers at London Life have done a decent job with this fund. The goal is to use a value approach to scout for opportunities within the mid-to-large-cap market, represented by the TSE 300 Index. With about 60 stocks in the portfolio, there is plenty of blue-chip exposure, with solid representation from such sectors as technology, financial services, oil and gas, and utilities. This is not what we would classify as a great fund, but it is a very serviceable one, especially for those who have RRIF assets with London Life. Long-term returns have been above average while risk is about on a par with the Canadian Equity category, but substantially less than that of the TSE/S&P 60 Index. This fund deserves its $$$ grade; however, we wouldn't advise anyone to switch business to London Life just to get access to it. The fund is available through the company's sales representatives.

MACKENZIE CUNDILL CANADIAN SECURITY FUND $$$$ ↓ G #/* RIF CE

Manager: Alan Pasnik and Peter Cundill, since September 1998
MER: "C" units 2.47%   **Style:** Core Value
Suitability: Low-risk investors.

This used to be classed as a small-cap fund, but now the mandate has been expanded and it invests in all types of stocks. Like with all the funds in the Cundill line, the managers take a deep value approach to investing. That means they buy only stocks that are trading at deep discounts to their underlying value. It's an approach that can produce indifferent results when stock markets are raging, but works wonders in bear markets. No surprise then that this fund did well after the fall of high tech, which was the prelude to the bear market of 2000–01. You need to be careful about reading the historical results, however. The "A" units have the longest record and the best numbers, but they are no-load units with a lower MER and were phased out after Mackenzie took over the Cundill operation. The "C" units, which are the only ones now available, are sold on an optional front- or back-end load and have a significantly higher management charge. So returns will be slightly lower, although that's not a big deal when the fund is doing so well. Risk is on the low side for a Canadian stock fund. Foreign content is maximized, and there will probably be a lot of names among the top holdings that you don't recognize. However, don't let that put you off. Although the management style is somewhat out of the ordinary (the fund held a big weighting in Japan when that country was out of favour with just about everyone), we regard this as a good RRIF choice because of its fine safety record and above-average long-term returns. A segregated version is also available if you prefer.

MACKENZIE IVY CANADIAN FUND $$$ ↓ G #/* RIF CE

Managers: Jerry Javasky and Chuck Roth, since June 1997
MER: 2.47%   **Style:** Value/Growth
Suitability: Low-risk investors.

Mackenzie officially says the style of this fund is a value/growth blend, and that's a good description. Co-manager Jerry Javasky is known in the financial community as an ultra-conservative value manager, but Chuck Roth brings a growth orientation to the portfolio. It's a mix that has worked well for investors, both in terms of risk (about half that of the average fund in the Canadian Equity category) and return (better than average over the long haul). The managers aim for a core of about 25 positions, each representing about 4 percent of the total assets. The objective is to provide above-average returns at below-average risk, and the fund does that job quite well. The combination makes it especially attractive for RRIFs. Consider using this one as the basis for a systematic withdrawal plan. It's one of the better entries in the Mackenzie stable.

MAXXUM CANADIAN VALUE FUND $$$ ↓ G #/* RIF CLC

Manager: Bill Procter, since November 1996
MER: 2.48% **Style:** Large-Cap Value
Suitability: Middle-of-the-road investors.

This was formerly the Mackenzie Industrial Horizon Fund. The name was changed in January 2002, but the mandate and manager remain the same. Bill Procter assumed responsibility for the portfolio of this long-time laggard in November 1996 and immediately started to implement changes. The underperforming natural resource component of this fund was pared down while the financial services and industrial products sectors were boosted. The number of stocks held was cut in half, from 80 to about 40. The mandate was clearly defined to focus on large-cap companies in established industries. Procter is a bottom-up manager who chooses stocks on the basis of fundamentals. The fund did well in the first full year under his mandate, gaining 14.7 percent in 1997. But it slumped in 1998 and 1999, before recovering during the bear market of 2000–01. In other words, it's been all over the place in performance terms since Procter took charge. However, when you take all those ups and downs and factor them together, it's doing well and has been very effective at preserving capital when times are tough. The style is officially listed as a value/growth blend, but the performance and the portfolio suggest that value is really in the ascendancy. What you're getting here is a middle-of-the-road large-cap fund. This fund has displayed a little more volatility than we like to see in a RRIF, but compared to the rest of its category, overall risk is relatively low. This is a well-managed fund that deserves consideration. If it comes down to a choice between this and Ivy Canadian (above), however, we'd go for the Ivy fund because of a superior safety record.

MCLEAN BUDDEN CANADIAN EQUITY
GROWTH FUND $$$$ → G NO RIF CLC

Manager: Team
MER: 1.30% **Style:** Large-Cap Growth
Suitability: Growth-oriented investors prepared to take additional risk.

This fund invests primarily in shares of the largest 100 companies on the TSE 300 Index. The managerial team has gradually increased the foreign-content component of the portfolio in recent years, by adding units of the companion American Equity Fund and International Equity Fund. So you are getting a lot of international exposure here, which can be an advantage if the Canadian dollar is weakening. This fund has a fine record of consistency. It is a first- or second-quartile performer almost every year, which means it constantly outperforms the majority of funds in its peer group. The fund's growth style caused it to suffer a setback in the bear market of 2000–01, although it still managed to do better than the category average and the benchmark index. However, if you're considering this fund for your RRIF, be aware that it will not do as good a job at preserving capital in rough markets as many of the conservatively managed value funds you'll find listed in this book. On the other hand, profit potential in good times will be greater here. So this might be a good fund to use to provide a value/growth portfolio balance. The minimum initial investment for all McLean Budden funds is $10,000. You can buy units on a no-load basis directly from the company if you live in Alberta, British Columbia, Ontario, or Quebec (call 1-800-884-0436 for details). Some brokers also have access to these units, although you may be charged a fee if you go that route.

MCLEAN BUDDEN CANADIAN EQUITY
VALUE FUND   NR → G NO RIF CE

Manager: Team
MER: 1.30%   **Style:** Large-Cap Value
Suitability: Long-term conservative investors.

McLean Budden made its reputation as a growth manager. The addition of a value team marks a departure for the company, but a welcome one because it gives the investor the option of style diversification. There are four members in this value group: Brian Dawson, Alan Daxner, Susan Shuter, and Ted Thompson. This fund is their collective baby. It did not have a three-year track record at the time we went to press, but we like what we have seen thus far and believe it offers a useful alternative for RRIF investors. The emphasis is on large-cap value stocks, although some mid-cap stocks may also be held (market valuation between $500 million and $1 billion). Performance and risk have been better than average thus far, which is a good combination for a registered income fund. This fund held up extremely well during the bear market of 2000–01, so it will do a good job of preserving capital in difficult markets. This would be a good complement to the companion Canadian Equity Growth Fund. The same purchase conditions apply.

NORTHWEST GROWTH FUND $$$ → G #/* RIF CE

Manager: Richard Fogler (Kingwest and Company), since 1997
MER: 2.89%   **Style:** Value
Suitability: Conservative investors.

Richard Fogler took over this fund in 1997, and it has been an above-average performer ever since. He is a veteran money manager with more than 25 years of experience, but he's not well known to investors. He uses a disciplined stock selection style called EVA (economic value added), which was developed in the 1970s by Joel Stern of the New York investment house Stern Stewart. The objective of the complicated analysis process is to identify companies that consistently add shareholder value, thereby improving the price of their stock. Essentially, Fogler uses this approach to analyze what a company will be worth in the future, and buys stocks in the firms with the best potential. If he doesn't see the prospect of 40 percent to 50 percent growth within two years, the stock doesn't make the buy list. The portfolio is kept small (about 35 stocks) and turnover is minimal, which is good from a tax-efficiency perspective if the fund is held outside a registered plan—something you might want to consider if you have both a RRIF and a non-registered portfolio. This fund has displayed a propensity to hold its ground very well in tough markets, which is another reason for liking it in a retirement account. It's one of those hidden gems that deserves more attention. You can buy units through brokers and financial advisors, although you may find that the person you're dealing with isn't familiar with the company. If you want to do some research on your own, check out their good Web site (**www. northwestfunds.com**). By the way, if you're wondering about the name of this group, which is not based anywhere in the northwest but in Toronto, it refers to what is known as the northwest quadrant on a risk-return chart. The funds that show up in that quadrant are those that combine the best returns with the lowest degree of risk.

O'SHAUGHNESSY CANADIAN EQUITY FUND $$$ → G NO RIF CLC

Manager: James P. O'Shaughnessy, since inception (November 1997)
MER: 1.60%   **Style:** Value
Suitability: Conservative investors.

This fund has everything you want in a large-cap Canadian equity fund. It has a skilled and experienced manager, a relatively low MER for the category, a transparent investment strategy, and a great record. The portfolio holds about 50 Canadian stocks, which are chosen by combining both value and growth measurements. James O'Shaughnessy is a U.S. money manager who is quite well known in that country because of a couple of best-selling books he has written. Royal Funds did a deal with him a few years ago to create three funds for Canadian investors that employ his proprietary style. All the O'Shaughnessy funds use what might be called an "active/passive" approach. Many of the same principles used by index funds are employed, but his system modifies this by actively selecting key stocks using specialized criteria that he developed. The system works; this fund has produced above-average returns and stood up very well against the battering ram of the 2000–01 bear market. Most RRIF investors have probably never heard of the manager or this fund, but it is well worth looking into, especially since you can acquire units without any sales commission. You can buy it through Royal Bank or any of its affiliated brokerage firms.

OPTIMA STRATEGY CANADIAN EQUITY
VALUE POOL $$$ → G #/* RIF CE

Manager: Daniel Bubis, since 1994
MER: 3.13%   **Style:** Value
Suitability: High-net-worth investors prepared to tolerate higher volatility.

This fund uses a disciplined value investing approach in its stock selection, looking for out-of-favour companies that trade at a low price/earnings multiple. That normally signals a fund with low volatility, but this one has experienced some unusually high performance swings in recent years as value investing went out of favour in the late 1990s and then came roaring back with the high-tech collapse. So you have to be prepared to live with more risk here than you might normally expect to find in a value fund. The portfolio makes good use of foreign content with a selection of U.S. stocks and is well diversified by sector. The main problem is that you need a minimum of

$25,000 to buy in; however, if you have RRSP assets with Assante Asset Management or one of its subsidiary companies, that should not be a barrier. This fund is sold by representatives of Assante and certain other financial planning groups. Note: Each investor is charged an annual management fee, which is included in the MER shown here. The base rate for equity funds is 2.5 percent a year. Investors who use the company's Asset Management Service receive a discount of 0.25 percent a year; however, you must have a total of $100,000 with Optima Strategy to qualify. Those who invest more than $250,000 get additional reductions. This is an unusual pricing mechanism, so be sure that you understand exactly what you'll be paying and what services you will receive for your money.

PHILLIPS, HAGER & NORTH CANADIAN
EQUITY FUND $$$ → G NO RIF CE

Manager: Team, headed by Ian Mottershead
MER: 1.14%   **Style:** GARP
Suitability: High-net-worth, conservative investors seeking a Canadian-content-only fund.

This is a pure Canadian stock fund with no foreign content (the companion Canadian Growth Fund holds foreign stocks). It is a growth-oriented fund but, as with all funds in this group, the managers will not overpay for stocks. The main holdings are in medium- to large-size companies. Over time, the fund has been a consistent above-average performer, with a brief dip to the third quartile in 1998 the only blemish in recent years. Risk is about average. Bottom line: Steady above-average returns at an acceptable degree of risk, which make it a good RRIF choice. The low MER and no load charges add to the fund's attractiveness. However, you'll need to have a fair-sized RRIF to get into this fund. The minimum initial investment is $25,000, but the total value of your RRIF must be in excess of $50,000 if you are opening a new RRIF account with the firm (if you already have an RRSP with them, this minimum does not apply). You can buy units on a no-load basis by contacting the firm directly; call 1-800-661-6141 for information. Note: Some investors are purchasing PH&N fund units through discount brokerage firms. In some cases, large amounts of money are involved. We were informed of one case in which a gentleman said he had paid several hundred dollars in commissions by going this route, even though these are supposed to be no-load funds. Although we generally support the idea of discount brokers, we advise against buying PH&N funds in this way if you are going to be charged any sort of commission, either when you make the purchase or when you sell. Set up an account directly with the company and save all sales charges.

PHILLIPS, HAGER & NORTH CANADIAN
GROWTH FUND $$$ → G NO RIF CE

Manager: Team, headed by Ian Mottershead
MER: 1.19%   **Style:** GARP
Suitability: High-net-worth, conservative investors looking for foreign content.

The performance pattern here is similar to the company's Canadian Equity Fund, so the same broad comments apply. The portfolios are also similar; the main difference is that a chunk of this fund's holdings (about one-quarter of the assets) is in U.S. and international securities, thus providing global diversification. Like its Canadian Equity Fund stablemate, this fund is also a consistent above-average performer. However, results have tended to lag behind those of the Canadian Equity Fund over the long term. But if you prefer your Canadian fund to have some foreign content in it, perhaps for purposes of currency diversification, this is the one to choose. It doesn't make much sense to hold both in the same portfolio, so pick one or the other, depending on your needs. Formerly known as the Canadian Equity Plus Fund, and prior to that as the RSP/RIF Equity Fund. See above listing for purchase details.

ROYAL CANADIAN VALUE FUND $$$ → G NO RIF CLC

Manager: Christina Poole and Ina Van Berkel, since March 1998
MER: 2.15% **Style:** Bottom-up Value
Suitability: Conservative investors.

All the bank fund families tend to be spotty. They have some very good funds available, but you have to search them out among a bunch of mediocre performers. This is one of the better selections from Royal Funds. The managers use classic, value-based fundamental analysis to select companies, and they are doing a good job. The fund turned in decent (although not spectacular) returns in the late 1990s and held up well under the relentless pounding of the 2000–01 bear market. This fund is a good candidate for a Royal Bank RRIF because it will not expose your capital to undue risk. When times get really tough, the managers will increase the cash position significantly to cushion the shock of market drops (at one point during the 2000–01 bear, about a quarter of the portfolio was in cash). This is the type of fund that is unlikely to do serious damage to your RRIF when times are tough, while providing respectable returns when things are going well. Available through Royal Bank branches and subsidiary brokerage firms.

SAXON STOCK FUND $$$$ ↓ G NO RIF CLC

Manager: Richard Howson, since 1989
MER: 1.75% **Style:** Bottom-up Value
Suitability: Low-risk investors.

Most investors are unfamiliar with the small Saxon organization, which is their loss. This Toronto-based shop, established in 1985, uses a disciplined value approach to its stock selection and is widely known for its expertise in the small-cap sector. Management of the company's line of five mutual funds is under the direction of the company's principals, Richard Howson and Robert Tattersall. Although its no-load funds are now available across Canada, the company has found it difficult to attract money to its funds despite several advantages: no load charges, very low MERs, and some very good performance numbers. The family is a model of consistency and transparency. Nothing fancy, no special features or confusing name changes or shifting objectives. Instead, what we see is good old-fashioned performance–high returns and relatively low volatility. This particular fund is one of their winners and is a good choice for a RRIF. The stock-selection criteria encompass not only bottom-up research but also top-down analysis in the never-ending search for Canadian stocks of all capitalization classes. Besides small companies, this fund also holds some blue-chip Canadian stocks for steady long-term appreciation. Stocks are held for the long term, between three and five years, but the manager may sell if the stock reaches its price target. Long-term results beat the averages by a mile, and the fund even managed to make a profit for investors in the bear market of 2000–01. Plus, all of this was achieved with a way-below-average standard deviation and, surprisingly, a low beta (both measures of risk). This fund is well worthy of a $$$$ rating and would be an excellent holding for the equity portion of your RRIF. Minimum initial investment is $5,000. If you live in Ontario, you can buy units direct from the company by calling 1-888-287-2966. Residents of other provinces will have to use a broker. Note: We've had reports from a few people who said they had difficulty in acquiring the Saxon funds through a discount broker. If you are told initially that the funds are not available, ask why not. Request to speak to a supervisor to determine if the firm does not offer them, or if the original sales person simply made an error. If you are told you cannot acquire the funds through your company of choice, call Saxon's toll-free number. Tell them about the problem, and ask which companies in your area offer their funds for sale.

SPECTRUM CANADIAN INVESTMENT FUND $$$$ ↓ G #/* RIF CLC

Managers: Kim Shannon and Gaelen Morphet, since June 1999
MER: 2.53%   **Style:** Value
Suitability: Low-risk investors.

This is the oldest continuously operated fund in Canada, running under the name Canadian Investment Fund since 1932. It had become almost moribund until Kim Shannon, then of AMI Partners, grabbed hold of it in 1996 and turned it around. The investment style is a conservative buy-and-hold value approach, with a focus on blue-chip stocks within the TSE 100 Index. This is designed to be a low-volatility fund that will tend to lag behind when markets are strong (as happened in the late 1990s) but will outperform when times get rough (as we saw in the 2000–01 bear, when it actually made a profit). This fund is a good choice for a conservative investor who prefers a low-risk approach and it is especially well-suited for a RRIF.

STANDARD LIFE EQUITY FUND $$$ → G #/* RIF CE

Manager: Standard Life Investments Inc.
MER: 2.19%   **Style:** Bottom-up Value
Suitability: Middle-of-the-road investors prepared to accept some risk.

This fund offers a large portfolio that includes a mix of small, medium, and large companies. It has produced some very good returns for its investors in both good and bad markets and consistently outperforms the category average. However, the risk level here is somewhat higher than in some more conservatively run funds such as

Spectrum Canadian Investment (above). In this case, it's about average for the Canadian Equity category. That's not bad, but you need to give it careful consideration if capital preservation is your top priority. Note that the company requires a minimum investment of $5,000 for opening a RRIF account. The Standard Life mutual funds used to be available only through Standard Life representatives. However, the company has opened up its distribution network to allow stockbrokers, financial planners, and dealers to sell its funds. This makes access to the family much easier.

TRIMARK CANADIAN FUND $$$ ↓ G #/* RIF CE

Managers: Ian Hardacre and Carmen Veloso, since 1999
MER: 1.63%/2.52%   **Style:** Value/Growth
Suitability: Conservative investors.

The late 1990s were rough on this one-time favourite, as value investing went out of style and returns foundered. But what goes around comes around and this entry looked very good when the high-tech bubble burst and value came back into style. You have to give the Trimark managers credit. They stuck by their traditional style of buying great companies at attractive prices and holding them, even when performance went into the tank. Unfortunately, the company itself didn't survive the battering it took in the late 1990s; it was bought out by the big AIM organization, which is foreign-owned. Trimark's brand name and its managerial team were retained, however, and that turned out to be a wise move by AIM's management. The team of Ian Hardacre and Carmen Veloso run the show here and their results are good. They employ a value/growth style blend, with a tilt towards value. The portfolio is well-diversified with a significant foreign-content holding. Performance over all time periods is above par for the category, and the safety rating is better than average. Note the two purchase options carefully. The back-end load (DSC) version carries a much higher MER that will cut deeply into your net returns. We recommend the front-end units. Try to persuade your advisor to sell them to you at zero commission. If you're a good client, it may work.

TRIMARK CANADIAN ENDEAVOUR FUND $$$ ↓ G */# RIF CE

Manager: Geoff MacDonald, since 1998
MER: 2.14%   **Style:** Value
Suitability: Conservative investors.

The distinctions between the various Trimark Canadian equity funds are somewhat difficult for the average investor (and even the professional advisor) to discern. This one takes a somewhat more value-oriented approach than Trimark Canadian (above) although, rather surprisingly, its risk level is a tad higher. Manager Geoff MacDonald is doing a good job with this one, and he piloted it well through the turbulence of the 2000–01 bear market. That kind of performance in tough times gives us the confidence to recommend it for RRIFs. The thrust of the portfolio is towards mid- to large-cap stocks; however, the manager has extensive small-cap knowledge, so some smaller companies may also show up here. Formerly known as the Trimark RSP Equity Fund.

TRIMARK SELECT CANADIAN GROWTH FUND $$$ ↓ G #/* RIF CLC

Manager: Heather Hunter, since 1999
MER: 2.52%   **Style:** Value/Growth
Suitability: Conservative investors.

This is another Trimark entry that struggled through the late 1990s but experienced a renaissance with the re-emergence of value investing. It's run by Heather Hunter, who moved over to Trimark from the Ontario Teachers' Pension Plan and came with the fund when AIM bought the company. She favours large-cap stocks that offer long-term growth potential. The portfolio is well-diversified, and Hunter is not averse to moving to a defensive posture by raising cash in rough markets. She prefers a buy-and-hold approach, typically retaining a stock for three to five years. Many of the top holdings in this portfolio also show up in other Trimark funds, but there is obviously enough differentiation to have an impact on returns. Another decent RRIF choice from this group.

Dividend Income Funds

BMO DIVIDEND FUND $$$ → G/FI NO RIF DIV

Manager: Michael Stanley (Jones Heward), since inception (1994)
MER: 1.77%   **Style:** Value
Suitability: Income investors with an equity bias.

If you want a top-performing Canadian dividend fund that looks for capital growth over regular income, this may be your choice. The core portfolio is composed of shares in value-oriented, large-cap, high-yielding companies such as banks, utilities, and pipelines. But since the fund pays only quarterly distributions, it is not recommended for RRIF investors seeking steady monthly income. Compared to the average Canadian dividend fund, this one has a strong focus on common shares, which account for about 84 percent of its assets. Other comparable funds offer more of a mix of common shares, preferred shares, trust units, and bonds. Returns have been generally high across the board. The fund is recommended as a relatively lower-volatility equity holding in a RRIF. The name change from BMO Dividend Income Fund reflects the capital appreciation bias. Available through branches of the Bank of Montreal.

CANADA LIFE ENHANCED DIVIDEND FUND (S-39) $$$ → G * RIF S DIV

Manager: Philip Wooten (Laketon), since 1997
MER: 2.00%   **Style:** Bottom-up Value
Suitability: Income-oriented equity investors with Canada Life accounts.

This fund is off to a strong start. In managing this portfolio, manager Philip Wooten focuses on high-yield common and preferred shares as well as income trusts. He has succeeded in balancing this blend very well, to the point where this has been one of the top-performing funds in the Dividend Income category in recent years. Wooten takes an interest rate anticipation approach in selecting securities, which means he tries to maximize returns when rates are falling and minimize the losses normally associated with interest-sensitive stocks and trusts when rates are on the rise. Stocks focus on mid- to large-cap companies, and you can expect to find the big banks prominently featured. Investments are kept within specific ranges: Canadian stocks 50 to 100 percent; Canadian preferred shares 0 to 30 percent; income trusts 0 to 30 percent; cash and short-term securities 0 to 30 percent. We won't give this fund a $$$$ rating as yet, since we look for consistent superior results over a longer period. But we are prepared to give it a $$$ rating and to recommend that you add it to your portfolio if you are a Canada Life RRIF client. This is a segregated fund that offers a guarantee that you will receive at least 75 percent of your principal at maturity (10 years), but we don't expect that guarantee will ever be needed, given the conservative nature of the portfolio. Available from Canada Life representatives.

CI SIGNATURE DIVIDEND FUND $$$ ↓ FI/G #/* RIF DIV

Manager: Eric Bushell, since October 1999
MER: 2.00%   **Style:** Value
Suitability: Low-risk, income-oriented investors.

We would prefer to be recommending the companion CI Signature Dividend Income Fund here because of its better cash flow, but it was closed to new investors in late 2001. So this is the only option now available, albeit a decent choice nonetheless. It's run by the same manager as Dividend Income and employs a similar portfolio approach, with a strong position in preferred shares. The combination of preferreds and dividend-paying common stocks generates good cash flow for investors seeking steady income—monthly distributions have been running at $0.04 a unit. Total return has generally been above average for the Canadian Dividend category since the launch of this fund in 1996. The safety record is better than average for the category, due in large part to the preferred share section of the portfolio, which doesn't carry the market risk associated with common stock. This fund is a solid RRIF choice if you're looking for a combination of dividends and modest capital gains.

CLARICA SUMMIT DIVIDEND GROWTH FUND $$$ → G/FI */NO RIF DIV

Manager: Mackenzie Investment Corp.
MER: 2.98%   **Style:** Bottom-up Value
Suitability: Investors seeking monthly cash flow.

The objective of this fund is to provide reasonable returns using high-yielding common stocks and preferred shares. However, the portfolio may also hold income trusts (e.g., Westshore Terminals) and REITs (e.g., Riocan). Blue-chip common stocks make up the bulk of the assets, however. As we're seeing with an increasing number of dividend funds, U.S. stocks have appeared in the portfolio, representing close to 15 percent of the assets at the time of writing. Returns are about average to slightly above; risk is about average as well. Distributions are paid monthly and have been running at about $0.60 a year, so this fund is a good source for steady cash flow within a RRIF. Although Clarica is an insurance company, this is not a segregated fund. However, units can be purchased only through Clarica Investco agents. Call 1-888-864-5463 for more details. All in all, this is an average dividend fund, but the good cash flow makes it worthy of consideration and is just the little extra it needs to boost it into the $$$ category. Investment tip: This fund, as with most of the Clarica funds except for the Leader series, offers both a no-load and a DSC (back-end load) purchase option. If you choose the DSC units, you will have to pay a sales charge of up to 6 percent if you cash in prior to the seventh year after purchase. The no-load units are exactly that, with no sales commissions at any time. The catch is that the no-load units carry a higher management expense ratio (MER)–the annual expense deducted from the fund's assets. It's not a big difference, however–in most cases 10 basis points (0.1 percent) or less. Your sales representative may press you to choose the DSC units because he or she won't get any commission if you opt for the no-load version. The rep will receive annual trailer fees in both cases. However, our preference is for the no-load units. The MER difference isn't significant and is a small price to pay for the freedom to be able to move your money out quickly and cost-free if you don't like the results you're getting and you don't have any alternatives you like within the company. We should also comment that the MERs on these funds are quite high–above the industry norm in many cases. You may wish to consider that when making an investment decision. The MERs shown for this and other Clarica funds in this book are for no-load units.

DESJARDINS DIVIDEND FUND $$ → G NO RIF DIV

Manager: Elantis Management Team
MER: 2.12%   **Style:** Value
Suitability: Middle-of-the-road investors.

The objective of this fund is to generate above-average dividend income that is eligible for the dividend tax credit, so if you hold it in your RRIF you will lose that tax advantage. If you also have a non-registered portfolio, better to park this fund in it. The portfolio is a mixture of preferred shares and high-yielding common stocks. Distributions are paid quarterly. Longer-term results are about average for the Dividend Income category, as is the risk level. We would classify this as a serviceable fund. It's not great by any means, but it won't be out of place if you are a client of this company.

EMPIRE DIVIDEND GROWTH FUND $$$ → G * RIF S DIV

Manager: Vince Zambrano, since 1998
MER: 2.39%   **Style:** Bottom-up Value
Suitability: Empire Life investors.

This fund concentrates on high-dividend, large-cap Canadian common and preferred shares, although there may be some small-cap issues in the mix as well for added growth potential. Manager Vince Zambrano has done a good job with it, guiding the fund to returns that have been well above average since he took charge of the portfolio in 1998. Risk is about average for the category. If you are an Empire Life RRIF client, this is certainly one to include in your plan, but don't open an account with the company just to get it.

GGOF GUARDIAN MONTHLY DIVIDEND FUND $$$ → FI #/* RIF DIV

Manager: John Priestman, since 1988
MER: 2.22% (Mutual Fund units)   **Style:** Income
Suitability: Income-oriented investors.

After being closed for more than five years, this fund was re-opened to investors in early 2001. That was good news because this is one of the best dividend funds around in terms of cash flow (though not total return). Also, it is a true dividend fund, with the bulk of the portfolio in preferred shares. There are also some royalty trusts in the mix to boost yields. Monthly payout has been running at $0.035 a unit for some time. We like this fund a lot, especially in a RRIF context, but you need to understand what you are getting. When you look at total return over time and compare it with other funds in the Dividend Income category, the results may seem unimpressive. But that's because of the heavy emphasis on preferred shares here. Most dividend income funds are actually common stock portfolios, which gives them more profit potential but usually results in reduced cash flow and a lot more risk. The risk level here is about half that of the category as a whole (the fund performed very well during the bear market of 2000–01), and the cash flow record is excellent. So, while your capital gains potential is limited and the advantage of the dividend tax credit is lost in a registered plan, there are important trade-offs that make this a worthwhile RRIF candidate. Investing tip: This and other GGOF funds are sold in two types of units. Classic units are offered on a front-end load basis only. They have a lower MER (in this case, the Classic units come in at 1.59 percent). Mutual Fund units can be purchased on either a front- or back-end load basis. Minimum initial investment in both cases is $500. Although in most cases the Classic units are the better choice, that isn't necessarily the case here. Since the payout is the same for both types, the difference in the MER shows up in the net asset value, which will be lower for the Mutual Fund units. That means the yield on the Mutual Fund units will be higher. For example, in late 2001 the NAV of the Mutual Fund units was $8.20. With an annual distribution of $0.42, that produced a cash-on-cash yield of 5.1 percent. At the same time, the yield on the Classic units, priced at $8.53, came in at 4.9 percent. So if cash flow is the priority, as it is likely to be in a RRIF, buy Mutual Fund units.

HSBC DIVIDEND INCOME FUND $$$ → G/FI NO RIF DIV

Manager: HSBC Asset Management (Canada) Ltd., since 1994
MER: 1.96%   **Style:** Value
Suitability: Balanced investors.

This fund is designed to produce a combination of long-term capital gains plus dividend income, using a mix of preferred shares and high-yielding common stocks, with a focus on large-cap issues. It's doing well on the first count, with better-than-average returns over the long haul. However, quarterly distributions are on the low side (annual yield has been running below 2 percent), so if you're seeking strong cash flow, take that into account when considering this fund as a RRIF option. Safety record is about average for the category. The fund uses covered call writing from time to time to lock in profits and enhance income. This is a no-load fund that can be purchased in branches of HSBC banks across Canada.

LONDON LIFE DIVIDEND FUND (LLIM) $$$ → G/FI * RIF S DIV

Manager: London Life Investment
MER: 2.30%   **Style:** Value
Suitability: Conservative investors.

This fund concentrates on earning above-average dividend income through high-quality common and preferred shares. That makes it better suited for a non-registered portfolio, but it can be considered for a RRIF if you're looking for what amounts to a blue-chip stock fund that will generate some income as well. This is not a pure dividend fund—most of the assets are in common stock rather than preferred shares. You'll find lots of banks and other high-profile corporate names in the mix. Total return since the 1998 launch is above average. Risk is slightly on the high side for the Dividend Income category but relatively low when compared to an ordinary Canadian equity fund, which this is in reality. Note there are two funds that carry the same name. This one is managed by London Life Investment Management (LLIM). The other is run by Mackenzie Financial's Maxxum team. Units are available through London Life representatives.

MAXXUM DIVIDEND GROWTH FUND $$$ ↑ G #/* RIF DIV

Manager: Bill Procter, since December 1994
MER: 2.47%   **Style:** Yield and Growth
Suitability: Investors seeking a combination of income and growth.

This was formerly the Mackenzie Industrial Dividend Growth Fund. The name was changed in January 2002, but the manager and the basic objectives remain the same. This is not a classic dividend fund. The portfolio is heavily weighted towards dividend-paying common stocks, rather than preferreds, with the big banks and large conglomerates among the major holdings. Plus there is a relatively large U.S. stock component that does not fit in a genuine dividend fund. However, if you're looking for a fund for your RRIF that provides a combination of income and growth, rather than a pure income fund, this one will work. The fund pays a monthly distribution of $0.05 per share and overall returns are respectable. However, be aware that the risk factor here is somewhat higher than you'd expect from a true dividend fund. It's really more of a blue-chip stock fund with a steady cash flow aspect. A segregated version is also available.

NATIONAL BANK DIVIDEND FUND $$$ ↓ FI NO RIF DIV

Manager: Jacques Chartrand, since 1992
MER: 1.73% **Style:** Value
Suitability: Conservative, income-oriented investors.

This relatively small fund has a portfolio that is in keeping with a true dividend fund, with the majority of the investments in preferred shares. As a result, longer-term performance numbers tend to lag behind those of other dividend funds because the blue-chip common stocks held by many "dividend" funds actually make them large-cap stock funds in disguise. However, this fund makes up for that deficiency by offering a fine safety record and excellent cash flow. This is a good choice for National Bank customers looking for steady quarterly income payments at minimal risk, although the benefits of the dividend tax credit will of course be lost inside a RRIF. If you also have a non-registered portfolio, you may prefer to hold it there. Available only in Ontario, New Brunswick, and Quebec.

PHILLIPS, HAGER & NORTH DIVIDEND
INCOME FUND $$$$ ↓ FI NO RIF DIV

Manager: Team, headed by Ian Mottershead
MER: 1.21% **Style:** GARP
Suitability: Conservative investors.

The portfolio concentrates on high-yielding common stocks, rather than preferreds (in fact you'll be hard pressed to find a preferred share here). However, the stock selection process puts a high degree of emphasis on safety (there are no cyclicals in this portfolio). As well, only new stocks with a dividend yield that exceeds the average of the TSE are added. The fund has a great performance record but cash flow is not its strongest suit, so keep that in mind if you're an income-oriented investor. However, on a total return basis, this fund is one of the consistent leaders in the Dividend Fund category and is usually a first-quartile performer, meaning it is in the top 25 percent of all funds in the group. Over the long term, this fund is always at or near the top of the list in terms of performance numbers in its category. Just remember, this is not a conventional dividend fund. It's more like a blue-chip stock fund and, as such, it will be especially vulnerable to developments like a big pull-back in bank share prices. Still, you won't do much better if you're seeking a conservative, well-managed Canadian stock fund for the equity section of your RRIF. You need a fair amount of money to get in, however; see the entry on the company's Canadian Equity Fund for details.

ROYAL & SUN ALLIANCE DIVIDEND
FUND (SERIES II) $$$ → G/FI NO/* RIF S DIV

Manager: Brad Cann, since January 2000
MER: 2.20% **Style:** Value
Suitability: Conservative investors.

This is a decent dividend fund that has been successful in its short existence in generating both income and capital gains. Manager Brad Cann invests mainly in common stocks, with an emphasis on financial services companies. However, the portfolio also holds a small number of preferred shares. Risk is about average for the category. What makes this fund appealing for a RRIF is the good cash flow it generates. Distributions are paid quarterly, and the annual cash-on-cash yield tends to be around 5 percent. While we like this fund, its future is somewhat uncertain. Royal and SunAlliance was purchased by Maritime Life in late 2001. Maritime told us it plans no changes in the Royal and SunAlliance fund family in 2002, but there may be mergers with other funds within the organization after that. Note: Like many other insurance companies, Royal & SunAlliance changed the guarantee structure on its segregated funds in 2000–01. For new investors, the maturity guarantee has dropped to 75 percent (from 100 percent). The death guarantee remains at 100 percent to age 80, after which it drops to 75 percent. With the change, the company closed its original line of seg funds to new investors and launched new versions, known as Series II. They are the same in all respects except for the guarantees they carry. Those who had bought units in the original funds retain re-investment privileges.

ROYAL DIVIDEND FUND $$$$ → G/FI NO RIF DIV

Manager: John Kellett, since 1993
MER: 1.88%   **Style:** Value
Suitability: Balanced investors.

The stated goal here is to maximize tax-advantaged income through the use of the dividend tax credit, as well as to generate capital gains. In both cases, it has excelled. Like many dividend funds, this one is heavily invested in interest-sensitive bank and utility stocks. This makes the fund vulnerable to rising interest rates—a fact that should always be at the back of your mind when deciding to buy. On balance, this fund is more aggressive than dividend funds that lean towards preferred shares, so the risk will be somewhat higher, although it is about on a par with the category average. Returns over longer time frames are well above average, so the higher risk pays off with good gains. Cash flow can be variable, however. The fund pays distributions quarterly and does not offer a steady return, such as you'll find, for example, with the GGOF Guardian Monthly Dividend Fund. So don't choose this one if predictable income is a top concern of yours. However, if that's a secondary consideration, then this is a terrific fund to own, as long as you don't lose sight of the sensitivity of this fund to interest-rate movements. Available through the Royal Bank and subsidiary companies. Other discount brokers may offer it as well.

SCOTIA CANADIAN DIVIDEND FUND $$$ → G/FI NO RIF DIV

Manager: Paget Warner
MER: 1.14%   **Style:** Yield; Moderate Growth
Suitability: Conservative investors.

Despite being classified as an income fund, this has been one of the best-performing Canadian equity funds in Scotia's stable. The focus is to provide favourable, tax-advantaged income to unit holders, along with capital appreciation, so it is better held outside your RRIF if you also have a non-registered portfolio. It is the most conservative fund in Scotia's Canadian equity line-up and has the lowest volatility in the Scotia equity family. This is achieved by holding the majority of its assets in common stocks, with the remainder in preferred shares and income trust units. This makes the fund very sensitive to rising interest rates. Performance numbers have been good, with long-term results well above average for the category in terms of total return. However, quarterly distributions are somewhat low when compared to dividend funds that focus on preferred shares, and are not predictable. So this fund is not the best choice if steady cash flow is a main concern. Otherwise, it's a useful option. Sold in Scotiabank branches and through affiliated brokerage firms.

SPECTRUM DIVIDEND FUND $$$$ ↓ FI #/* RIF DIV

Managers: Peter Kotsopoulos, since January 1995, Cort Conover, since January 1996, and Tony Magri, since February 2001 (McLean Budden)
MER: 1.79% **Style:** Blend
Suitability: Conservative, income-oriented investors.

This is a genuine dividend fund, not a large-cap fund with "dividend" as part of the name. The focus is on high-quality preferred shares. Only the top-ranking preferreds (P-1 and P-2 ratings) are used. For common stocks, the managers avoid the more cyclical sectors of the market and concentrate on stable businesses like pipelines, utilities, and banks. Total returns tend to be below average for the Dividend Income category because of the defensive nature of the portfolio. Cash flow is very good, which is what really counts in a fund of this type. Distributions are paid monthly, at a rate of $0.04 per unit. Yield is usually in the 4 percent range. This fund is a good choice for RRIF investors, although the advantages of the dividend tax credit are lost inside a registered plan. The safety record is one of the best for its category.

STANDARD LIFE CANADIAN DIVIDEND FUND $$$ ↑ G #/* RIF DIV

Manager: Standard Life Investments Inc.
MER: 1.60% **Style:** Bottom-up Value
Suitability: Growth-oriented investors.

This is really more of a blue-chip stock fund than a dividend income fund. The portfolio is invested almost exclusively in common shares, with no preferreds, royalty trusts, or the like. As a result, returns will tend to be more volatile than you'll find in a more conventional dividend fund that holds a lot of preferred shares. This is an important consideration in a RRIF if you want to keep risk to an absolute minimum. That said, this fund has been a standout performer in its category in terms of total return—in fact, over the long haul, it's one of the best. The main weakness in the past has been cash flow—this fund is not a great choice if steady income for your RRIF is a prime need. Distributions are paid only quarterly and they have tended to be meagre.

The exceptions occur in years when there are large year-end capital gains distributions, as happened in 2000, when the fund paid out a total of $2.05, of which $1.79 was as a result of realized capital gains. Nice, but unpredictable, and you can't base an income stream on that. However, if you want a conservative stock fund for your RRIF and cash flow is not a concern, this is a first-rate choice.

STRATEGICNOVA CANADIAN DIVIDEND FUND $$$ → G/FI #/* RIF DIV

Manager: Canadian Stock Markets Team (CDP Global Asset Management), since September 2000

MER: 2.66%   **Style:** Value

Suitability: Conservative, income-oriented investors.

This was previously the Strategic Value Dividend Fund, under the direction of Mark Bonham, who was president of SVC O'Donnell before it was acquired by Montreal-based Nova Bancorp, which then changed the fund family name to StrategicNova. Bonham was shuffled out after the takeover and a new managerial team is in place. Under Bonham's direction, the twin objectives of this fund were capital growth and dividend income, and he made a concerted effort to enhance the cash yield with a goal to produce a fixed payout of between 4 percent and 5 percent annually. Distributions were on a monthly basis, set at $0.05 a unit ($0.60 a year). The new managers have maintained that monthly distribution, but they have changed the composition of the portfolio somewhat. Previously, the typical portfolio mix was 40 percent preferred shares, 40 percent high-yielding common stock, 15 percent bonds, and 5 percent cash, which gave the fund a more defensive tone in rough markets. Now, however, the preferred share portion of the fund has been reduced in favour of more common stock positions, so this fund has come more into line with others in its category in terms of asset composition. Of course, that increases the risk factor. The structure of the fund under Bonham was much more defensive in nature. Now, the fund will be more vulnerable to market swings. What we are uncertain about is whether the managers will be able to maintain the high monthly payment rate, given this new approach. If the monthly payments are a prime reason for selecting this fund, ask detailed questions about future policy before making a purchase. As things stand at the time of writing, this is a still a good choice for a RRIF, although the tax advantages of the distributions will be lost.

TD DIVIDEND GROWTH FUND $$$ ↑ G NO RIF DIV

Managers: Doug Warwick, since 1993, and Paul Harris, since 1996

MER: 2.17%   **Style:** Blend

Suitability: Growth-oriented investors.

The word *growth* was added to this fund's name in 2000—it was previously the Green Line Dividend Fund. The goal is to provide investors with superior after-tax income and steady growth, but you can forget about the income part. Distributions are very small. If cash flow is what you need, don't choose this one. The fund invests primarily in large-cap, high-yielding common stocks and, to a lesser degree, in bonds, trust units, and preferred shares. The portfolio holds a small core group of around 35 to 40 stocks, mainly in the traditional dividend-paying sectors of financial services, utilities, and pipelines. In terms of risk, this fund is a tad more aggressive than the average Canadian dividend fund because of its significant bias towards common stocks and its lower holdings in bonds and preferred shares. The compensating factor is that long-term returns are better than average for the category. Although TD funds are normally no-load, the company recently introduced "A" units of this fund, which are sold on an optional front- or back-end load basis and carry a somewhat lower MER. They're available through financial advisors. Overall, this is an above-average fund for capital appreciation, but cash flow is not its strong suit. The fund is therefore not recommended for RRIF investors who need regular income, but is suitable if you are looking to increase your capital base.

TD DIVIDEND INCOME FUND $$$ ↑ FI NO RIF DIV

Managers: Doug Warwick and Mike Lougl, since October 2000
MER: 2.00 %   **Style:** Generally Value
Suitability: Conservative income investors.

This fund was the Canada Trust Dividend Income-Inv Fund prior to the TD and Canada Trust merger. It is geared for investors seeking monthly income and the opportunity for moderate capital gains. Since its inception in 1994, the fund has generally been an above-average performer compared to its peer group. Cash flow is good and distributions are paid monthly; however, the amount may vary considerably from one month to the next, which makes planning somewhat difficult. The bond side of the portfolio consists of government and corporate bonds and is very low-risk. The safety rating is better than average for a fund of this type. The overall defensive-ness of the fund and the decent cash flow makes it a good vehicle for RRIF investors, as long as you don't mind the fact that income is not predictable.

U.S. Equity Funds

MCLEAN BUDDEN AMERICAN EQUITY FUND $$$$ → G NO £ USE

Manager: Team
MER: 1.30%   **Style:** Large-Cap Growth
Suitability: Growth section of a RRIF.

McLean Budden offers several high-quality growth funds. This is one that brings a fine record of consistency to the table. Since 1994, it has been below second quartile in only one calendar year, 1999, when it dipped to third quartile despite a respectable gain of 11.9 percent. That means you can depend on it to be in the top half of its cate-gory virtually all the time. The goal of this fund is long-term growth by investing in a diversified portfolio of 40–50 U.S. stocks selected from the S&P 500. Emphasis is on large companies like Pepsico, Colgate Palmolive, Microsoft, and General Motors, although you will find a few unfamiliar names in the mix. Over the long haul, very few U.S. equity funds have done better than this one. The fund did not record a losing calendar year from 1994 to 2000, and held up very well in the bear market of 2000–01. This is a very good selection if a U.S. growth fund fits into your RRIF profile. This will eat up foreign-content room because there is no clone available, but it's worth it. See the entry on the McLean Budden Canadian Equity Growth Fund for purchase details.

MUTUAL BEACON FUND $$$ ↓ G #/* £ USE

Manager: Lawrence Sondike (Franklin Capital Advisors), since 1998
MER: 2.67%   **Style:** Value
Suitability: Low-risk investors.

One of the factors that gets high priority when we are looking at equity funds for RRIFs is the risk aspect. This is not a time in your investing career when you can afford big losses. You want equity funds that will minimize risk while still providing respectable growth potential. This one, which is offered through the Franklin Templeton organization, fits the bill. It is the only fund in the "Mutual" series offered by the company in Canada, although there are several in the U.S. The name Templeton says value investing, but this offering goes beyond that. Manager Lawrence Sondike is what is known as a "deep value" investor, which means his criteria for stock selection are even more demanding than those normally associated with the Templeton funds. He is a disciple of legendary value manager Michael Price and seeks his stocks from among out-of-favour companies, particularly those in financial distress. Prudence dictates all selections, and the fund focuses on capital preservation, in good times and bad. Long-term growth is the aim, with income a secondary goal. The value approach was out of favour in the period that followed the launch of this fund in 1997, so it did not fare well immediately. But it looked much better in the bear market of 2000–01, beating the group average and the S&P 500 by incredible margins. This fund is unlikely to soar to the heights of some of the go-go growth funds in hot markets, but it's a good safe haven in troubled times. A clone fund, the Mutual Beacon RSP Fund, is available for RRIF investing; however, its return has been lower than that of the parent fund. If foreign-content room is not a problem for you, stick with the original.

O'SHAUGHNESSY U.S. VALUE FUND $$$$ → G NO £ USE

Manager: James P. O'Shaughnessy, since November 1997
MER: 1.60%   **Style:** Value
Suitability: Growth investors looking for some income from equity funds.

There are two O'Shaughnessy funds offered by the Royal Bank group. The Growth Fund is somewhat more aggressive, so we recommend this Value Fund for a RRIF. Manager James O'Shaughnessy uses a U.S. Value Strategy Index, which he devised, to identify firms with high dividend yields and higher-than-average sales and capitalizations. After a slow start, the fund rebounded strongly after the high-tech collapse, and its longer-term results are well above average. Another advantage is that it makes quarterly distributions, unusual in an equity fund, so it will enhance your cash flow. Risk is about average for the category. As with the McLean Budden entry, this fund will eat up some of your foreign-content room, but it's also worth it.

Global and International Equity Funds

AGF INTERNATIONAL VALUE FUND $$$$ ↓ G #/* £ GE

Managers: Charles Brandes, since November 1994, and Chris Richey, since October 2001

MER: 2.80%   **Style:** Bottom-up Value

Suitability: Conservative investors.

This is one of the stars in the AGF firmament and should be high on a RRIF investor's shopping list. Charles Brandes is one of America's great value investors, regarded by many as a successor to the legendary Benjamin Graham. He has written his own book on the subject, *Value Investing Today*, and is frequently quoted in the U.S. media. The 20/20 Group, which has since been absorbed into AGF, scored a major coup in getting him to take over this fund in 1994, even though they had to change the fund's original mandate to do it. Brandes and his San Diego-based team scour the world for good values and the result is a well-diversified portfolio that has churned out returns that are well above the average since he took charge. The fund had never lost money over a calendar year since he and his team assumed responsibility up to and including 2000. The portfolio is well diversified geographically, with an emphasis on North America. Risk is better than average for the Global Equity category but about on a par with the MSCI World Index. This is a very good choice for the international equity section of a RRIF. There's a RRIF-eligible clone available but it has not been tracking the parent fund as closely as we would like, so stick with the original if possible.

BISSETT MULTINATIONAL GROWTH FUND $$$ ↓ G NO £ GE

Manager: Jeffrey Morrison, since 1999

MER: 2.48%   **Style:** Bottom-up Growth

Suitability: Conservative investors.

The mandate of this fund is somewhat unusual. The manager seeks out European and North American companies that operate on a multinational level and offer a growing dividend stream. So you'll find both traditional blue-chip stocks and major firms on the rise in the mix. We like the history here. The fund consistently outperforms the category average and the benchmark MSCI World Index. It also has a good safety record in relation to other funds in the Global Equity category. That combination of decent retains and below-average risk makes it a good choice for a RRIF. Investing tip: The "F" units are no-load and have a lower MER, but you probably won't be able to acquire them, although it never hurts to ask. The new "A" units were launched after

Franklin Templeton acquired the Bissett funds. They carry an optional front- or back-end load and the MER is about a percentage point higher. There is a clone version available if foreign-content room is a problem.

MACKENZIE IVY FOREIGN EQUITY FUND $$$$ ↓ G #/* £ GE

Manager: Jerry Javasky, since April 1999 (previously 1992–97)
MER: 2.49%   **Style:** Value/Growth
Suitability: Low-risk investors.

Mackenzie Financial offers two global equity funds that would look good in a RRIF—this one and the Mackenzie Cundill Value Fund. However, this one is our choice because it has a more consistent performance record and a better safety rating. We also feel the conservative, capital preservation style of manager Jerry Javasky serves RRIF investors well. He ran this fund from 1992 to 1997 before handing over portfolio responsibility to Bill Kanko. Now Kanko is running the Trimark Fund for AIM (see below) and Javasky is back in charge. This fund's main emphasis is on U.S. stocks, but there are several other countries represented as well, with Europe quite prominent. Javasky will also hold a lot of cash during times of market turbulence to preserve assets. Returns are generally above average for the Global Equity category. Historically, the fund has a better-than-average safety rating, and it did not record a losing year from 1994 to 2000. It also held up very well during the bear market of 2000–01. In early 1999, Mackenzie launched a RRIF-eligible clone of this fund, the Ivy RSP Foreign Equity Fund. It's an option to look at if foreign-content room is a problem in your plan. There is also a segregated version and a tax-advantaged Capital Class version, although the latter would not be useful in a RRIF. Recommended.

TRIMARK FUND $$$$ ↓ G #/* £ GE

Manager: Bill Kanko, since 1999
MER: 1.62%/2.50%   **Style:** Value/Growth
Suitability: Conservative investors.

We're delighted to report that this long-time favourite is back on track after running into a rough patch in the late 1990s. Lead manager Bill Kanko, who took over in May 1999 from Robert Krembil who had run this fund since it was created back in 1981, restored it to first-quartile status in 2000 and retained that top ranking through the worst of the bear market when his value approach paid off by protecting the asset base. Kanko can invest around the world, although he tends to favour the U.S. market. The risk level is quite low for a global equity fund, an important consideration in a retirement fund. Note that we recommend the purchase of front-end load units (try to get them at zero commission) because of the high MER attached to the back-end load (DSC) units. There is no clone version so the units will come under the foreign-content rule.

TRIMARK SELECT GROWTH FUND (CLASS) $$$ ↓ G #/* £ GE

Manager: Bill Kanko, since 1999
MER: 2.50%   **Style:** Value/Growth
Suitability: Conservative investors.

This started out as an optional front- or back-end load companion to the front-end Trimark Fund. However, now that the Trimark Fund also offers two purchase options (albeit with different MERs), we wonder how long the two funds will remain separate. This fund features the same manager (Bill Kanko), the same style, and a similar, but not identical, portfolio. Nominal returns should generally be slightly below those of the original Trimark Fund SC units because of the higher MER. This fund originally grew more rapidly because of the public preference for back-end load funds, but that distinction no longer holds. If you're going to buy one of these funds on a back-end load basis, it really doesn't matter which you pick, but our preference is for the SC units of Trimark Fund. However, this one offers the advantage of a RRIF-eligible clone, in the event you are bumping against the foreign-content ceiling. Returns for the clone tend to be slightly lower, however. Yet another version of this fund, Trimark Select Growth Class, was launched in June 2001 as part of the umbrella AIM Global Fund Inc., but it is more suitable for investors with non-registered portfolios who make frequent switches.

Canadian Balanced and Tactical Asset Allocation Funds

ABC FULLY-MANAGED FUND $$$$ ↓ G NO RIF CBAL

Manager: Irwin Michael, since inception (1988)
MER: 2.00%   **Style:** Value
Suitability: Conservative investors.

You'll need a pretty big RRIF to include this fund on your shopping list. Minimum initial investment is $150,000. But if you have that kind of juice, then you should certainly take a look at this one. It has been a consistent above-average performer, except for a brief slump in 1997–98 (1998 was the only year it actually lost money). During the 2000–01 bear market, it not only protected capital but actually made money for its investors. The fund is run by Irwin Michael, an MBA from the prestigious Wharton School of Finance, who has established a reputation as one of Canada's top value managers. He is highly disciplined in his approach and doesn't stray from it, even when the financial tides are flowing strongly against him as they were in the late 1990s. During that period, which he describes as the most difficult one he has ever encountered for his fundamental value approach, his funds languished and investors became restless. But the collapse of the high-tech juggernaut brought value investing back into style, and it wasn't long before this fund was back among the top performers in its category. Michael and his colleagues spend most of their working hours poring over balance sheets and income statements, looking for hidden value within a company. They have shown themselves to be especially adept at identifying companies that are ripe for takeover bids—his funds were heavily into Gulf Canada Resources, which was taken out in the spring of 2001 for a fat premium. None of the funds in the group has ever used options, futures, or other derivatives. The fund's risk ranking is about average but it actually has a first-rate safety record. If value investing, low risk, and steady returns are what you're looking for in your RRIF and you have the money in your plan, this is the answer. Units can be purchased through the management firm; call 1-888-OPEN-ABC or 416-365-9696. The company maintains its own Web site (**www.abcfunds.com**), as well as a new one it recently launched, called The Value Investigator (**www.valueinvestigator.com**). There you'll find a detailed analysis of many of the stocks in the ABC portfolios. It's useful reading.

AGF CANADIAN HIGH INCOME FUND $$$ ↓ FI #/* RIF CBAL

Managers: Clive Coombs, since inception (May 1989), and Tristan Sones, since June 2000

MER: 1.74%   **Style:** Interest Rate Anticipation

Suitability: Investors looking for low risk and steady cash flow.

This fund has been difficult to classify because of its unusual asset mix: mainly short-term bonds but with a large holding in preferred shares. AGF describes it as a short-term bond fund, but it really doesn't fit comfortably there. What we can say with certainty is that this is a low-risk fund that offers decent cash flow with monthly distributions, making it a useful holding for RRIF accounts. There is no real growth potential here, so if you're looking for a balanced fund that offers an income/growth mix, this is not it. But if you need something that will keep the income flowing while protecting your asset base against loss, then this fund should be on your shopping list.

BEUTEL GOODMAN BALANCED FUND $$ ↓ FI/G #/NO RIF CBAL

Manager: Denis Marsh, since 1991

MER: 1.11%   **Style:** Value

Suitability: Conservative investors.

If a low-risk balanced fund would fit well in your RRIF, this one may be for you. Its performance has been slightly above average throughout its history, as you might expect from a fund of its conservative nature. The equities side has a value orientation that favours large-cap stocks with fairly good yields; however, small caps are added for some growth potential. The fixed-income side is conservatively managed, and federal and provincial bonds comprise the bulk of the bond portfolio. The overall portfolio risk is low versus the market, and the fund held up very well in the bear market of 2000–01. In all, this is a lower-risk/average-return fund that would suit conservative investors. See the entry on the Beutel Goodman Canadian Equity Fund for purchase details.

BMO ASSET ALLOCATION FUND $$$ ↓ FI/G NO RIF CTAA

Manager: Mary Jane Yule (Jones Heward), since 1989
MER: 2.09%   **Style:** Tactical Asset Allocation
Suitability: Conservative investors.

This is a conservatively managed fund on both its equity and fixed-income sides. The equity component is well diversified, with a large-cap value orientation. It holds a relatively large portfolio of over 150 stocks, while the fixed-income side is concentrated mainly in government bonds and relatively short-duration fixed-income securities, resulting in below-average interest-rate risk. The fund's performance has been steadily improving and returns are now above average for the category. The safety record is quite good for a fund of this type. A good RRIF choice if you're a Bank of Montreal client, although it's not worth opening an account there to acquire it.

CLARICA SUMMIT GROWTH AND
INCOME FUND $$$ ↓ G/FI */NO RIF CBAL

Manager: Mackenzie Investment Corp.
MER: 2.99%   **Style:** Value
Suitability: Conservative investors.

This balanced fund leaves full discretion to the managers (who we believe to be Mackenzie's Ivy group) to determine the asset allocation. They tend to take a fairly conservative approach, not overweighting the portfolio dramatically in any one direction. The value approach hurt returns in the initial years after the June 1997 launch, but saved the fund from disaster when markets plunged in 2000–01. Overall result is above-average performance with below-average risk—a good RRIF pairing. The major weakness of this fund for a retirement income plan is its lack of cash flow. Distributions are paid only once a year, in late December, and tend to be on the low side. So this fund is really better suited to those seeking balanced growth. See the entry on the Clarica Summit Dividend Growth Fund for purchase details and advice on whether to buy no-load or DSC units.

CLARINGTON CANADIAN BALANCED FUND $$$ ↓ FI/G #/* RIF CBAL

Manager: Peter Marshall (Seamark), since inception (1996)
MER: 2.90%   **Style:** Value
Suitability: Conservative investors.

This is one of those sound little funds that too few people know about. It has produced consistent high-return/low-risk results ever since its launch back in 1996. The fund maintains a fairly balanced mix of equities/fixed-income securities. Manager Peter Marshall uses the foreign-content allowance liberally, with about a quarter of the assets held outside Canada. The MER is a bit above average, but with results like these, we don't think we'll be hearing any complaints. One disadvantage from a RRIF perspective is that distributions are paid only once a year and tend to be on the low side. If cash flow is important, look at the companion Canadian Income Fund instead.

CLARINGTON CANADIAN INCOME FUND $$$$ ↓ FI #/* RIF CBAL

Manager: Peter Marshall (Seamark), since inception (1996)
MER: 2.51%   **Style:** Value
Suitability: Income-oriented investors.

This is officially classified as a balanced fund, but it operates more like a dividend income fund. The objective is to provide a reliable monthly income stream of $0.08 per unit, along with some capital gains potential. So the portfolio is a mix of stocks, bonds, income trusts, etc. Results have been very good and risk is low—the fund has never lost money over a calendar year since it was launched in late 1996. But income is where the fund really shines. It has spun off $0.96 a unit for each of the past four years, as advertised. If the fund is held outside your RRIF, a significant portion of that payment is received on a tax-deferred basis. But that does not mean you shouldn't include it in your retirement income plan if you don't have a non-registered portfolio option. If you need cash flow in the RRIF, this fund will provide it. However, be aware that some of that money may come at the expense of a reduced net asset value. In other words, this fund works something like a systematic withdrawal plan. If the assets don't generate enough profits to cover the distributions, you will effectively get some of your capital back. That's not necessarily a bad thing in a RRIF context—a lower NAV reduces the minimum withdrawal requirement next year. But it's a twist you need to know about before investing.

ELLIOTT & PAGE MONTHLY INCOME FUND $$$ → FI/G #/* RIF CIT

Manager: Alan Wicks, since 2000
MER: 2.43%   **Style:** Top-down
Suitability: Income-oriented investors.

This is a fund that can generate very healthy cash flow for your RRIF, albeit with more risk than you'd experience in, say, a government bond fund. The portfolio contains a lot of income trusts and REITs, as well as common stocks, bonds, and other income-generating securities. Distributions are paid monthly, an important consideration if you rely on your RRIF for steady income. The rate can vary, but it was running at $0.055 per unit through 2001. The safety level is about average for a fund in the Canadian Income Trusts category, but by nature most funds in that group will tend to be higher risk than a regular balanced fund because of their large holdings in royalty trusts. If that extra risk isn't acceptable in your RRIF, then pass.

FIDELITY CANADIAN ASSET
ALLOCATION FUND $$$$ → FI/G #/* RIF CTAA

Manager: Dick Habermann, since inception (December 1994)
MER: 2.49%   **Style:** GARP
Suitability: Core fund for conservative RRIF investors.

This big fund operates using a team approach with Dick Habermann as lead manager, along with input from Alan Radlo on the equities side and Jeff Moore on the bond side. That's a formidable team and the fund's results show how well they work together. The fund consistently generates above-average rates of return, with moderate risk. The portfolio's "neutral" weightings are 65 percent stocks, 30 percent fixed-income, and 5 percent money market, but they are constantly monitored and change to reflect market conditions, so check the current weightings if you're considering an investment. The fund's diversified group of stocks is conservatively managed, with many large-cap, dividend-paying issues. The bond portion has average risk. Weakness is the frequency of distribution—only one payment is made each year, in December. So you can't use this fund for cash flow purposes. If that is not a problem, then this is a good Canadian balanced fund for your RRIF.

GREAT-WEST LIFE GROWTH & INCOME FUND (M) $$$ ↓ FI/G */NO RIF S CBAL

Manager: Mackenzie Financial Ivy Team
MER: 2.37%   **Style:** Value/Growth
Suitability: Conservative investors.

This fund is operated along the same lines as the Mackenzie Ivy Growth and Income Fund, which has the same management team. However, the mandate here is more aggressive as it doesn't limit the amount that can be held in stocks or bonds. So you could have 100 percent of the fund in a specific category, which makes it similar to a tactical asset allocation fund. We don't really expect that the portfolio will see such extremes as long as the Ivy team is running the show, however. And the results show that. Despite the ability to make large bets, historically this is one of the lower-risk alternatives within GWL's stable of balanced funds. Of course, lower risk usually comes with a price. In this case, it was lower-than-average returns through the late 1990s. But that's all changed, and now long-term results are better than average for the peer group and for the benchmark indexes. Overall, this is a conservative balanced choice for a RRIF. See the entry on the Great-West Life Dividend/ Growth Fund for advice on which units to choose, no-load or back-end load.

GREAT-WEST LIFE INCOME FUND (G) $$$ ↓ FI/G */NO RIF S CBAL

Managers: Terry Parsonage and Patricia Nesbitt (GWL Investment Management)
MER: 1.94%   **Style:** Blend with a Fixed-Income Bias
Suitability: Conservative investors.

Of Great-West's balanced funds, this is the most conservatively managed in terms of both its equity and bond sides. The majority of the portfolio is invested in bonds, but there are some stocks and income trusts in the mix as well. The fund is geared for those seeking more interest and dividend income, with minimal risk. Returns will generally fall between those of a bond fund and a balanced fund. All in all, it's a good fit for a RRIF, and very low risk.

GREAT-WEST LIFE INCOME FUND (M) $$$ ↓ FI/G */NO RIF S CBAL

Manager: Mackenzie Financial Maxxum Team
MER: 2.10%   **Style:** Blend
Suitability: Balanced investors.

This fund is designed for those seeking a regular income stream along with capital appreciation. The mandate allows up to 40 percent of the assets to be held in stocks, thus making this relatively conservative as balanced funds go. In fact, this fund is officially within the Canadian Bond category. However, that is misleading. While the majority of the holdings are in fixed-income securities, of which up to 30 percent can be corporate bonds, there is a large percentage of the portfolio in common shares, REITs, and royalty trusts. So this is actually a balanced fund despite what the newspapers or Web sites may tell you. Returns are respectable and risk is on the low side for a balanced fund.

ICM BALANCED FUND $$$ ↓ FI/G #/NO RIF CBAL

Managers: Gryphon Investment Counsel and Lincluden Management, since inception (1987)
MER: 1.75%   **Style:** Value/Growth
Suitability: Conservative investors.

There are two teams involved in running this and several other ICM portfolios. Each employs a different style for its half of the assets. Gryphon uses a top-down investing approach, which involves identifying key sectors of the economy that are expected to do well and selecting large-cap stocks that will profit as a result. Lincluden takes a value-oriented, bottom-up approach, selecting stocks on the basis of their intrinsic value without reference to overall trends. The managers can shift freely between asset classes to maximize returns. Results have shown steady improvement in recent years, although the figures published in the media do not reflect the full impact of the expense charges that are levied against individual unit holders—most of that cost is assessed directly. As a result, historic comparisons are difficult for ordinary investors, who may be left with a misleading impression. The good news here is that the risk level is very low—the fund rarely loses money over a calendar year. If safety is your primary concern, then this fund is worth considering. Distributions are paid quarterly. Minimum investment is $5,000. Units must be purchased directly from the company. Call 1-877-799-1942 for information.

LEITH WHEELER BALANCED FUND $$$ → FI/G NO RSP CBAL

Manager: Leith Wheeler Investment Committee, since inception (1987)
MER: 1.10%   **Style:** Bottom-up Value
Suitability: Conservative investors.

The story here is similar to that of the companion Canadian Equity Fund, which is included in these recommendations. For a few years both funds wandered in the value wilderness of the late 1990s, but both did well once the high-tech bubble burst and the bear market of 2000–01 appeared. The portfolio of this fund is well constructed and makes good use of U.S. stocks to add foreign content and boost returns. The investment parameters of this fund have narrowed somewhat in recent years. In the past, the managers enjoyed a fairly wide latitude in determining their asset allocation; the fund could hold between 25 percent and 75 percent in equities. Now, however, the equity range is usually limited to between 45 percent and 65 percent of the total portfolio. Longer-term results are comfortably above par. Risk is slightly better than average for the category. Distributions are paid quarterly. Like the Canadian Equity Fund, this one is defensive in nature, which makes it a sound choice in turbulent markets. See the entry on that fund for purchase details.

LONDON LIFE BALANCED FUND (BG) $$$ ↓ C * RIF S CBAL

Manager: Beutel Goodman
MER: 2.45%   **Style:** Tactical Asset Allocation
Suitability: Moderate-risk investors.

The value-oriented Beutel Goodman group is in change of the managerial work here and they use a tactical asset allocation approach in managing this fund. This means they will adjust the asset category weights with their view of changing conditions and outlook, so the fund may be heavily overweighted towards stocks or bonds at any particular time. Beutel Goodman has an excellent reputation, but if you invest here you should be prepared for below-average returns in strong markets because of the defensive approach they take. On the other hand, this fund will protect your asset base in tough times. Risk is low, and results since the 1998 launch have been above average. Note that there are other London Life products that also have the word *Balanced* in the name; look for the initials *BG* at the end to distinguish this fund from the rest. Sold by London Life agents.

MACKENZIE CUNDILL CANADIAN
BALANCED FUND $$$ → G #/* RIF CBAL

Managers: Alan Pasnik and Peter Cundill, since inception (September 1998)
MER: "C" units 2.53%   **Style:** Core Value
Suitability: Conservative investors seeking a value style.

The Cundill equity funds have generally had a good record, so it is hardly a surprise that this relatively new balanced fund (launched in late 1998) has also turned in some impressive numbers. The same deep value stock-picking philosophy that characterizes the older stock funds is at work here. The equity portfolio is similar to that of the Canadian Security Fund (same management team), and you'll find all kinds of securities in the mix from major banks to small-cap companies you've never heard of. This fund is likely to show the same pattern as the other Cundill entries, with the best results in down markets. Risk is about average. The fund pays quarterly distributions, but they usually aren't very large so don't look here for cash flow.

MACKENZIE INCOME FUND $$$ ↓ FI/G #/* RIF CBAL

Managers: Tim Gleeson, since 1992, and Bill Procter, since 1998
MER: 1.93%   **Style:** Relative Value
Suitability: Conservative investors.

This is not a true fixed-income fund, despite the name, hence its inclusion in the balanced section. Federal government bonds are the core holding, but the manager may invest a portion of the fund's assets in stocks, and the fund also holds some REITs. The "A" units are the original ones, and pay an annual distribution of $1 each. The "B" units pay an annual distribution of about $0.40 each. Both the "A" and "B" units are otherwise the same. Mackenzie warns that "A" unit holders who receive distributions in cash will deplete their investment in the fund over time, which will lead to "administrative complexities." The company encourages Class "A" unit holders to make a non-taxable switch to Class "B" shares to avoid this problem, and no longer offers "A" units for sale. As far as total returns are concerned, the fund will tend to be below average for the Canadian Balanced category over the long haul because of the dominant position of bonds in the portfolio. But risk will be much lower than the category norm as well. Distributions are paid quarterly and usually run around $0.10 a unit. A useful choice in a RRIF context. This fund comes in a segregated version as well.

MACKENZIE IVY GROWTH AND INCOME FUND $$$ ↓ FI/G #/* RIF CBAL

Manager: Jerry Javasky, since June 1997
MER: 2.20%   **Style:** Value/Growth
Suitability: Growth-oriented investors.

This fund has no set asset allocation parameters, so the ratios could swing dramatically in any direction at any time. In fact, Mackenzie specifically warns that the relative weighting of stocks and bonds "may vary widely," so if that is a potential problem for you, look for an alternative balanced fund that operates with set ranges. That said, this fund is conservatively managed and a good choice for growth-oriented RRIF investors. Long-term results are well above average for the Canadian Balanced category. Good safety record. But as with the companion Maxxum Pension Fund, cash flow is not a strong point here–distributions are made only once a year. Otherwise, this is a sound balanced fund with growth potential. Also available in a segregated version.

MAWER CANADIAN BALANCED
RETIREMENT SAVINGS FUND $$$$ ↓ FI/G NO RIF CBAL

Manager: Donald Ferris, since inception (January 1988)
MER: 1.10%   **Style:** Strategic asset allocation
Suitability: Conservative investors seeking both income and growth potential.

This fund is fully RRIF-eligible, while the companion Canadian Diversified Investment Fund is not, so it's our choice for this book. It's a high-quality balanced fund, investing in short-term notes, bonds, and Canadian and foreign equities within the foreign-content limit. It also holds positions in other Mawer funds, including the New Canada Fund, World Investment Fund, and U.S. Equity Fund. Performance has been good, with above-average returns over all time frames. The safety record is very good as well—this fund has not had a calendar year loss since 1994. The portfolio is well-diversified, and manager Don Ferris has been around for more than 10 years, so there's real stability at the top. MER is low. Plus this fund offers monthly distributions, great for cash flow in your RRIF. All-in-all, a top-notch combination; in fact, you can't ask for much more than this from a fund. If you're not familiar with Mawer, it is a Calgary-based company that has been in business since 1974. Its investment style is a modified GARP. Normally, this is an acronym for Growth At a Reasonable Price; however, the Mawer people prefer the term Growth At the Right Price. The distinction, as they see it, is that their version is somewhat more conservative in its approach. The "right" price to their managers means a stock that is trading at a discount to its intrinsic value. Their funds are registered for sale in all provinces. However, the minimum investment required will vary, depending on where you live and from whom you buy. Residents of Alberta and Saskatchewan can buy units directly from the company. In that case, there's an initial minimum of $25,000 per account, although the company has the discretion to waive that. Residents of other provinces can also buy direct from Mawer, but in that case, the minimum initial investment rises to $100,000. Alternatively, you may purchase the funds through a licensed dealer, in which case the minimum is $5,000 per fund (note the distinction between "per fund" and "per account"). Although the funds are no-load, a dealer or broker may levy some kind of fee for the service.

MAXXUM PENSION FUND $$$ → G/FI #/* RIF CBAL

Manager: Bill Procter, since March 1995
MER: 2.48% **Style:** Value
Suitability: Growth-oriented investors.

This was formerly the Mackenzie Industrial Pension Fund. When Mackenzie over-hauled its fund line in January 2002 to eliminate the Industrial name, this fund moved into the Maxxum camp. However, the manager and mandate stayed the same. This fund invests mainly in stocks, with a small bond component tossed in (about one-quarter of the assets). So this is a fund to choose if you're looking for a Mackenzie entry that emphasizes growth through equities while offering some fixed-income exposure as well. Long-term results are excellent and the managerial responsibilities are in very capable hands. However, there is no monthly cash flow here, so if that's your need look to Mackenzie Income Fund as the better choice. There's a segregated version if you prefer.

MCLEAN BUDDEN BALANCED GROWTH FUND $$$ → FI/G NO RIF CBAL

Manager: Team
MER: 1.00% **Style:** Large-Cap Growth
Suitability: Long-term, balanced investors.

This fund employs a conservative investment strategy, combining stocks of large companies (e.g., conglomerates, banks) with bonds and debentures with at least an "A" safety rating. On the equities side, McLean Budden's trademark large-cap growth approach is used. On the fixed-income side, the company employs a number of active bond strategies to maximize returns, including interest rate anticipation, yield enhancement (overweighting provincial and corporate issues), special feature bonds, and U.S.-pay bonds. The managers maintain a truly balanced portfolio with the equity component between 40 percent and 60 percent. Results have been good in recent years, and the fund consistently shows above-average returns. Risk is slightly high for the category, but not unduly so. Income distributions are paid quarterly with a capital gains distribution at year-end. A good choice for a RRIF because of its income/growth combination. See the entry on the McLean Budden Canadian Equity Growth Fund for purchase details.

NORTHWEST BALANCED FUND $$$ → G/FI #/* RIF CBAL

Manager: Richard Fogler (Kingwest and Company), since 1997
MER: 2.78%   **Style:** Value
Suitability: Growth-oriented investors.

This is a conservatively managed balanced fund that uses a "sleep at night" approach to investing, in the words of Northwest president Michael Butler. Domestic stocks are selected using the same EVA analysis that manager Richard Fogler employs in the companion Northwest Growth Fund (see that entry for details). There is also a very good foreign component to this fund, with both U.S. and global stocks (those stocks are selected by OpCap, which runs the companion International Fund). The fixed-income side consists mainly of short-term bonds, which provide some income while reducing overall volatility. There may also be large cash holdings, especially when markets are in a downturn. Results of this blend since Fogler took charge at the end of 1997 are good, with returns that are comfortably above average. There's no cash flow here, however; distributions are paid only once a year, in mid-December. So this is a better choice if you're looking for growth potential with about average risk.

PERIGEE ACCUFUND $$$ ↓ FI/G NO RIF CTAA

Manager: Team
MER: 1.04%   **Style:** Top-down Growth
Suitability: Conservative investors.

The Perigee organization has been in business for almost 30 years. It was recently acquired by the U.S. money management firm Legg Mason, and some of its funds now use that name. Perigee's funds were previously available to pension plans and Perigee's own high-net-worth clients. However, they are now open to the general public, with a minimum initial investment of $2,500. This is Perigee's lowest-risk balanced fund. Like all Perigee funds, this fund is managed using a team approach. In this case, the managers follow a conservative asset mix, split about 70/30 between debt instruments and equity. Securities in the mix include government bonds, mortgages and mortgage-backed securities, T-bills, and U.S. and Canadian stocks, so you have broad diversification here. Returns are usually above average for the fund's peer group. Distributions are paid quarterly. This fund is an excellent low-cost choice for conservative investors and would fit well into a RRIF. If you want more growth potential, look at one of the other two Perigee balanced offerings, but this offers the best combination of risk and return in our opinion. Investing tip: Although Perigee's funds are no-load, they can no longer be acquired directly through the company, which is a departure from past practice. This means you must buy through a dealer or online, and you may be assessed some type of charge. Be sure to clarify this before you place an order. Sales people receive a trailer fee of 0.5 percent annually from Perigee so you may be able to negotiate a no-charge arrangement. Note that the "B" units are the ones sold to the general public.

PHILLIPS, HAGER & NORTH BALANCED FUND $$$ → FI/G NO RIF CBAL

Manager: Team
MER: 0.92%   **Style:** GARP
Suitability: Conservative investors.

This is a well-diversified fund, with a portfolio made up of a carefully chosen mix of Canadian stocks; U.S. stocks; federal, provincial, and corporate bonds; plus a 25 percent foreign-content holding. Up to and including 2000, it never recorded a losing calendar year, going all the way back to its launch in 1991, although that streak was broken in 2001. Historically, this fund tends to be a second-quartile performer, which means it does slightly better than the average for the Canadian Balanced category. This one won't shoot the lights out, but you won't toss and turn at night worrying about your money either. Distributions are paid quarterly. Good choice for a RRIF.

ROYAL & SUN ALLIANCE
BALANCED FUND (SERIES II) $$ → FI/G NO/* RIF S CBAL

Managers: Rob Rublee, since 1990, and Brad Cann, since January 2000
MER: 2.40%   **Style:** Value/Interest Rate Anticipation
Suitability: Conservative investors.

The fund's mandate puts a cap of 75 percent on the proportion of the assets that can be in stocks or bonds at any given time, but usually the ratios are kept in closer balance. The equity section has a large-cap value bias while being well diversified across industries. On the fixed-income side, default risk is low with the majority of assets held in federal bonds and high-quality corporate debt. However, interest-rate risk is above average. The fund uses an "interest rate anticipation approach." Overall portfolio risk is average. Results have been generally good, with longer-term returns slightly above the norm for the category. This is one of those funds that manage to produce profits most of the time with a modest level of risk. However, don't buy this one if steady income is needed, as distributions are paid only once a year. See the entry on the Royal and SunAlliance Dividend Fund for more information about this family, which was acquired by Maritime Life in late 2001.

ROYAL MONTHLY INCOME FUND $$$ ↓ FI/G NO RIF CIT

Manager: John Varao, since 1997
MER: 1.26%   **Style:** Tactical Asset Allocation
Suitability: Income investors.

This fund invests in high-yield fixed-income securities including corporate bonds, preferred shares, and income trusts, as well as holding some common shares. It's more conservatively managed than many funds in the Canadian Income Trusts category, but there's more risk here than, for example, in a government bond fund. If you add this to your RRIF, expect some possibly dramatic swings in unit value. On the plus side, this fund is a good choice for steady cash flow. Distributions are paid monthly and have been running at a rate of $0.0425 per unit. The MER is very low for a fund of this type, which means most of the profits flow to you, the investor. As a bonus, there are no sales commissions. All-in-all, this is a very good choice if above-average cash flow is a priority need, as it usually is in a RRIF, and you can handle the somewhat higher risk factor.

ROYAL SELECT INCOME FUND $$ ↓ FI/G NO RIF CBAL

Manager: John Varao and Mark L. Arthur, since 1999
MER: 1.93%   **Style:** Tactical Asset Allocation
Suitability: Conservative investors.

There are three "Select" funds, each of which fulfills a specific investing goal. All invest in units of other funds within the family. This is the Select fund for those who are conservative and seek income versus capital growth—a good RRIF combination. In terms of volatility, it has the lowest risk of any of Royal's balanced funds, due to its large weighting towards fixed-income securities. The neutral weighting for this fund is about 67 percent in income funds and 33 percent in equity funds. However, the emphasis on bonds means that long-term results are only about average for the category. Distributions are paid quarterly and are not as high as those of the companion Monthly Income Fund, above. You would choose this one if steady income is less important to you and you want to avoid the potential higher volatility of the Monthly Income Fund.

SAXON HIGH INCOME FUND $$$ → FI/G NO RIF CIT

Manager: Richard Howson, since 1997
MER: 1.25%   **Style:** Bottom-up Value
Suitability: Aggressive income investors.

This fund is designed to earn high income through a portfolio of Canadian dividend-paying stocks, income trusts, and fixed-income securities. Howson's concentration on income, royalty, and real estate trusts produces above-average cash flow (distributions are paid quarterly), which makes it useful if above-average income is a requirement for your RRIF. However, be aware that some of the income will be tax-deferred if received outside a registered plan. If you have a non-registered portfolio as well, you may want to hold these units there. Risk level is about average for a fund of this type. But don't lose sight of the fact that a fund like this will normally be more volatile (therefore more risky) than a regular balanced fund. The trade-off is the higher cash flow potential. See the entry on the Saxon Stock Fund for purchase details.

SCOTIA CANADIAN BALANCED FUND $$ → FI/G NO RIF CBAL

Manager: Britton Doherty
MER: 1.63%   **Style:** Biased toward Growth
Suitability: Conservative investors.

This is a conservatively managed fund on both the equity and fixed-income sides. Stocks have a blue-chip orientation, with strong valuation and dividends. Risk is minimized through both industry and foreign stock diversification, including a heavy weighting of U.S. stocks. The bond side is conservative, with lots of federal and corporate issues and below-average interest-rate risk. Bonds chosen must have an "A" rating or better. Longer-term results are average to slightly above. Safety record is also about average for the category. Distributions are paid quarterly. In sum, this is a decent RRIF fund for Scotiabank clients, but not exceptional.

SPECTRUM DIVERSIFIED FUND $$ → FI/G #/* RIF CBAL

Managers: Brian Dawson, Susan Shuter, and Peter Kotsopoulos (McLean Budden), since November 1997
MER: 2.32%   **Style:** Blend
Suitability: Conservative investors.

This is a conservatively managed fund that invests mainly in blue-chip stocks and government bonds. It is run by McLean Budden, a top-notch money management company that is owned partly by Sun Life, which is also the parent of Spectrum. This fund is a good choice for risk-averse investors who want some growth potential but don't like big asset class bets. That makes it a sound choice for RRIFs. Returns tend to be average to slightly above. Weakness is the distribution policy. The fund makes semi-annual income distributions, but they don't amount to much. Capital gains distributions are made once a year, in December. Not a great fund, but not bad.

STANDARD LIFE IDEAL INCOME
BALANCED FUND $$$ ↓ FI/G */NO RIF S CBAL

Manager: Standard Life Investments Inc.
MER: 2.40%   **Style:** Bottom-up Value
Suitability: Conservative income investors with a Standard Life account.

This fund has been especially designed to meet the needs of investors who require steady income along with modest growth potential and relatively low risk. In other words, it would be very well suited for a RRIF. The portfolio tends to be fairly evenly divided between stocks and bonds/cash, with no undue risk. The term to maturity of the bonds is kept relatively low to meet the needs of income-oriented investors. This segregated fund is quite new (launched in December 1998), but we like it a lot. It looks like an excellent choice for low-risk Stardard Life clients. However, you'll need $10,000 if you want to open a RRIF account with this company.

STRATEGICNOVA CANADIAN
BALANCED FUND $$$ → FI/G #/* RIF CBAL

Manager: StrategicNova Asset Allocation Team, since August 2000
MER: 2.58%   **Style:** Value
Suitability: Income-oriented investors.

This fund differs from the companion Canadian Asset Allocation Fund (which is not recommended for a RRIF) in that the management team here uses a value approach to stock selection. The Asset Allocation Fund approach is growth-oriented. That makes this fund more suitable for conservative investors. The focus is on medium to large companies that are undervalued. The fund has been an above-average performer, but what really makes it useful for a RRIF is the monthly distribution policy, which provides for steady cash flow. Payments have been running at a rate of $0.035 per unit. Formerly known as the Centrepost Balanced Fund and renamed Nova Balanced Fund. The Strategic Value Canadian Balanced Fund was the absorbed into the Nova Balanced Fund, and the new name applied.

TD BALANCED INCOME FUND $$$ ↓ FI/G NO RIF CBAL

Manager: Margot Ritchie (Jarislowky Fraser), since 1988
MER: 2.12%   **Style:** Blend
Suitability: Conservative income investors.

This fund is the survivor of the merger between the Green Line Balanced Income Fund and the Canada Trust Retirement Balanced Fund. The mandate here is to generate income through a combination of high-quality fixed-income securities, money market instruments, and stocks. In terms of portfolio risk, both the equities and fixed-income side are conservatively managed. The equity side is well diversified and maximizes its foreign content. Over time, this fund tends to trail the companion TD Balanced Growth Fund in terms of return, but it is more conservatively managed, which makes it a better choice for a RRIF. Income distributions are paid quarterly but often don't amount to much, so don't count on this one to produce a lot of cash flow. If that's okay with you, then this is a good choice.

TRIMARK INCOME GROWTH FUND $$$ → FI/G #/* RIF CBAL

Managers: Patrick Farmer, since 1997, G. Keith Graham, since 1999, Rex Chong, since 2000, and Vince Hunt, since 2001
MER: 1.67%/2.44%   **Style:** Value/Growth
Suitability: Conservative investors.

The recovery of value investing revived the fortunes of this fund in 2000–01 after several years wandering in the wilderness. The portfolio is broadly diversified, although the bond holdings can sometimes be on the low side. Stock selection tends more towards value than growth, with emphasis placed on issues that are attractively priced in relation to historical earnings and valuations. Long-term results are well above average. Risk tends to be slightly better than the norm for the Canadian Balanced category. This fund comes with two purchase options, and we strongly recommend the "SC" (front-end load) units, which have a much lower MER. That makes a big difference to your net return. See if you can get them from your broker at zero commission.

Global Balanced and Tactical Asset Allocation Funds

AGF AMERICAN TACTICAL ASSET ALLOCATION FUND $$$$ ↓ FI/G #/* £ GBAL

Manager: Barclays Global Investors, since inception (1988)
MER: 2.51%   **Style:** Quantitative Value
Suitability: Conservative investors.

The portfolio of this fund is adjusted between U.S. bonds, stocks, and short-term notes according to the dictates of a computerized asset allocation formula developed by the manager, a San Francisco-based company that runs hundreds of billions of dollars in assets worldwide. Results have been very good; the fund never had a losing calendar year all through the turbulent 1990s, and even managed to earn a small profit for investors in 2000. Over the long haul, this is an excellent holding for conservative investors who want exposure to U.S. markets. Returns have been way above average for the Global Balanced category, despite occasional short-term weakness, such as in 2001. Distributions are made only annually, so this is not an appropriate choice if steady cash flow is a need. On the other hand, this fund is a good way to hedge some of your RRIF assets against future declines in the value of the Canadian dollar. The RRIF-eligible clone of this fund, called the AGF RSP American Tactical Asset Allocation Fund, tracks the parent quite closely, although its returns are slightly lower. The parent fund is preferred if foreign-content room in your registered plan is not a concern.

AGF WORLD BALANCED FUND $$ → G/FI #/* £ GBAL

Managers: John Arnold and Rory Flynn, since June 1996
MER: 2.50%   **Style:** Top-down Country/Bottom-up Value
Suitability: Growth-oriented investors.

The managers of this fund are based in Dublin, which has become something of a mini financial capital in recent years. The fund uses a three-way asset allocation approach, taking asset class, currency mix, and geographic allocation into account. Individual stocks are selected using value criteria, which places special emphasis on companies with a low p/e ratio and above-average yield and earnings growth. Geographic exposure may be heavily weighted to one specific region at times, with Europe often a favourite. The fund's "neutral" position is 40 percent stocks,

40 percent bonds, and 20 percent cash, but the managers can be much more aggressive at times. In fact, this fund is run more like an asset allocation fund than a balanced fund, so if heavy weightings to one asset class or another are a problem for you, look elsewhere. Returns are usually above average for the Global Balanced category. Risk is about average. Cash flow is negligible, so this is not one to pick if income is a major priority. Be especially wary of the RRIF-eligible clone; it has performed much more poorly than the parent fund.

CLARINGTON GLOBAL INCOME FUND $\qquad$ NR → FI/G #/* £ GBAL

Manager: Peter Marshall (Seamark), since inception (January 2001)

MER: 2.88% $\qquad$ **Style:** Value

Suitability: Investors seeking a combination of steady income and capital gains potential.

This is one of the few global balanced funds that offers monthly distributions, which makes it a fine choice for RRIF investors who need regular cash flow. Portfolio responsibility is in the capable hands of Peter Marshall of Seamark Asset Management. Although this is a new fund (launched in early 2001), Marshall and his Seamark team have already proven their abilities by guiding older Clarington funds to excellent results. We like the prospects for this fund, and we believe it is especially well-suited for a retirement income plan because of Marshall's conservative value style, the regular distributions, and the international diversification it provides.

Canadian Bond Funds

AGF CANADIAN BOND FUND $\qquad$ $$ → FI #/* RIF CB

Managers: Clive Coombs, since January 1990, and Scott Colbourne, since December 1997

MER: 1.88% $\qquad$ **Style:** Interest Rate Anticipation

Suitability: Income investors.

This fund has been a dependable performer for many years, never sensational but with decent, steady returns. This is a conservative fund from a portfolio safety perspective, investing almost exclusively in government or government-guaranteed issues. Long-term results are about average. Distributions are paid monthly so this fund works well from a cash flow perspective. A sound choice in the AGF line-up.

BEUTEL GOODMAN INCOME FUND $\qquad$ $$$ → FI #/NO RIF CB

Manager: David Gregoris, since 1992

MER: 0.67% $\qquad$ **Style:** Term Structure Analysis

Suitability: Long-term income investors.

As far as bond funds go, this is one of the steadier performers in its peer group, with returns consistently in the top 25 percent of its class. This performance has attracted plenty of new capital into this actively managed fund. Default risk—always a concern in a bond fund—is low, as evidenced by the portfolio's composition of mainly Government of Canada bonds and high-quality corporate debt, with the latter rated at least "A" by a recognized bond credit agency. In terms of interest-rate risk, the fund is relatively defensive in its approach. Add a low MER and you have a decent fund for fixed-income RRIF investors. Distributions are paid quarterly. See the entry on the Beutel Goodman Canadian Equity Fund for purchase details.

BMO BOND FUND $$ ↓ FI NO RIF CB

Manager: Mary Jane Yule (Jones Heward), since 1996
MER: 1.59% **Style:** Term Structure Analysis
Suitability: Conservative income investors.

This fund is managed more conservatively than the average Canadian bond fund. A large percentage of the bonds are Government of Canada issues, with a secondary focus on provincials and high-quality corporate issues. Performance has been reasonably good, and risk is slightly better than average. Monthly distributions provide steady cash flow. If you want a conservative, no-nonsense, low-risk bond fund for your RRIF, you may want to look here.

CI CANADIAN BOND FUND $$$ → FI #/* RIF CB

Manager: Jeffrey Herold, since inception (1993)
MER: 1.68% **Style:** Term Structure Analysis
Suitability: Income investors.

Jeffrey Herold has made this into one of the better-performing bond funds. It has easily beaten the average for its category the majority of the time and is a top-quartile performer over its life. Holdings consist mainly of Government of Canada bonds, with the remainder in high-quality corporate issues and provincial debt. As such, default risk is low in this fund. You'll get steady income from the monthly distributions, always useful if you are drawing cash regularly from the plan. This fund is recommended as a core holding for the fixed-income section of your RRIF portfolio.

CIBC CANADIAN BOND INDEX FUND $$ ↓ FI NO RIF STB

Manager: Jacques Prevost, since July 1999
MER: 0.96% **Style:** Index
Suitability: Conservative investors.

The fund is very similar to the Canadian Short-term Bond Index Fund (below). It tries to emulate the return of the Scotia Capital Markets Universe Bond Index by investing in various securities that comprise the Index, primarily federal government bonds and high-quality corporate debt. Over the long term, we expect that to result in returns that are close to average, and a risk level that is also near the norm for the category. So far, that's exactly what the fund has delivered. Distributions are paid quarterly. This is a sound core bond fund for a RRIF, nothing flashy but very serviceable.

CIBC CANADIAN SHORT-TERM
BOND INDEX FUND $$$ ↓ FI NO RIF STB

Manager: Jacques Prevost, since July 1999
MER: 0.90%   **Style:** Index
Suitability: Low-risk income investors.

If you are very risk conscious but want higher returns than money market funds or T-bills, this fund may be the solution. The fund tries to emulate the return of the Scotia Capital Markets Short-Term Bond Index by investing in various securities that comprise the Index. This means a focus on federal bonds, followed by high-quality corporate debt. With the majority of investments in short-term bonds, this fund has minimal interest-rate risk. Returns have been consistently above the average for its peer group, the Canadian Short-Term Bond category. Risk is about average for the category but low in relation to bond funds generally. Over time, the companion CIBC Canadian Bond Index Fund should give higher returns, but this one will protect your capital more effectively in rising interest-rate environments. The cash flow is also better here as distributions are paid monthly. This is a very good choice for a low-risk RRIF.

FIDELITY CANADIAN BOND FUND $$ → FI #/* RIF CB

Manager: Jeff Moore, since October 2000
MER: 1.54%   **Style:** Credit Analysis; Yield Curve Strategies
Suitability: Core bond fund.

Canadian Jeff Moore took over this fund in October 2000. He's a graduate of the University of Waterloo and the University of Western Ontario, so he brings a home-grown touch to this portfolio. The fund offers a mix of federal, provincial, municipal, corporate, and agency bonds, and is slightly higher in risk than its benchmark index (RBC Dominion Canadian Bond Market Index). The fund's duration (a measure of risk) will typically be longer than that of the companion Canadian Short-Term Bond Fund (below), which Moore also manages, so it would be the preferred choice for risk-averse investors. This one offers greater long-term profit and income potential, however. Distributions are paid quarterly. It's not the top Canadian bond fund around, but respectable for a RRIF portfolio.

FIDELITY CANADIAN SHORT-TERM BOND FUND $$$ ↓ FI #/* RIF STB

Manager: Jeff Moore, since October 2000
MER: 1.34%   **Style:** Credit Analysis
Suitability: Risk-averse income investors.

Canadian Jeff Moore took over the direction of this fund in the fall of 2000, but the conservative, low-risk style remains the same. Unlike the companion Canadian Bond Fund (above), this fund avoids all exposure to higher-risk long bonds in order to preserve capital. This fund is geared towards those who need regular monthly income, and has a good record for payouts. That makes this fund an especially good choice for a RRIF—the combination of steady returns and low risk is perfect for that situation. Moore's strategy focuses more on fundamental research than the state of interest rates. As with the Bond Fund, bonds of cyclical companies are avoided to minimize risk. Corporate and federal bonds comprise the majority of the portfolio. The risk here is far less than in the Bond Fund. Returns are generally above the peer group, which is the Canadian Short-Term Bond category. This fund used to be known as the Fidelity Canadian Income Fund. A very good choice for your income plan.

GREAT-WEST LIFE GOVERNMENT
BOND FUND (G) $$ ↓ FI */NO RIF S STB

Manager: Terry Parsonage (GWL Investment Management)
MER: 1.83%/2.05%   **Style:** Interest Rate Anticipation
Suitability: Low-risk investors.

This fund is geared towards very conservative investors who want returns that are generally between those of a money market fund and a regular bond fund. Default and interest-rate risk are minimal, as the portfolio invests primarily in federal bonds, followed by mortgage-backed securities. The average term of the portfolio will range from two to five years, so this is a short-term bond fund that will underperform in strong markets but protect your money when bond prices fall. However, for some reason it has been placed in the broader Canadian Bond category, which means that comparative return and risk measures against the peer group are not appropriate. Treat this for what it really is, a short-term bond fund, and you'll be on target. We think the MER is too high, given the nature of this fund, but it's a decent choice for those with a Great-West Life RRIF. The DSC version has a lower MER and is the better choice.

HSBC CANADIAN BOND FUND $$$ → FI NO RIF CB

Managers: HSBC Asset Management (Canada) Ltd., since 1994
MER: 1.18%   **Style:** Credit and Term Structure Analysis
Suitability: Income investors.

This portfolio favours government bonds, mainly federal, along with some Ontario and New Brunswick issues. The fund also has about a third of its assets in high-quality corporate securities. Performance has been better than average over all time periods, and risk is about the norm for the category. Distributions are paid monthly, so you have a good income stream. A decent choice for a RRIF.

ICM BOND FUND $$$ ↓ FI NO RIF CB

Managers: Gryphon Investment Counsel and Lincluden Management Ltd., since 1990
MER: 1.30%   **Style:** Interest Rate Anticipation/Credit Analysis and Yield
Suitability: Conservative investors.

This fund has been a consistent above-average performer, even after discounting the returns to take the full management fee into account. It invests mainly in Government of Canada issues, with a few provincial and corporate bonds tossed in. The management style is conservative. Very good safety profile, as is the case with almost all ICM funds. The fund has not shown a calendar year loss since it was started. Distributions are paid quarterly. The minimum initial investment is $5,000. See the entry on the ICM Balanced Fund for purchase details.

JONES HEWARD BOND FUND $$$ ↓ FI #/* RIF CB

Manager: Jones Heward Investment Team
MER: 1.75% **Style:** Risk Management
Suitability: Conservative investors.

This is a pretty good bond fund, with above-average returns in recent years. Performance has been either first or second quartile since 1999. Government bonds represent the largest portion of the assets. The portfolio is conservative in nature and the strategy is defensive, to protect capital. That pulled down the long-term results to slightly below average, but also gives the fund an above-average safety rating. This fund is best suited for investors seeking a conservatively managed bond fund for the fixed-income side of their portfolio, and who don't mind sacrificing a bit of return for greater safety—a trade-off that may be desirable in the context of a RRIF. Distributions are paid quarterly.

LEITH WHEELER FIXED INCOME FUND $$$ ↓ FI NO RIF CB

Manager: Leith Wheeler Investment Committee, since inception (1994)
MER: 0.75% **Style:** Value
Suitability: Conservative investors.

This portfolio invests mainly in government issues, but the portion of corporate bonds in the portfolio has been steadily increased in an effort to boost returns. The fund is an above-average performer over all time periods, due in part to its low MER. Until 1999, this fund had a great safety record—it was one of the few bond funds we'd encountered that had never been in the red over any calendar year since its inception. But that changed in a falling bond market as the fund slipped about 2 percent. It has bounced back nicely since, however, and has again become one of the top performers in its category. Distributions are paid quarterly. The big stumbling block for many people is the high entry charge; you need at least $50,000 to buy in. Also, the fund is not available in all provinces. See the entry on the Leith Wheeler Canadian Equity Fund for more purchase details.

MAWER CANADIAN BOND FUND $$$ → FI NO RIF CB

Manager: Gary Feltham, since February 1993
MER: 1.13% **Style:** Enhanced Core
Suitability: Income investors.

This is one of those steady performers that never gets much attention but turns in above-average results year after year. In fact, it's been a second-quartile performer every single year since 1994. You can't ask for greater reliability than that. Government of Canada bonds make up about half the portfolio, with corporate issues accounting for about a third. The rest comprises provincials and municipals. The manager closely tracks the Scotia Capital Markets Universe Bond Index in duration terms, within a 0.5 percent range on either side. Returns are above average for all time periods. Safety rating is good. Distributions are paid monthly so cash flow is first rate. Put it all together and you have a very tidy RRIF package. See the entry on the Mawer Canadian Balanced Retirement Savings Fund for purchase details.

MAWER CANADIAN INCOME FUND $$$ ↓ FI NO RIF STB

Manager: Gary Feltham, since February 1993
MER: 1.37% **Style:** Bottom-up Value
Suitability: Very conservative investors.

This fund was included in the balanced category until 1999, but it is now officially classified as a Canadian short-term bond fund. This category switch explains why the fund does not show a long-term historic rate of return. Actually, the fund has been an above-average performer in its new category since the change. It's now a pure bond fund that focuses on the short to medium term. No securities are held with maturities beyond 10 years. This greatly reduces the risk inherent in the portfolio, which had been quite high in its previous incarnation because of the inclusion of royalty trusts. The portfolio tilts towards government bonds but there is a large percentage in corporate issues to increase overall yield. You can arrange for regular distributions from this fund on a monthly or quarterly basis, which is useful for retirees. The low risk and good cash flow make this a fine holding for a RRIF. The only thing that troubles us is the fact that this fund has a higher MER than the companion Canadian Bond Fund for reasons that are not obvious. Still, a good choice.

MCLEAN BUDDEN FIXED INCOME FUND $$$ → FI NO RIF CB

Manager: Team
MER: 0.70% **Style:** Multiple
Suitability: Conservative investors.

This small fund specializes in high-quality government and corporate bonds. It generally produces very good results and has never been below second quartile since 1994. Returns over all time periods are well above average for the Canadian Bond category. The low MER is a big help here. Distributions are paid quarterly. Another good choice in this sound family. See the entry on McLean Budden Canadian Equity Growth Fund for purchase details.

OPTIMA STRATEGY CANADIAN
FIXED INCOME POOL $$$ → FI #/* RIF CB

Manager: Nestor Theodorou, since 1994

MER: 2.62%   **Style:** Yield Curve Analysis

Suitability: Clients of Assante Asset Management.

This fund invests mainly in Government of Canada bonds with varying maturities, as well as some provincial issues and a few corporate bonds. Returns have been consistently above average over all time periods. However, the spread between the average returns for the Canadian Bond category and the historic results of this fund are not as great as they look in the media because the Optima funds do not deduct fees and expenses before publishing their results. To get an accurate assessment of how this fund is doing in relation to others, insist on receiving a report that shows historic returns with all fees and expenses deducted. That said, if you have a big RRIF with Assante Asset Management, this fund should be part of it. See the entry on the Optima Strategy Canadian Equity Value Pool for purchase details.

OPTIMA STRATEGY SHORT-TERM INCOME POOL $$$ ↓ FI #/* RIF STB

Manager: Nestor Theodorou, since 1994

MER: 1.97%   **Style:** Yield Curve Analysis

Suitability: Conservative investors.

This fund is designed for investors who want less risk in their bond holdings. The portfolio holds government and corporate issues with maturity dates of no more than five years. In fact, the average duration of the portfolio (a measure of risk) has been much less than that for some time. This type of fund will typically underperform when bond markets are strong, but will protect your asset base when bonds hit the skids. In fact, the risk level here is very low even for a short-term bond fund. A high MER cuts into returns, but the average annual compound rate of return is still above average (but see our comments on this in the above entry). This is a good choice if capital preservation with modest returns is your goal.

PERIGEE ACTIVE BOND FUND $$$ ↑ FI NO RIF CB

Manager: David L.H. Yu, since 1996

MER: 0.75%   **Style:** Interest Rate Anticipation

Suitability: Investors seeking above-average returns who are willing to accept more risk.

For this fund to perform well, the managers have to guess right on the future course of interest rates. The emphasis of the portfolio is constantly shifting, depending on whether they expect rates to rise or fall. So far, they've been pretty good in their forecasts. Bonds chosen for the portfolio must have a safety rating of "BBB" or higher. One advantage of this fund is its attractive MER, which becomes especially important during times of low interest rates. Returns are superior and this fund generally outperforms the companion Perigee Index Plus Bond Fund. Distributions are made monthly, so cash flow is good. However, the risk will be slightly higher than in the Index Plus Bond Fund, an important consideration in a RRIF.

PERIGEE INDEX PLUS BOND FUND $$$ → FI NO RIF CB

Manager: David L.H. Yu, since 1996
MER: 0.75%   **Style:** Index
Suitability: Long-term conservative investors.

The goal of this fund is to track the Scotia Capital Markets Universe Bond Index, with slight variations to provide added value. Most of the bonds in the portfolio are government issues, with some corporate issues added for extra return potential. Performance has been very good over all time periods. The low MER is a big help in producing the good numbers. Risk is about average and somewhat lower than in the companion Active Bond Fund. Cash distributions are paid monthly. Overall, this fund is an excellent low-cost alternative for your RRIF.

PHILLIPS, HAGER & NORTH BOND FUND $$$$ → FI NO RIF CB

Manager: Team, headed by Scott Lamont
MER: 0.58%   **Style:** Interest Rate Anticipation plus Active Trading
Suitability: Conservative investors.

This is one of the better bond funds around. Results are usually well above average, even in tough bond markets. Over a decade, this fund ranks among the top 10 percent of bond funds in Canada. The portfolio is weighted to government securities, with some corporate issues, foreign bonds, and mortgages also in the mix. An extra benefit is the very low management expense ratio, which makes this one of the best values you'll find in bond funds from that point of view. The fund tracks the Scotia Capital Markets Universe Bond Index, with some leeway in terms of the managers' duration call. That means they may increase or decrease the risk level slightly from that of the Index, depending on their views of where the bond market is going. They also do some active trading. The risk rating is about average for the category. Distributions are paid quarterly and usually run about $0.15 a unit. If you're looking for a long-term buy-and-hold bond fund, they don't come much better than this one. However, the high entry price may be a barrier; see the entry on the PH&N Canadian Equity Fund for details.

PHILLIPS, HAGER & NORTH SHORT-TERM
BOND AND MORTGAGE FUND $$$$ ↓ FI NO RIF STB

Manager: Team, headed by Scott Lamont
MER: 0.62%   **Style:** Defensive
Suitability: Low-risk investors.

This is a halfway house between the company's successful Bond Fund and its money market funds. The idea is to generate a better return than you'll get from money funds, but with less risk than a conventional bond fund would carry. To achieve that, the fund invests in bonds that mature within five years as well as conventional mortgages. This means the safety record is very good in relation to an ordinary bond fund, as you would expect; however, it is only about average for the Short-Term Bond category. Although the fund usually ranks as a top-quartile performer in its category, returns will normally be lower than you might expect from the Bond Fund. Distributions are paid quarterly. If you're looking for a defensive fund with decent returns, this one will work well. A useful holding for a conservatively managed RRIF, as long as you don't mind the relatively low returns.

SCEPTRE BOND FUND $$$ → FI NO RIF CB

Manager: Richard L. Knowles, since March 2000
MER: 1.03%   **Style:** Value, Modest Timing
Suitability: Conservative investors.

The portfolio of this fund is divided into three distinct components. Federal and provincial government securities account for slightly more than half the assets, providing security and liquidity. Corporate bonds make up about 40 percent of the total, generating higher yields. Finally, foreign-currency bonds may be used when appropriate. The net result is a fund that consistently turns in above-average results. In fact, it has been a first- or second-quartile performer every year except one since 1994. At a time when Sceptre has very few funds to feel good about, this one stands out as a notable exception. The main disadvantage for RRIF investors seeking regular cash flow is that distributions are made only semi-annually, in June and December. The minimum initial investment is $5,000. You can buy units directly from the management company if you live in B.C., Manitoba, Ontario, New Brunswick, or Saskatchewan: call 416-360-4826 or 604-899-6002 or 1-800-265-1888 for details. If you buy from Sceptre there are no sales commissions. Elsewhere, you may be able to acquire units through a broker but a fee may be levied.

SCOTIA CANADIAN INCOME FUND $$$ → FI NO RIF CB

Manager: Romas Budd
MER: 1.16%   **Style:** Interest Rate Anticipation
Suitability: Moderate-risk income investors.

This is a strong entry from Scotia Securities. It's conservatively managed but at the same time produces above-average returns, aided by a low MER. Interest rate anticipation (a style in which the manager projects rate movements and adjusts the holdings accordingly) directs its strategy. The fund invests primarily in Government of Canada bonds, with provincial and corporate bonds rounding out the remainder. All bonds must be rated "A" or higher by a major Canadian rating agency, thus there's little default risk here. Interest-rate risk is minimized through a conservative holding of long bonds. Returns are usually better than average. Risk is about normal for the category. Distributions are paid monthly, so you can rely on this fund for steady income. All in all, a good bond fund for your plan.

SCOTIA CANADIAN SHORT-TERM INCOME FUND $$ ↓ FI NO RIF STB

Managers: Bill Girard and Nicholas van Sluytman

MER: 1.32%   **Style:** Credit Analysis

Suitability: Low-risk income investors.

As far as risk and return go, this fund lies on the spectrum between the companion Money Market Fund on the low end and the Canadian Income Fund higher up. This fund invests primarily in high-quality corporate bonds, followed by government bonds. It has a longer time horizon than a money market fund but a shorter one than most bond funds, thus reducing its volatility during times of sharp interest-rate movements. During a period of declining interest rates, a fund like this will underperform most conventional bond funds. But when rates are rising, it will do much better and protect your capital. Returns have been better than average for the Canadian Short-Term Bond category. The risk level is low compared to a regular bond fund, such as the companion Canadian Income Fund, but is only about average in relation to the peer group. Distributions are paid monthly. Recommended as a haven for your bond content when rates rise or if you're an ultra-cautious investor. Don't expect anything exciting in the way of returns, but your trade-off is safety and steady income.

SPECTRUM MID-TERM BOND FUND $$ → FI #/* RIF CB

Managers: Peter Kotsopoulos, since January 1995, Curt Conover, since January 1996, and Tony Magri, since February 2001 (McLean Budden)

MER: 1.78%   **Style:** Duration Management

Suitability: Middle-of-the-road income investors.

This fund focuses on mid-term bond issues, which means bonds maturing in five to ten years. That places it squarely in the middle of the three funds in the Spectrum bond fund grouping, both in terms of risk and potential return. So it's for investors who want some fixed-income exposure without undue risk. That would make it most suitable for use in a RRIF, and the monthly distributions provide good cash flow. The portfolio can hold all types of bonds but the emphasis is on government issues. Formerly known as the Spectrum Interest Fund.

SPECTRUM SHORT-TERM BOND FUND $$ ↓ FI #/* RIF STB

Managers: Peter Kotsopoulos, since January 1995, Curt Conover, since January 1996, and Tony Magri, since February 2001 (McLean Budden)

MER: 1.58%   **Style:** Duration Management

Suitability: Low-risk income investors.

This is the most defensive of the three Spectrum Canadian bond offerings and, therefore, the fund that combines the lowest risk with the lowest potential returns. It was previously the United Canadian Mortgage Fund. The mandate was amended in August 1996 to allow investment in bonds and other debt securities that mature in five years or less, as well as in conventional first mortgages. It's only one step removed from a money market fund, but returns are higher than you'll normally get from a money fund. Risk and return are about average for the Canadian Short-Term Bond category. Distributions are paid monthly.

STANDARD LIFE BOND FUND $$ → FI #/* RIF CB

Manager: Standard Life Investments Inc.
MER: 1.61%   **Style:** Interest Rate Anticipation
Suitability: Conservative investors.

This is a decent choice from the underrated Standard Life group. This fund invests almost entirely in government issues. The bulk of the portfolio is in federal government bonds, but there are also some top-rated provincial securities (Alberta, Ontario) and a few corporates. So the quality of the assets is excellent. Returns have been about average for the Canadian Bond category over longer time periods. The risk level is about average for a bond fund. Distributions are made quarterly.

TALVEST INCOME FUND $$$ ↓ FI #/* RIF STB

Manager: Jeff Waldman, since November 1998
MER: 1.69%   **Style:** Top-down/Index
Suitability: Income investors.

Jeff Waldman took over this fund in 1998, replacing long-time manager John Braive. He has done a decent job, producing slightly above-average returns for the Canadian Short-Term Bond category. The fund is geared towards investors who want high monthly income and capital preservation. The bond portfolio is conservatively managed with minimal interest-rate risk and is composed mainly of corporate bonds, followed by mortgage-backed securities and federal bonds. Returns tend to be higher than a money market fund but lower than a regular bond fund because of the short duration of the portfolio. A good choice if reducing risk is an objective in your RRIF, but you will sacrifice some return when bond markets are strong. Distributions are paid monthly, so this fund is a good source of regular income.

TD CANADIAN BOND FUND $$$ → FI NO RIF CB

Manager: Satish Rai, since inception (1988)
MER: 1.00%   **Style:** Credit and Term Structure Analysis
Suitability: Conservative income investors.

This fund is the product of the merger between the Green Line Canadian Bond and the Canada Trust Bond Funds. This is a very steady bond fund and, since 1994, has beaten both the average of its peer group and the Scotia Capital Markets Universe Bond Index the majority of the time. To achieve this, the fund manager has overweighted the portfolio towards high-quality corporate bonds, with the remainder in various government bonds. The fund is conservatively managed as far as interest-rate risk goes. Risk is slightly better than average for the Canadian Bond category. Distributions are paid monthly. Put all that together with a low MER and no sales commissions, and you have a very good RRIF choice.

TD CANADIAN BOND INDEX FUND $$$ → FI NO RIF CB

Managers: Lori MacKay and Kevin LeBlanc, since October 2000
MER: 0.89%   **Style:** Index
Suitability: Conservative income investors.

TD offers a wide range of bond funds, and in some cases the distinctions are very small. This one uses the Scotia Capital Markets Universe Bond Index as its benchmark. The portfolio is a mix of government and corporate issues. The fund doesn't quite match the Index's returns, but it generally outperforms the category average. Distributions are paid monthly, so this fund will provide steady cash flow for your RRIF. Investing tip: Buy the "e" units of this fund over the Internet and you'll benefit from a lower MER (0.47 percent versus 0.89 percent for the regular units). That will translate into a little more money in your pocket.

TD CANADIAN GOVERNMENT BOND INDEX FUND $$$ → FI NO RIF CB

Managers: Lori MacKay, since 1996, and Kevin LeBlanc, since 1993
MER: 0.86%   **Style:** Index
Suitability: Conservative investors.

This fund is structured to track the Canadian government bond portion of the Scotia Capital Markets Universe Bond Index and was the first such bond index fund marketed in Canada. Unlike the companion Canadian Bond Fund, this fund is predominantly composed of federal bonds, followed by a mix of provincial and municipal bonds. As a result of this more conservative approach, the fund tends to have lower returns on average than the companion Canadian Bond Fund. But having said that, this index fund beats the return of the average Canadian bond fund more times than not. Distributions are made only quarterly, so cash flow is not as good as that offered by the Canadian Bond Fund. Note that "e" units are also available here (see above entry).

TD MONTHLY INCOME FUND $$$ ↓ FI NO RIF STB

Manager: Doug Warwick, since 1998
MER: 1.27%   **Style:** Credit Analysis
Suitability: Low-risk income investors.

This fund's objective is to earn consistent monthly income, and it does so with a relatively low-risk portfolio of short-term bonds and high-grade income trusts like Superior Propane. Its performance record is strong for its type, although there's a bit more risk here than in the average short-term bond fund. Distributions are paid monthly, as you would assume from the name. A good choice for a RRIF if you don't mind sacrificing some return potential for a higher measure of safety than you'd find in a regular bond fund.

TD REAL RETURN BOND FUND $$$ → FI NO RIF CB

Manager: Satish Rai, since 1994
MER: 1.64% **Style:** Duration Matching
Suitability: Investors seeking inflation protection.

With inflation nowhere to be seen over most of the 1990s, it's not surprising that this inflation-hedged bond fund wasn't very popular. But when inflation picks up a bit, as it did in 2000, this fund looks much more attractive, and in fact was the top performer in its category for a while. The fund's mandate is to generate yields based on the "real interest rate," which is the nominal rate plus inflation. Default risk is minimal due to the fund's 100 percent investment in Government of Canada guaranteed real return bonds (RRBs). Interest payments on these bonds are adjusted according to movements in the consumer price index. As well, the value of the bond at maturity is adjusted to protect investors from a loss of buying power due to inflation. These provisions make RRBs one of the best ways to invest in fixed-income securities when interest rates are on the rise. Quarterly cash distributions are made. Consider using this fund in special economic situations when it is likely to perform to best advantage.

TRIMARK CANADIAN BOND FUND $$$ ↓ FI #/* RIF CB

Managers: Patrick Farmer, since inception (1994), Rex Chong, since 2000, Vince Hunt, since 2001
MER: 1.31% **Style:** Credit Analysis/Interest Rate Anticipation
Suitability: Conservative income investors.

This is a very respectable fixed-income entry from the Trimark family, which is now part of AIM Funds. The managers also run the companion Advantage Bond Fund (see the entry under Canadian High-Yield Bond Funds) but this fund's mandate doesn't include the high-yield component that drives its stablemate and makes it somewhat more risky. The safety record here is very good and the portfolio mix suggests it should stay that way. Returns are usually above average for the Canadian Bond category. The portfolio is a mixed bag of federal and provincial bonds, corporate issues, mortgage-backed securities, asset-backed securities, and even a few preferred shares. Distributions are made monthly, so the income stream is good. A fine choice for any RRIF.

TRIMARK GOVERNMENT INCOME FUND $$$ ↓ FI #/* RIF STB

Managers: Patrick Farmer, since inception (1993), Rex Chong, since 2000, Vince Hunt, since 2001
MER: 1.31% **Style:** Value/Interest Rate Anticipation
Suitability: Low-risk income investors.

This is a defensive bond fund. The securities are all government or government-guaranteed issues, and all have relatively short maturities, not exceeding five years. Some mortgage-backed securities are included in the mix. A portfolio such as this will produce below-average returns in strong markets, but will preserve capital when bond markets weaken. In the past, this fund suffered by being compared to the total bond fund universe. Now it has been placed in the Short-Term Bond category, where it fits more comfortably and shows rates of return that are average to slightly above. Distributions are paid monthly. This one is for RRIF investors who don't want to take on as much risk as you'd find in the companion Canadian Bond Fund or Advantage Bond Fund.

Canadian High-Yield Bond Funds

GGOF GUARDIAN CANADIAN
HIGH-YIELD BOND FUND $$$ ↓ FI #/* RIF HYB

Manager: Stephen D. Kearns, since inception (January 1999)
MER: 2.21%   **Style:** Credit Analysis
Suitability: Income investors willing to accept higher risk.

This is a junk-bond fund, to put it crudely. But, so far in its young life, it has been a very impressive one, with well-above-average returns. However, that return is somewhat misleading because this is not a pure bond fund. Some of the assets are invested in royalty trusts, such as PrimeWest and Superior Propane, and real estate investment trusts, such as Royal Host. There are also some preferred shares in the mix. So, although this is technically classified as a high-yield bond fund, it is more akin to a high-yield balanced fund in its composition. However, the risk is below average for the High-Yield Bond category, which is important for a RRIF portfolio. Distributions are paid monthly and have been running at a rate of $0.04 a unit, so there is good cash flow here.

TRIMARK ADVANTAGE BOND FUND $$$ ↓ FI #/* RIF HYB

Manager: Patrick Farmer, since inception (1994), Rex Chong, since 2000, Vince Hunt, since 2001
MER: 1.30%   **Style:** Credit Analysis
Suitability: More aggressive bond investors.

This is a somewhat unusual bond fund in terms of its portfolio structure. The managers hold a core of federal government bonds for stability and then blend in high-yield issues (about 70 percent of the portfolio) to boost returns. So the fund is included in the High-Yield Bond category, although it is not a pure junk-bond portfolio. Results have been well above average when compared to the peer group but lower than from a regular bond fund. Offsetting that are the higher monthly distributions, which at times can be as much as one-third more than you'll receive from the Trimark Canadian Bond Fund. That is obviously an important consideration in a RRIF context. Given the fact that corporate bonds make up most of the portfolio, you'd expect this fund to have a higher-than-normal risk level, but in fact it has never yet suffered a loss over a given calendar year. The risk level shown here is low, but keep in mind that this is in relation to other funds of the same type. Compared to a standard bond fund, the potential for an above-average loss at some point is always present. So you have to make a decision here: Are you prepared to take on a higher degree of risk in return for more cash flow? It's not an easy call, but if you're going to do it, this is certainly a good fund to choose.

Foreign Bond Funds

BMO U.S. DOLLAR BOND FUND $$$ ↓ FI NO £ FB

Manager: Maureen Syagera (Harris Investment Management), since inception (1998)
MER: 1.59%   **Style:** Term Structure Analysis
Suitability: Conservative income investors seeking currency diversification.

This fund's objective is to provide current income in U.S. dollars while preserving capital. The portfolio invests in U.S. Treasury bonds, Fannie Maes (mortgages), corporate bonds, etc. Although the fund has been in existence only since 1998, returns so far have been well above average for the Foreign Bond category while risk is very low. The fund makes monthly distributions, so you have excellent U.S.-dollar cash flow here. This is one to look at if you want to hold U.S. currency securities in your RRIF, although it will eat up foreign-content room.

CI GLOBAL BOND RSP FUND $$$ ↓ FI #/* RIF FB

Managers: Kent Osband and William Sterling, since July 2000
MER: 2.47%   **Style:** Term Structure Analysis
Suitability: Conservative investors.

This is a foreign bond fund that is 100 percent RRIF-eligible. This is achieved by using bond futures contracts of different countries. The portfolio focuses primarily on developed countries but may hold some emerging market securities for added growth. The fund holds its primary assets in Canadian dollars, avoiding any significant currency risk, but of course this also means that you don't get a lot of currency diversification either. If that's your objective in seeking a foreign bond fund for your RRIF, look elsewhere. Returns have been consistently above average within its peer group, while risk is on the low side. One significant disadvantage if steady income is important is the fact that distributions are made only once a year.

GREAT-WEST LIFE GLOBAL INCOME FUND (A) $$$ → FI */NO RIF S FB

Managers: Clive Coombs and Scott Colborne (AGF)
MER: 2.43%/2.65%   **Style:** Interest Rate Anticipation
Suitability: Great-West Life clients seeking foreign currency exposure.

This foreign bond fund offers full RRIF eligibility, so it won't eat up your foreign-content room. The fund invests mainly in foreign-currency denominated bonds that are issued or guaranteed by the Government of Canada, provincial governments, or corporations. The key risk here is foreign currencies and their movements against the Canadian dollar. At least half of the issues in the fund will have a credit rating of "AA" or higher. Returns have been good for the Foreign Bond category, and risk is about average. You won't get rich here, but if you want to hold some foreign currency in your registered plan it's an acceptable choice.

PERIGEE GLOBAL BOND FUND $$$ → FI NO RIF FB

Manager: David L.H. Yu, since 1996
MER: 1.41%   **Style:** Index
Suitability: Investors seeking income and foreign currency diversification.

On the whole, foreign bond funds have been weak performers over the years. The main attraction of these funds is that they provide fixed-income currency diversification in a portfolio. This fund does well on that score, and also has produced better-than-average gains over all time frames. As a bonus, it is RRIF-eligible, meaning that you will not impinge on foreign-content restrictions when purchasing units. Foreign bond funds generate the best results when the Canadian dollar is falling and interest rates are declining. But even if those conditions don't currently exist, this can be a useful fund if you like the idea of having some exposure to foreign currencies in your RRIF, perhaps because you will need U.S. dollars. Distributions are made monthly, so cash flow is good. See the entry on the Perigee Accufund for investing tips.

SCOTIA CANAM U.S. $ INCOME FUND $$$ → FI NO RIF FB

Manager: Bill Girard
MER: 1.89%   **Style:** Yield Curve, Credit Analysis
Suitability: RRIF investors seeking U.S. currency exposure and steady income.

You may be investing in so-called Yankee Bonds and not even be aware of it. Quite simply, these are just foreign companies or governments (Canadian in our case) that issue debt denominated in U.S. dollars and sold in the U.S. In this way, this Yankee bond fund offers investors full U.S.-dollar exposure while being fully eligible for registered plans. The fund is a bet on the direction of the U.S. versus the Canadian dollar. When the Canadian dollar weakens, the fund gains, and vice versa. The risk comes from holding U.S.-denominated securities. The fund invests mainly in federal and corporate bonds and has minimal interest-rate risk. Performance over its life has been solid, with above-average returns. Risk rating is average. Monthly distributions provide excellent cash flow. Investors who want more U.S.-dollar exposure in their retirement plan without having to sacrifice foreign-content room may want to look at this no-load fund.

Canadian Mortgage Funds

BMO MORTGAGE FUND $$ → FI NO RIF M

Manager: Mary Jane Yule (Jones Heward), since 1996
MER: 1.50%   **Style:** Interest Rate Anticipation
Suitability: Conservative income investors.

For pure mortgage investment, this has long been a decent performer within its group. Since inception in 1974, this fund has had only one losing calendar year, in 1994, when it was down 0.5 percent. A major plus is its MER, which is about 25 basis points lower than the average for its group. The safety profile of this fund over the longer term is somewhat erratic, however, producing an overall rating of average within the Canadian Mortgage category. However, default risk is virtually non-existent because the Bank of Montreal has undertaken to repurchase any defaulting mortgages from the fund, at no penalty to unit holders. Returns are average compared to other mortgage funds of this type. Distributions are paid monthly. Conservative investors may like this fund. It's a decent choice for a RRIF because of the reasonable risk and the monthly cash flow.

CIBC MORTGAGE FUND $$ → FI NO RIF M

Manager: John W Braive, since December 1999
MER: 1.81%   **Style:** Credit Analysis
Suitability: Conservative income investors.

This fund has a respectable record despite the fact that it has the highest MER of any fund of its type offered by the five major banks. The portfolio is made up almost entirely of high-quality NHA-insured mortgages. The fund will suit ultra-conservative RRIF investors who want higher returns than those of money market funds and who need steady income–distributions are made monthly. Performance and risk are about average for the category.

DESJARDINS MORTGAGE FUND $$ ↓ FI NO RIF M

Manager: Elantis Management Team
MER: 1.83%   **Style:** Term Structure Analysis
Suitability: Conservative income investors.

This is steady mortgage fund that produces average returns at slightly below-average risk. Although residential mortgages make up the bulk of the portfolio, a portion of the fund is invested in bonds. The big attraction here is a great safety record: This fund has never recorded a losing 12-month period in its history, and that goes all the way back to 1965. That and the monthly distributions make it an excellent core holding for a conservatively managed RRIF.

HSBC MORTGAGE FUND $$ ↓ FI NO RIF M

Managers: HSBC Asset Management (Canada) Ltd., since 1992
MER: 1.56%   **Style:** Credit Analysis
Suitability: Conservative income investors.

This fund offers relatively low risk and decent returns for this low-paying category. There's nothing particularly exciting about it, but it is a solid and serviceable choice for a RRIF if you have an HSBC account. Distributions are paid monthly. This is a useful fund as long as you don't expect big profits from it.

IRIS MORTGAGE FUND $$ → FI NO RIF M

Manager: Gilles Shouinard (BLC-Edmond de Rothschild), since September 2000
MER: 1.94%   **Style:** N/A
Suitability: Conservative income investors.

Mortgage funds haven't been exciting places to be in recent years, but they are usually solid and dependable. This one holds a fairly high percentage of bonds in its portfolio as well as first mortgages, so it is not a pure mortgage fund. However, it is a respectable choice in its category and would fit comfortably into a conservatively managed RRIF. Distributions are paid monthly. The IRIS funds are available through Laurentian Bank of Canada.

NATIONAL BANK MORTGAGE FUND $$ → FI NO RIF M

Manager: Gilles Tremblay, since inception (1991)
MER: 1.68%   **Style:** Term Structure Analysis
Suitability: Conservative income investors.

This fund is a decent choice in the Mortgage category. Recent returns have shown improvement and longer-term results are about average. Plus, the safety record is unblemished. This fund has never gone through a 12-month period with a loss, although shorter-term volatility is higher than normal for a mortgage fund. This fund even managed to stay in the black in 1994, when many mortgage funds recorded small losses. A worthwhile option if you're looking for a mortgage fund, but don't expect it to make you rich, especially in times of low interest rates. Distributions are made monthly.

SCOTIA MORTGAGE INCOME FUND $$ ↓ FI NO RIF M

Managers: Nicholas Van Sluytman and Bruce Grantier
MER: 1.56%   **Style:** Credit Analysis
Suitability: Conservative income investors.

This fund was formed from the merger of the National Trust Mortgage Fund and the Scotia Excelsior Mortgage Fund. It invests primarily in residential first mortgages, with all the mortgages in the portfolio being guaranteed by the bank. Prior to the merger, the returns were about average for both funds, so it's not surprising to see continued average returns for the new fund. All in all, this is a low-risk choice for fixed-income investors. Distributions are paid monthly.

Canadian Money Market Funds

ALTAMIRA SHORT TERM CANADIAN
INCOME FUND $$$$ ↓ C NO RIF CMM

Manager: Edward Jong, since 1997
MER: 0.60%   **Style:** Index
Suitability: Low-risk income investors.

This is what RRIF investors like to find—a number one performer in its first three years, with rock-bottom volatility, low MER, and no fees. If there's a downside, it's the minimum deposit to get into this fund: $5,000. The fund invests primarily in Treasury bills and other short-term debt instruments issued or guaranteed by the Canadian federal or provincial governments, the U.S. government, Canadian chartered banks, or Canadian corporations. Short term is just what it means. The portfolio will maintain an average term to maturity of less than one year. Edward Jong manages the fund actively, trying (and apparently succeeding) to anticipate changes in short-term interest rates. The manager can go up to 30 percent in U.S.-dollar securities while maintaining full RRIF eligibility. This is a first-rate money fund and deserves its $$$$ rating.

ALTAMIRA T-BILL FUND $$$ ↓ C NO RIF CMM

Manager: Edward Jong, since 1998
MER: 0.39%   **Style:** Index
Suitability: Low-risk income investors.

Manager Edward Jong seems to have a touch for anticipating short-term interest-rate movements. This T-bill fund, which invests in Canadian Treasury bills and other short-term federal and provincial debt instruments, has been a consistent top performer. However, it doesn't do quite as well as the companion Short Term Canadian Income Fund, hence the difference in the rating. This is Altamira's most conservative fund. The portfolio generally has an average term to maturity of between 90 and 180 days. The attractive results are matched by low volatility, no fees, and a very nice MER.

BEUTEL GOODMAN MONEY MARKET FUND $$$$ ↓ C #/NO RIF CMM

Manager: Team
MER: 0.61%   **Style:** N/A
Suitability: Low-risk income investors.

Since inception, this fine money market fund is batting 1000–beating the average in every year since 1991. This consistent top-quartile performer is conservatively managed, mixing government T-bills with higher-yielding short-term corporate debt, all with a maturity of under one year. The volatility is below average as well. A recommended fund for your temporary cash as well as your RRIF. One of our favourite money market funds. See the entry on the Beutel Goodman Canadian Equity Fund for purchase details.

CI MONEY MARKET FUND $$$ → C #/* RIF CMM

Manager: Wally Kusters, since September 1999
MER: 0.85%   **Style:** Value
Suitability: Low-risk income investors.

This is a strong performer in the Money Market category. With a significant bias towards short-term corporate debt, this fund has continued to shine among its peers by beating the average in most years. The main risk is derived from the fact that this fund has an unusually high percentage of its assets in corporate debt as compared to other Canadian money market funds. We recommend this fund as a temporary haven for your excess cash. Tip: Don't buy this or any other money market fund on a back-end load basis. Try to get the front-end load waived as well.

CLARINGTON MONEY MARKET FUND $$ ↓ C #/* RIF CMM

Manager: Peter Marshall (Seamark), since inception (1996)
MER: 0.80%   **Style:** Credit Analysis
Suitability: Low-risk income investors.

This fund is invested in a range of securities, including Canada T-bills, provincial and municipal notes, bankers' acceptances, etc. Returns are about average; risk is better than average. Monthly distributions.

GGOF GUARDIAN CANADIAN
MONEY MARKET FUND $$$ → C #/* RIF CMM

Manager: Stephen D. Kearns, since 1998
MER: 0.86% (Classic)   **Style:** N/A
Suitability: Low-risk income investors.

This fund invests entirely in short-term, high-grade corporate notes. That should produce above-average returns for this category, and indeed that's been the case for the Classic units, over all time periods. But that's because they have a much lower MER (0.86 percent) than the Mutual Fund units (1.55 percent), which are optional front- or back-end load. The latter produce sub-par results because of their high management fee. So consider the $$$ rating as applicable to the Classic units only. They are front-end loaded, so we don't recommend this purchase unless you can get them with zero commission. Don't buy this fund on a back-end load basis, whatever you do! Previously called Guardian Short-Term Money Fund.

HSBC CANADIAN MONEY MARKET FUND $$$ ↓ C NO RIF CMM

Managers: HSBC Asset Management (Canada) Ltd., since 1988
MER: 0.96% **Style:** N/A
Suitability: Low-risk income investors.

Nothing fancy here, just a sound money market fund that is a good choice for HSBC clients. Returns have been slightly above average for the money market category, while the safety rating is good. Monthly distributions.

ICM SHORT-TERM INVESTMENT FUND $$ ↓ C NO RIF CMM

Managers: Gryphon Investment Counsel and Lincluden Management, since inception (1992)
MER: 0.75% **Style:** Multi-style
Suitability: Low-risk income investors.

Pick up the newspaper and check the monthly mutual fund performance numbers. This fund will stand out in the Money Market category. Its average annual return is either right at the top of the list or close to it. But, like its sister ICM funds, it quotes returns before deducting the management fees. For example, if the paper says you earned an average of 4 percent annually in this fund, knock off three-quarters of a percentage point if you're a retail investor (institutions and group RRSPs get a reduction), and you're down to 3.25 percent. Take that into account before you invest. That doesn't mean this is a bad fund—it's not. It just means you have to know how to interpret all the numbers. Distributions are monthly.

JONES HEWARD MONEY MARKET FUND $$$ → C # RIF CMM

Manager: Dorothy Biggs, since 1994
MER: 0.54% **Style:** N/A
Suitability: Low-risk income investors.

The 1998 cut in the MER of this fund from 1 percent to 0.5 percent provided a nice boost to returns. Since then, the fund has been returning almost half a percentage point more on an annualized basis than the average Canadian money fund. Only a few funds of this type offer as low an MER, and most of them require very high minimum investments. You can get into this one for as little as $1,000. The fund is sold only on a front-end load basis, with a maximum commission of 2 percent. If you can get that waived, you've got a real bargain here. The portfolio is a mix of government and corporate notes. Distributions are made monthly.

LEITH WHEELER MONEY MARKET FUND $$$ ↓ C NO RIF CMM

Manager: Leith Wheeler Investment Committee, since inception (1994)
MER: 0.60%   **Style:** Value
Suitability: Low-risk income investors.

This fund is consistently among the better performers in the Canadian Money Market category, helped by its low MER of 0.6 percent. It invests primarily in high-grade corporate notes, with slightly less than a third of the portfolio in T-bills. See investment purchase details in the entry on the Leith Wheeler Canadian Equity Fund.

MACKENZIE CASH MANAGEMENT FUND $$$$ ↓ C # RIF CMM

Manager: Mackenzie Team, since 1986
MER: 0.54%   **Style:** N/A
Suitability: Low-risk income investors.

This is one of the better money market funds in the country. It combines above-average returns with a high degree of safety (the entire portfolio is normally invested in Government of Canada T-bills). Returns are well above average, thanks in part to a very low management expense ratio. Try to get it without paying any load fee (maximum is 2 percent). The name has been changed from Industrial Cash Management Fund and some of the terms are different, so check it out.

MAWER CANADIAN MONEY MARKET FUND $$$ → C NO RIF CMM

Manager: Bill MacLachlan, since September 1993
MER: 0.87%   **Style:** N/A
Suitability: Low-risk income investors.

This fund invests mainly in corporate notes, with a few government T-bills tossed in. Returns are consistently above average, thanks in part to the low management fee.

MCLEAN BUDDEN MONEY MARKET FUND $$$$ → C NO RIF CMM

Manager: Team
MER: 0.60%   **Style:** Maximizing Risk-Adjusted Returns
Suitability: Low-risk income investors.

This fund invests in a mix of Canadian T-bills, banker's acceptances, and corporate short-term notes. The team seeks to add value in several ways, including credit quality management aimed at generating the best possible return on a risk-adjusted basis. The results speak for themselves: The fund has been a first-quartile performer every year since 1995. The low MER is a big plus. This is one of the best money funds you'll find.

PERIGEE T-PLUS FUND $$$$ → C NO RIF CMM

Manager: Owen D. Phillips, since 1986
MER: 0.48%   **Style:** Index
Suitability: Low-risk income investors.

This is a first-rate money market fund with good returns. It is consistently in the first quartile of its category, and we're going back more than a decade here. The good numbers are helped by the low MER, although the fees and costs have been inching up in recent years. The portfolio is invested mainly in Treasury bills, with a few bankers' acceptances in the mix to provide higher yields. Safety profile is excellent.

PHILLIPS, HAGER & NORTH
CANADIAN MONEY MARKET FUND $$$$ → C NO RIF CMM

Manager: Team, headed by Scott Lamont
MER: 0.48%   **Style:** N/A
Suitability: Low-risk income investors.

The portfolio invests mainly in high-grade corporate notes, which enhances return with slightly more risk. Major advantage: one of the lowest management fees in the business, which contributes significantly to the above-average performance numbers. In fact, it is a first-quartile performer in its category almost every year. Consistently good returns, timeliness, and no-load status earn it a top rating.

ROYAL & SUNALLIANCE MONEY
MARKET FUND $$$ → C NO/* RIF S CMM

Manager: Steve Locke, since 1999
MER: 1.20%   **Style:** N/A
Suitability: Low-risk income investors.

This is a money market fund with above-average returns. To achieve this, the fund invests predominantly in higher-yielding corporate debt. The absence of government securities adds slightly to the risk level, although we don't regard that as a major concern. Distributions are paid monthly. This fund group was sold to Maritime Life in late 2001. No changes are expected in 2002, but beyond that nothing is certain.

ROYAL CANADIAN MONEY MARKET FUND $$$ → C NO RIF CMM

Manager: Walter Posiewko, since 1999
MER: 1.00%   **Style:** N/A
Suitability: Low-risk income investors.

It's amazing what a lower MER can do for a fund's return, especially in this category where a slight variation in the MER can lead to quite different results. Case in point: Prior to reducing its MER by 33 basis points, this fund was an underachiever. With the lower fees, the fund has returned slightly above-average numbers, with less-than-average volatility. A decent choice.

SCEPTRE MONEY MARKET FUND $$$$ ↓ C NO RIF CMM

Manager: Richard L. Knowles, since March 2000
MER: 0.80%   **Style:** N/A
Suitability: Low-risk income investors.

This fund has a wonderful record of consistency. It has been an above-average
performer for as far back as we can remember, never sinking below second quartile
since at least 1994. The portfolio is about equally divided between government and
corporate notes, which provides a good combination of security and decent returns.
The low MER helps as well. The safety rating is among the best in the category.
Monthly distributions provide decent cash flow. See the entry on the Sceptre Bond
Fund for purchase details.

SCOTIA MONEY MARKET FUND $$ ↓ C NO RIF CMM

Managers: Cecilia Chan and Amanda Ford
MER: 1.00%   **Style:** N/A
Suitability: Low-risk income investors.

The fund was formed from the merger of the Scotia Excelsior Money Market Fund
into the National Trust Money Market Fund. The portfolio is invested in a mix of
corporate and government short-term notes. Returns are about average, while the risk
level is better than average. Monthly distributions.

SPECTRUM CANADIAN MONEY MARKET FUND $$ → C NO RIF CMM

Manager: Cort Conover (McLean Budden), since January 1996
MER: 1.05%   **Style:** N/A
Suitability: Low-risk income investors.

This is a standard money market fund, investing in a mix of government T-bills,
corporate short-term notes, and bankers' acceptances. Performance is average to
slightly above. Note that, although there is no sales charge for buying units in this
fund, you will be subject to normal commissions if you transfer into another fund
later. Formerly the Spectrum United Canadian T-Bill Fund.

STANDARD LIFE IDEAL MONEY
MARKET FUND $$$ → C */NO RIF S CMM

Manager: Standard Life Investments Inc.
MER: 1.00%   **Style:** Income
Suitability: Low-risk income investors.

With most of the assets invested in higher-yielding corporate debt, returns here have
been consistently above average from one to five years. The remainder is in T-bills and
provincial bonds. A good haven for idle cash. This is one of the few cases in which the
segregated fund version of a Standard Life fund is outperforming the mutual fund.

TALVEST MONEY MARKET FUND $$$ ↓ C #/* RIF CMM

Manager: Steven Dubrovsky, since 1994

MER: 1.00%   **Style:** Index

Suitability: Low-risk income investors.

The fund's low-risk portfolio consists mainly of corporate notes and government securities. Both the short- and long-term records are good, with the fund beating the averages virtually every year over the past 10. A good choice. If buying, try to negotiate for no load charge.

TD CANADIAN MONEY MARKET FUND $$$ ↓ C NO RIF CMM

Manager: Satish Rai, since inception (1988)

MER: 0.91%   **Style:** N/A

Suitability: Low-risk income investors.

This is the result of the merger between the Green Line Canadian Money Market Fund and the Canada Trust Money Market Fund. It has shown continued excellent performance since its launch in 1988, with consistently above-average returns. The portfolio invests primarily in commercial paper and short-term (less than one year) government notes.

TD CANADIAN T-BILL FUND $$$ ↓ C NO RIF CMM

Manager: Satish Rai, since inception (1991)

MER: 0.93%   **Style:** N/A

Suitability: Low-risk income investors.

An alternative money market fund from TD, this one invests exclusively in Government of Canada Treasury bills. This gives you a slightly higher level of safety. Returns tend to be lower than those of the Canadian Money Market Fund, but better than the average for the Canadian Money Market category.

TRIMARK INTEREST FUND $$$ → C #/* RIF CMM

Manager: Patrick Farmer, since 1993, Rex Chong, since 2000, Vince Hunt, since 2001

MER: 0.89%/1.87%   **Style:** Credit Analysis

Suitability: Low-risk income investors.

This fund invests almost entirely in commercial paper. This boosts return, but adds a slightly higher degree of risk. But a word of warning: The DSC units, which were launched in October 2000, carry a much higher MER, which will result in returns that are consistently below average. As a result, they are not recommended. Opt for the SC units only and insist on paying a zero front-end load. If your advisor won't go along, choose a no-load money market fund from another organization.

Foreign Money Market Funds

CI U.S. MONEY MARKET FUND (US$) $$$ ↓ C #/* RIF FMM

Manager: Wally Kusters, since September 1999
MER: 0.85%   **Style:** Value
Suitability: U.S. income investors.

This fund has outperformed the average of its group in each of the past five years by investing in any U.S.-dollar-denominated debt of less than 365 days, whether marketed by the U.S. or Canada. A relatively low MER helps with the returns here. The fund's risk is low and tracks that of the 30-day T-bill. Currency risk is derived from holding U.S.-denominated investments. The main holdings of this fund include short-term U.S.-dollar debt issued by such government organizations as the Export Development Corp. and U.S. T-bills. Note: If you can get this fund on a no-charge basis (front-end load option with zero commission), it's worth considering if it meets your needs. Note that this fund is fully eligible for registered plans.

INVESTORS U.S. MONEY MARKET (US$) FUND $$$ ↓ C NO RIF FMM

Manager: Patsy Rogers, since January 1999
MER: 1.21%   **Style:** N/A
Suitability: U.S. income investors.

If you are looking to park U.S. cash in your RRIF, this is a good choice. The MER is high, but performance has been well above average and the safety rating is good. If you have a RRIF with Investors Group, consider adding some of this one.

NATIONAL BANK U.S. MONEY MARKET FUND $$$ ↓ C NO RIF FMM

Manager: Richard Lévesque (Natcan Investment Management), since 1995
MER: 1.11%   **Style:** N/A
Suitability: U.S. income investors.

This is a fully RRIF-eligible fund that invests in Canadian debt securities denominated in U.S. dollars. The portfolio is mainly in Government of Canada T-bills. Returns are well above average. In sum: a good-quality portfolio with above-average returns and the second-lowest risk rating in its category. That makes it a good hedge against future declines in the Canadian dollar.

PHILLIPS, HAGER & NORTH
$U.S. MONEY MARKET FUND $$$$ → C NO RIF FMM

Manager: Team, headed by Scott Lamont
MER: 0.55%   **Style:** N/A
Suitability: U.S. income investors.

This is a solid U.S. money fund that offers the bonus of full RRIF eligibility. The managers invest in short-term notes issued by Canadian governments and corporations but denominated in U.S. currency. The fund offers one of the lowest management fees in this category, as well as being no load. It's been a first-quartile performer every year since it was launched in 1990. You don't get better consistency than that. A good choice, especially for those who want to hold U.S. dollars in their RRIFs.

ROYAL $U.S. MONEY MARKET FUND $$$ ↓ C NO RIF FMM

Manager: Walter Posiewko, since 1999
MER: 1.16%   **Style:** N/A
Suitability: U.S. income investors.

This fund invests primarily in high-quality, short-term debt that is denominated in U.S. dollars. The securities may be issued or guaranteed by Canadian or foreign governments, banks, or corporations. Holdings favour commercial paper and bankers' acceptances. Returns have generally been average. Risk is low for a fund of this type, but don't lose sight of the currency risk that comes with holding U.S.-dollar denominated securities. Full RRIF eligibility.

SCOTIA CANAM U.S. $ MONEY MARKET FUND $$$ → FI NO RIF FMM

Managers: Cecilia Chan and Amanda Ford
MER: 1.00%   **Style:** N/A
Suitability: Conservative investors seeking U.S. currency exposure.

The average annual return for this RRIF-eligible U.S. money fund is generally way above the average for the group. The portfolio is split fairly equally between Canadian corporate and provincial issues, denominated in U.S. funds. This is an excellent U.S.-dollar money market fund, and it's no load.

TD U.S. MONEY MARKET FUND $$$ ↓ C NO RIF FMM

Manager: Satish Rai, since inception (1988)
MER: 1.19%   **Style:** N/A
Suitability: U.S. income investors.

This fund invests in short-term securities denominated in U.S. dollars but issued by Canadian governments and corporations, which makes it fully RRIF-eligible. Returns have been higher than its Canadian counterpart in recent years. Factor in the strength of the U.S. dollar, and you're well ahead. This fund is recommended for investors who have a constant need for U.S. dollars and don't want the hassle of having to regularly convert from Canadian dollars. It is also a good choice for those who want to reduce Canadian currency risk in a registered plan.

Glossary

Amortization The gradual reduction of debt over a fixed period of time. For example, if a mortgage is amortized over 25 years, regular payments consist of a blend of principal and interest—early payments being mostly interest, later payments mostly principal—and the full amount of the debt will be retired in 25 years.

Annuitant A person who receives annuity payments.

Annuity A contract providing for a series of payments to be made or received at regular intervals. For retirement purposes, an annuity is an income vehicle that provides a guaranteed, regular income based on your age, the amount you invest, the type of annuity you buy, and interest rates at the time of purchase. *See:* cashable annuity, deferred annuities, guaranteed-term life annuity, income-reducing annuity, indexed annuity, insured annuity, joint-and-last-survivor annuity, life annuity, prescribed annuity, term-certain annuity.

Asset Any property or investment that has monetary value.

Asset allocation Mixing assets (cash, bonds, stocks) in a diversified portfolio. Most professional money managers agree that holding the right blend of investments can account for, on average, 80 percent or more of gains in the long term.

Back-end load A mutual fund purchase option. The buyer pays no sales commission at the time of purchase, but may be required to pay a redemption charge when the units are sold. Also known as deferred sales charge.

Balanced fund A mutual fund that invests in a balanced portfolio, including interest-bearing securities, such as bonds and mortgages, and equity investments, such as preferred and common shares.

Bear market A steadily falling stock market. A "bear" is a person who believes the market will drop.

Beneficiary The person designated as heir to the assets of a RRIF in the event of the death of the annuitant.

Blue-chip stocks Shares of large, well-known, established corporations with a history of good earnings and/or dividend payments.

Bond fund A mutual fund that invests in a widely diversified portfolio of bonds with varying maturities. A bond fund usually holds bonds issued by governments as well as by major corporations.

Bonds Certificates through which governments and large corporations borrow money. In return for borrowed capital, the borrower promises to pay the holder a fixed annual rate of interest for a specified term and to repay the principal at maturity.

Broker A person who acts as an intermediary in the purchase of securities or insurance. In this book, *broker* normally refers to a stockbroker unless otherwise indicated.

Bull market A steadily climbing stock market. A "bull" is a person who believes the market will rise.

Canada Deposit Insurance Corporation (CDIC) A Crown agency that provides insurance to banks and most trust companies to protect individual depositors against losses of up to $60,000 on specific deposit investments.

Canada Premium Bonds Long-term securities issued by the federal government, specifically designed for retirement plans and education savings plans.

Canada Savings Bonds (CSBs) Savings certificates issued by the Government of Canada for purchase by individual Canadian citizens. The interest rate is set with each new issue that appears.

Capital gains Profits realized on the sale of capital assets, such as stocks or property. Only one half of your capital gain is included in your income for tax purposes. The other half is, in effect, tax-free.

Cashable annuity Most annuity decisions are irrevocable, but the law has allowed cashable annuities since 1986. Not many companies offer this option, but most will at least consider paying an annuitant the "commuted value" of a term-certain annuity because it can be easily calculated at any time. Usually, a penalty is involved.

Common shares Also known as common stocks or equities, they represent a portion of ownership in a corporation. If the corporation is public, the shares can be bought or sold on a stock exchange.

Commutation payment A fixed or single lump-sum payment from an annuity equal to the current value (the

"commuted value") of all or part of your future annuity payments.

Deemed disposition Assets, including RRIFs, may pass tax-free to a spouse upon death. As well, rules introduced in 1999 now allow RRSP and RRIF assets to be passed on after death to financially dependent children or grandchildren and to be taxed as assets in their hands. However, other than when passed to these "qualified beneficiaries," all the assets in an estate are considered by the Canada Customs and Revenue Agency's "deemed disposition" rules to have been sold. Taxes must be paid in the year of death on RRSPs and RRIFs, and on capital gains in stocks, a business, or a cottage.

Deferred annuities You can buy an annuity to provide income in the future, rather than at the date of purchase. Such deferred annuities must begin by January of the year in which you turn 70, but can be put in place as much as 10 years in advance. This makes sense only at times when interest rates are high and you want to lock in at these rates ahead of the time you'll start collecting.

Deferred profit-sharing plans (DPSPs) Employer-sponsored pension plans, registered by the Canada Customs and Revenue Agency, in which the employer shares the profits of a business with all employees or a designated group.

Deferred sales charge A fee charged when units of a mutual fund purchased on a back-end load option are redeemed.

Defined-benefit pension plans Once the most common type of pension plan, defined-benefits have been falling in popularity among sponsors because of the difficulty of administration and reluctance to assume the responsibility for potential shortfalls. These plans provide pensions generally calculated on the basis of earnings and years of service. Under such plans, you know exactly what your pension payments will be.

Discretionary investment management A service provided by most financial institutions that takes the management of your investment portfolio off your shoulders and puts them onto those of a professional money manager. Normally, you need to have at least $100,000 in assets to make use of this type of service. Some organizations require even higher minimums.

Diversification Spreading risk by investing in a broad range of securities. A diversified portfolio would include both short- and long-term interest-bearing securities, as well as common or preferred stocks. A diversified portfolio would usually include investments in different industrial, as well as geographic, sectors.

Dividends Payments, as a share of profit, made to holders of common or preferred shares of corporations, or distributions of dividend mutual funds. If held outside a registered plan, such as a RRIF, dividend income is eligible for the dividend tax credit and represents a tax-effective way to receive investment income.

Dollar-cost averaging Buying securities (e.g., a mutual fund) with investments spread out over a period of time, on a regular basis such as monthly, so as to ensure the lowest average purchase price during that period. Also, the technique of using market corrections as bargain-hunting opportunities, adding to a portfolio at reduced prices. This generally lowers the average cost of securities in a portfolio over time.

Equities Another way of referring to common shares or stocks. An equity mutual fund, for example, is one that invests entirely in such shares.

Executor/Executrix The person or institution named in your will to represent you after death, to act on your behalf and carry out your wishes. Your executor not only distributes your estate, but also administers any trusts you may have set up.

Fair market value The accepted buying and selling price in an open market at any given time.

Financial dependent A person is generally considered financially dependent on a deceased annuitant if that person ordinarily resided with and depended on the annuitant prior to death, and his or her net income was below a certain level. If, prior to the annuitant's death, the dependent lived away from home while attending school, he or she is considered to have resided with the annuitant.

Foreign content The international portion of a RRIF or other registered plan. You are allowed to hold up to 30 percent of your RRIF in non-Canadian securities. Previously, the limit was 20 percent until 2000, when it was increased to 25 percent for that year, and subsequently to the current level.

Front-end load A sales commission charged up-front when buying units of a mutual fund.

Guaranteed investment certificates (GICs) Investment certificates issued by banks and trust companies, GICs repay principal and interest according to an agreed term and interest rate. An investor's money is generally locked in for the term. GICs are backed by the issuing institution and may also be insured by the CDIC.

Guaranteed-term life annuity Life annuities may be purchased with a guarantee of a minimum number of payments–commonly ranging between 5 and 20 years, but going up to a maximum of age 90. The decision on term must be made at the time of purchase. Any payments remaining (or their "commuted value"–the equivalent lump sum of future payments) under the guaranteed period upon your death are paid to your spouse or other beneficiary. Payments do not stop at the end of the guaranteed period if you are still alive– they continue on until your death, or that of your spouse in the case of a joint-and-last-survivor annuity.

Impaired annuity If your doctor's report shows a medical condition that could result in a lower life expectancy, you may qualify for an annuity (in the case of life annuities only) that will pay out as if you were older. Such impaired annuities result in higher payments because the actuarial tables used by life insurance companies project a shorter-than-normal life span.

Income-reducing annuity This form of joint-and-last-survivor life annuity provides higher monthly payments until the death of one spouse. Payments to the surviving spouse are then reduced. The rationale for this reduction is that one person will not require as much income as two people would.

Income splitting The division of income among family members for the purpose of minimizing tax.

Index fund A mutual fund constructed to track a particular stock market, such as the Toronto 300 or 35 Index and the U.S. Standard and Poor's 500. Index funds are passively managed in that they generally mirror market performance. These types of funds have often ranked in the upper 30 percent for performance among their peers.

Indexed annuity Annuities structured to provide protection from inflation in return for lower payments–in the beginning anywhere from 30 percent to 45 percent less than non-indexed annuities. Payments then increase every year, based on one of four formulas.

Individual pension plan (IPP) A registered pension plan designed for a specific individual, usually an owner/manager of a company.

Inflation Annual cost-of-living increases, usually defined as changes in the Consumer Price Index, a Statistics Canada measurement of such changes.

Insured annuity This combines two insurance products, a life annuity with no guarantee period and a term-to-100 life insurance policy. This product offers annuity payments with the additional feature of preserving capital for your estate. However, you must be in good enough health, i.e., able to pass a medical examination, in order to qualify for the life insurance.

Interest income The most common source of investment income in Canada. Interest is derived from bonds, GICs, CSBs, deposit accounts, and other interest-bearing investments. Such income receives no tax advantage, and investors pay tax on interest at their marginal rate (the rate paid on their last dollar).

Intestate Dying without a will, whereupon provincial regulations determine the distribution of the estate.

Joint-and-last-survivor annuity A variation on the life annuity theme, this pays between 10 percent and 15 percent less per month than a straight life annuity, but payments continue until the surviving spouse dies. This is the most common annuity option for married couples.

Laddering maturities Laddering, or staggering, maturities involves buying GICs (or bonds) so that 20 percent of the total portfolio matures each year. The maturing principal is then reinvested each year for a new five-year term. This enables an investor to benefit from any increase in interest rates and ensures that some money will be rolled over at the best interest rate available at the time. The process makes sense in a low-interest-rate environment.

Life annuity Sold only by life insurance companies, this type of annuity makes monthly payments—at the highest rates of all annuities—that continue for as long as the annuitant is alive; these payments stop on the day the annuitant dies.

Life Income Fund (LIF) A special kind of RRIF for proceeds from locked-in RRSPs and LIRAs, with specific limitations. As with all RRIFs, a minimum amount must be withdrawn each year, but there is also an annual ceiling on how much can be withdrawn up to age 80. The remaining money stays locked in, just as with a pension or locked-in RRSP. In many provinces, you must buy a life annuity with the remaining balance of funds in a LIF by December 31 of the year in which you turn 80. This life annuity must include a 60 percent survivor benefit,

unless this condition is waived by your spouse.

Life Retirement Income Fund (LRIF) A type of retirement income vehicle to which proceeds from a locked-in retirement plan or pension plan assets can be converted. An LRIF is like a regular RRIF in that a minimum amount must be withdrawn each year but, like a LIF, there is also a maximum withdrawal ceiling. The major difference with an LRIF, which is now available in Alberta, Manitoba, Newfoundland, Ontario, and Saskatchewan, is that it can continue after age 80; there is no requirement that the remaining proceeds be used to purchase an annuity, as there is for a LIF.

Load The commission charged when mutual fund units are bought (front-end load) or sold (back-end load).

Locked-in retirement account (LIRA) *See* locked-in RRSP.

Locked-in RRSP When you leave a company and opt to take your pension plan dollars along, the funds must be transferred directly into a locked-in RRSP, termed a locked-in retirement account (LIRA) in certain provinces. The funds are exactly that—locked in—and, unlike funds in ordinary RRSPs, cannot be withdrawn for any purpose, not even financial disaster, until retirement. At that point, you must convert to a Life Income Fund (LIF), or buy an annuity. For plans in Alberta, Manitoba, Newfoundland, Ontario, and Saskatchewan, you have the option of converting to an LRIF, which is similar to a LIF but can continue after age 80. (With a LIF, you must purchase a life annuity at age 80.)

Management fees Charges made against a mutual fund by the managers to compensate them for their services and expenses. These charges are usually made against the assets of the fund itself and are not charged directly to individual investors. However, the size of the management fee will affect a fund's overall performance, as the more it pays out in fees, the less profit the fund will realize.

Marginal tax rate A taxpayer's highest tax rate—what he or she pays on the last dollar earned in a given year.

Market correction A drop in value in a market that has been rising for some time.

Market-linked GICs Similar to regular GICs in that full security of the original amount invested is guaranteed, but, instead of being based on a set interest rate, returns are linked to how well a particular stock market performs over a specific period, generally two or three years.

Maturity The time at which principal and all interest owing on a debt or other obligation become due.

Minimum amount The smallest amount you may withdraw from a RRIF in any given year, based on federal government law. No withdrawals are required during the year the plan is created.

Money market fund A mutual fund that invests exclusively in money market securities, those involved in the short-term lending and borrowing of money.

Money-purchase pension plans Also known as defined contribution pension plans. These plans may pay out whatever level of pension income the accumulated contributions and return on investment in a Registered Pension Plan (RPP) will buy at retirement. Rather than receiving a pre-determined pension amount, employees make the decision—in the same way as they would for an RRSP—about retirement income options.

Mutual fund A mutual fund pools money from many individuals and invests, according to its specific mandate, in a broad range of securities. Mutual funds are managed by professional money managers and provide extensive diversification.

Net asset value (NAV) The value of a mutual fund unit at any given time. It is calculated by subtracting the fund's liabilities from its assets and dividing by the number of units outstanding. Open-end mutual funds are bought or sold at their net asset value.

Overcontribution allowance The amount of excess contribution permitted to RRSPs to provide a margin for error without incurring the overcontribution penalty of 1 percent per month. The 1995 federal budget reduced this allowance from $8,000 to $2,000 from 1996 forward.

Penalties Special assessments by the Canada Customs and Revenue Agency for violating RRIF rules, such as the foreign-content limit. The penalty usually takes the form of a special tax of 1 percent a month.

Portfolio The total of an individual's investments, including stocks, bonds, GICs, cash, and other holdings.

Preferred shares Preferred shares usually have prior claim over common shares to the assets of the corporation. They pay dividends at specific rates, and these must be paid before any dividends are paid on common shares. Preferred shares are usually bought for the potential dividend income they provide while common shares are purchased for their capital growth potential.

Prescribed annuity A prescribed annuity can be purchased only with non-registered funds—so the money cannot come from an RRSP. Payments consist of principal and interest, and only the interest portion received during a calendar year is taxable. This effectively spreads the tax impact out over the life of the contract by keeping the taxable portion—the interest—at the same level throughout the life of the annuity. It makes sense at times to use such an annuity in combination with a RRIF.

Present value The amount of money that, if invested at today's interest rates, would grow to a future amount in a specific time period.

Prime rate The lowest interest rate charged by chartered banks at a given time. Usually this rate is available only to a bank's largest customers. The prime rate is used as the basis for all other lending rates, including consumer loans, mortgages, and business loans.

Qualified investment One that is eligible for inclusion in a RRIF. Non-qualified investments (gold bullion is one example) may not be held in registered plans.

Registered Education Savings Plan (RESP) A vehicle for saving for a child's post-secondary education. Unlike RRSP contributions, money deposited to an RESP is not tax deductible, but the earnings are sheltered from tax until drawn out for the child's education, and then taxed at the child's marginal rate.

Registered Pension Plan (RPP) The basic company private pension plan for employees, sponsored by employers or unions, usually jointly funded by workers and the company. Contributions to RPPs are tax deductible; like RRSP withdrawals or income paid from RRIFs, the resulting pensions are taxable.

Registered Retirement Income Funds (RRIFs) A RRIF is basically a continuation of your RRSP, providing the same tax sheltering of principal and earnings, with one key difference: Instead of making contributions, you must take out a minimum amount every year. The amount is based on your age, with withdrawal rates increasing annually before levelling off at 20 percent for people age 94 and older. In effect, a RRIF takes the accumulated savings of an RRSP and spreads the income over retirement years while, at the same time, investing the monies not needed to cover the mandatory withdrawals.

Registered Retirement Savings Plans (RRSPs) Tax-sheltered retirement savings plans for individuals, including the self-employed. RRSP contribution limits are based on earned income, and RRSPs provide retirement income based on what the accumulated contributions and earnings will buy at conversion. This must take place no later than December 31 of the year in which you turn 69. Contributions to RRSPs are tax deductible, while withdrawals are taxable. RRSP contributors may also belong to a registered pension plan, but RRSP contribution limits are reduced by the amount of a pension adjustment, a measure of the benefits provided in the RPP. RRSPs set up to receive funds transferred from RPPs on the condition they be used solely for retirement income purposes are called locked-in RRSPs.

Retiring allowance A lump-sum payment made by an employer to an employee on termination, or an amount received on or after retirement in recognition of long service. This includes payment for unused sick leave as compensation for loss of employment. Such payments can be rolled over, or transferred, to an RRSP to defer tax, but only for years prior to 1996. Allowable amounts are up to $2,000 for each year of service, plus up to $1,500 for each year before 1989 in which no pension or DPSP benefits were earned—in addition to the normal limits for RRSP contributions. However, the 1995 federal budget eliminated this rollover provision for years of service after 1995, drastically reducing the amount of such a lump sum a person facing this situation will be able to shelter from taxes in the future.

Reverse mortgage A reverse mortgage allows people to generate income through the equity in their homes. The cash from such a mortgage may be invested or used to purchase an annuity that will pay a regular income. No payments are required on the mortgage. When the owner dies, the mortgage loan and interest are paid and the rest of the proceeds, if any, become part of the owner's estate. In most cases, reverse mortgages should be considered only by people in their 70s and 80s.

Segregated funds Investment vehicles offered by life insurance companies and by mutual fund companies with insurance company partners. They are similar to mutual funds but with several interesting differences, such as guarantees of principal on maturity and death benefits. In a way, they combine the growth aspects of a mutual fund with the guarantees of a GIC.

Spousal RRSP An RRSP to which contributions are made by the plan holder's spouse.

Spouse Technically, the law makes a distinction between a spouse and a common-law partner. While the term *spouse* refers to a person of the opposite sex to whom you are legally married, a common-law partner is a person of the opposite or same sex who is living with you in a common-law relationship. A common-law partner is generally defined as someone who is your child's natural or adoptive parent (legal or in fact); or who has been living with you in such a relationship for at least 12 continuous months; or who previously lived with you in such a relationship for at least 12 continuous months (including any period of separation of less than 90 days) and is living with you again. For tax purposes, a common-law partner is accorded the same rights as a spouse.

Staggering maturities *See* laddering maturities.

Successor annuitant A designation used to ensure that a RRIF will pass to your spouse undisturbed. Instead of naming your spouse the beneficiary of your RRIF, you can designate him or her as the "successor annuitant"—either in the fund itself or in your will. In this way, the RRIF will remain exactly the same, except that the name of the payee will be changed to his or hers. If you name your spouse as beneficiary of the RRIF, the assets may be cashed in and the proceeds rolled over into your spouse's RRIF. Tax forms must be filed, and investments must be made anew.

Switching Moving money from one mutual fund to another. Many mutual fund companies allow switching with little or no charge among their own funds.

Term-certain annuity Provides a fixed monthly income until you turn 90. If you die earlier, payments continue to your surviving spouse until what would have been your 90th birthday. If your spouse is younger, you can base this form of annuity on his or her age, thereby extending the payment schedule. If you do not have a surviving spouse, the remaining payments are cashed out according to the insurance company's "commuted value" formula and paid to your estate. Term-certain annuities are offered by banks and trust companies as well as by life insurance companies.

Timing the market Attempting to guess when a market will go up or down, and investing accordingly.

Treasury bills Short-term securities issued by governments and sold at retail by stockbrokers and banks. Those issued by the Government of Canada are regarded as excellent short-term investments because of their safety and good return.

Trust A legal arrangement under which title to property or assets is given to a third party who manages it for the benefit of a beneficiary or beneficiaries.

Unit A share in a mutual fund.

GENERAL INDEX

Fund Index